CU00868774

For George
Hope you enjoy
the story

Pete...
Trevor Wilson

www.united-pc.eu

TREVOR WILSON

THE ENGLISH CONFEDERATE

Chapter 1

It was dark in the room, a total blackness that seemed to smother me, I sat bolt upright and immediately started to sweat, the drops of moisture rolling quickly down from my head and face soaking into the cloth wrapped around my throat. My mouth was dry and my tongue felt too big for my mouth, threatening like it was going to stop me from swallowing. This thumping in my ears was getting louder and when I realised it was my own heart beating it frightened me, and I could feel myself panicking, that old familiar companion fear, in a lump now seeming to rise from my stomach and up into my chest.

The sheets around my legs were wet with my own sweat and there were bandages around my left thigh but the blood had come through and was wet and sticky as I touched it.

Suddenly the door opened and the light from the oil lamp made everything clearer. I was in my mother's farm house, my old room in our family home and the bearer of the lamp rushed in, the sound of her skirts swirling around as she pushed through the door to get to the bedside.

"Shush now," she said, "everything is going to be fine now." It was my younger sisters' friend Beth and as she fussed over me wiping my body with a cloth soaked in cool water, my memory started to clear and I started to calm down. At last my breathing had recovered and the pounding of my heart had slowed.

She told me I had been in a tormented sleep with a high fever for several days, and that this was the first time I had lifted my head from the pillow.

"You give us all a fright." It was the Captain and I strained to see his face beyond Beth's shoulders.

He came into the room now with a lighted candle and set it on the table. "It is time to tell you what has happened, and I only hope you are strong enough to take it." He went on to ask me if I could remember anything about our return to Georgia and the homecoming.

Well, I had trouble here as things were not making any sense, I could not remember being wounded and as this was my biggest concern then, I pressed him for the information. It worked out that we had returned from Virginia before the surrender of Lee. I could recollect our latest active service for we had joined with Mosby for those last months before everything was lost, but had mustered out a few weeks before. We were given leave of absence by our leader Mosby to go home as things were said to be unbelievable in the South, and that the civilian population had been forced to endure continual hardship beyond belief. We were informed by both our own company engaged in scouting and gathering information, and also the network of people engaged in the spying business, having far reaching contacts and eyes and ears everywhere. The enemy was operating to divide the confederacy in half making the situation in the South very serious. Mosby was convinced the end was near and that we could not serve much longer fighting.

As the night turned slowly and the light of dawn got stronger in the east, I learned of the fate of my family. I was quiet as the Captain told the story of how my mother and two sisters had been forced to take work in the factory in Roswell. The enemy action around Atlanta and the crossing of the Chattahoochee River had caused the damage in Roswell as it was here that the Federals outflanked us and forced a crossing. The mills were put to the torch as Sherman considered these legitimate military targets and should therefore be denied to the Confederate war effort. Unfortunately his twisted thinking extended to all the civilian workers employed in these factories, they were arrested and charged with treason. It didn't end there as they were ordered to be transported to the North via Marietta and then by train to Louisville.

Beth dressed my thigh wound and informed me it was on the mend, and that it was my sudden movement by sitting up that had caused the wound to open slightly, but the deepest part had started to close and there was no corruption. My head wound that had caused me to lose all consciousness for a while was almost gone and there was little need for the head bandage. I was left with a closing scab over the new, raw flesh but I was not suffering from delirium like before.

We had to make up our minds what the next course of action would be and the next day the Captain brought my uncle to my bedside. He was very quiet and I thought not very much like his usual self as far as I could remember. The Captain then was able to explain to me when my relative had gone outside, that he was filled with guilt for not being able to prevent my mother and my sisters being taken and transported to the North.

I couldn't believe the reality of this, and maybe it was because of my weakened condition but the facts simply would not sink in. I tried to swing my legs out of bed, as in my state of mind this was all a dream and they would surely be in the next room where mother would be preparing our midday meal. Had it not been for the Captain I think my injuries would have really suffered a turn for the worse but his restraining of me and the

7

gentleness with which he and Beth talked me through it, allowed me to come to terms with the fact they were gone and that I had to try and get to them, find out what had happened and if possible return them to the South and our family. We talked through most of the day and into the night, using the information from uncle to put together a plan. I was really worried by what he was telling us and the more information he delivered the more my mood changed to anger. If it hadn't been for my weakened state I knew I would have ridden north then and there, blind with fury and most likely to have ended my life in a senseless, blind search.

A day later uncle told us of the situation when just before the fall of Atlanta Federal troops were patrolling east probing our positions, searching for a route and crossing place where they could cross the Chattahoochee River and outflank our positions. The obvious place was the fords and bridge near to the town. After a brief skirmish our lads were forced to abandon their positions and retreat before they were outflanked. This left the town and its civilians without protection and completely at the mercy of the enemy.

The first enemy troops involved in taking the town were cavalry, under a Col. Adams and a Maj. Tompkins who were under a General Garrard. Uncle described how he and another irregular militia man had shadowed their movements, dodging their patrols and pickets, while constantly observing every manoeuvre. I can remember him saying that at first there seemed some order to the events involving all the townspeople and workers from the mills, but after a couple of days things changed for the worse and trouble broke out when a French national flag was flown from the roof of the Roswell mill. This was where my family worked and what he said next set me on the verge of panic. Wagons arrived the next day and all the workers mostly women with a few men, were loaded onto them. As many of the women were mothers with young dependent children these were given some priority for transport. There were others that were not and the Yankees seemed unprepared for the numbers involved that had to be accommodated and loaded for transportation. This resulted in many single unmarried women being unable to get any room on the wagon train. There were, as uncle says nearly 500 people, mostly women, but with a few men, to ship to the North. The Yankees were not prepared or equipped with enough transport to take them. Uncle now admitted that he was thoroughly ashamed at not being able to help these women and he began to cry taken for a moment deeply with grief. It was in this moment that he told us of the plight of my mother and sisters not being in the wagons but being forced to either walk or travel doubled-up on horseback with a cavalryman.

Uncle shadowed the transport train and those women who were at first allowed to continue walking on foot. They were making for Marietta but the progress was slow, and this must have angered the Captain in charge of the prisoners for after several hours there was a commotion and much shouting with women screaming. The women on foot were ordered to double-up on the cavalry horses to travel behind the troopers. My mind was immediately filled with horror, to the inevitable which was going to happen to some of the young girls. I was beside myself at this stage and the Captain had to restrain me for I was going for my revolver to blow uncles head off. That evening uncle revealed he was watching with his friend when there was a breakdown in military discipline. Resulting in several incidents where the women were subjected to rape and assault from the cavalrymen escort.

I was up from my bedside and like a mountain lion I leapt for uncle's throat, my fingers tightening around his windpipe and making his face change colour in his attempt to draw breath. I would have probably killed him but the others prised my fingers from around his throat. They sat me down again but by now I was beyond hearing them or even what the Captain was saying. Eventually my rage subsided and I caught some of the conversation between uncle and the Captain. He was pumping him for information on the officer's name and his regiment. Uncle managed to offer what he thought would ease my pain, by saying there was good discipline resumed and the women were finally separated from the troopers with strict security put in place. However the damage had been done and after another break down from uncle, when again he burst out crying but between sobs and trying to talk with a rasping, squeaky voice he finished the story that he had seen my sister Roseanne being brutally assaulted by a large Yankee Sergeant of the 1st Kentucky.

I again couldn't control myself and had suddenly snatched a revolver from under my pillow and before any of them could react I had cocked, levelled and fired it at him. The room was filled with smoke and still rang from the sharp explosion; everyone seemed frozen in the shock. The Captain had rounded on me and hit me under the chin knocking me unconscious. They told me afterwards that uncle had survived due to the .36 bullet hitting the cross belt buckle of his carbine sling belt and in so doing, when it finally entered his shoulder it contained hardly enough energy to penetrate further than just under the fleshy part of his shoulder.

By the time I regained consciousness, Joe had removed the bullet and Beth was bandaging his wound. I was not sorry and my feelings even after all these years are unchanged. Even when my uncle died recently it didn't totally subdue my hatred for the man who had done nothing to prevent or avenge my sister's fate; disregarding any consequences as such an attempt would have meant certain death. This for me would have been the only action to take as I would not have been able to stop myself had I seen what was happening that day.

I can remember that night the Captain stayed with me and we shared a jug of liquor drinking till the early hours of the morning. His experience with soldiers and the way he talked to me allowed me to come out of the dark place I had gone to and listen to what he was saying. I enjoyed his stories and could listen without uttering a sound to his tales of combat in the British Army. We were back in England now and my imagination pictured up visions of a regiment in a training camp and under instruction in cavalry tactics. He had explained many times about how he wanted to keep us alive and the only way he knew was by routine manoeuvres in all aspects of cavalry tactics and fighting. This was true as here most of us, apart from Clem and Squirrel, were still together after nearly 5 years of war, safe only because he had shown us how to stay one step ahead of our enemy and fight better than they could. He went on to talk about there were always some men who were weak and at any opportunity when discipline was not as strict as it could be, would take advantage of soft officers or Sergeants and try to disrupt leadership. He would not tolerate any behaviour that seemed would threaten his command and I had once seen him beat a trooper half to death with his fists for insubordination. Afterwards when we were again in action that same trooper had not questioned his leadership or resented the Captain's swift discipline, but had done his duty for his comrades and a leader he respected.

 I am wandering now which at this time in my life I can be forgiven, but the story must return to England and the Captain's regiment.

There were such incidents in the regiment, he told me, and as ever there were individuals that would never fully accept the army and the harsh routine and unforgiving discipline and military justice. He explained about this trooper in his own troop who fitted this description. The Captain was involved in an incident of this man's insubordination and crime but could not step in to help save him or lessen his sentence. The trooper was marched into the horse exercise area where there stood a gun limber. The Commanding Officer of the regiment a Lord Cardigan was present and there was a swift hearing where evidence both for and against the accused was offered. Several high ranking officers voted on the man's fate and they were all in agreement of his guilt. The Captain had given evidence to the man's previous record of good service, and that he was a good soldier who had served with him for several years. This was not accepted and the fate of the soldier was, being secured to the spokes of a gun limbers wheel and there to receive 30 lashes. The sentence was carried out to the beat of a drum, the only other sound being the sound of the lash through the air and the sickening noise of it striking flesh. The man's collapse into unconsciousness was probably a blessing for this soldier but he did recover. After a month in the infirmary and light duties the following month he was returned to active duty in time, as the regiment was to embark for the Crimean.

Chapter 2

He was quiet for several minutes and his face had taken on an expression as though he was not in the same room as me but far away. I had seen this look before and had no doubt he was back with his men. Suddenly he started talking and had taken hold of my arm above the wrist. As he told me of that day, the same one I had remembered from other nights, when he would go into one of these trances where his eyes would be focused far away in the distance.

"We were in line of advance with the Lancers in the vanguard, we were the last in line and the order had come down to advance at the trot, sabres were drawn and then, regiment will canter. The line was straight and discipline held the men to control their mounts so as when the impact with the enemy finally came we would be still together. Before the charge was sounded on the bugles we were being shelled and shrapnel was exploding above us as the Russians got the range. They were good, and knew what they were doing exactly as the shells followed us down the valley accurately even as the range decreased. Horses and men were hit, and I saw the line start to open but the troop commanders were shouting for them to close up and soon I heard the bugle. We kicked the horses into a gallop and they knew, as that sound was routine, because they were just as well trained as their riders. The ground seemed to blur as we galloped even closer to those guns but we were taking heavy casualties now as the guns were firing round shot and our lines were opened wide where men and horses had been turned into bloody pulp. I tried to find the gaps where the guns had been spaced, and where their shot was not slamming into our ranks. My troop was close to another which belonged to my friend, who had tried to help me after my house arrest and we took the same line to converge on the guns around 150 yards to our front. They had changed to grape shot now and all I could hear above the sound of screaming horses and their regular volleys was my own voice screaming orders to close into a ragged column rather than line abreast. We were then suddenly amongst them and I had images through the thickening smoke of gunners being cut down and my troop and that of my friends inflicting a savage but practised sword play. We rode in from the flank giving them no advantage to shoot in volley at a large amount of horsemen. I wouldn't like to say how many we accounted for, but we suddenly came under rifle fire from other infantry in positions that were covering their gunners. I had no idea what had happened to the rest of the regiments, because of the thick cloud of gun smoke covering the ground. When we went in we numbered around 600 but I had less than 40 now with me and my friend probably the same. I turned my horse and was greeted by my fellow officer as he came up to my blind side. Together we rallied our troop and were successful in leading another ragged charge toward the Russian riflemen. Many of my men had been wounded but were still able to wield a sword, and we rode into the muskets. Again I led them down the line and we slaughtered them where they stood. It was about this time when I felt a vicious blow to my left shoulder and after some minutes I lost complete control of my arm, it dangled uselessly, but I grabbed hold with my stiffening fingers, to the pistol boot on the saddle and was able to stop it flapping about. My fellow officer now took over and he rallied the remaining men to regroup and retreat. The only problem being we were now being attacked by Russian cavalry and constantly receiving rifle fire on our flanks. I managed to get the lads to realise independent action was our only chance and would not give the infantry as easy a shot and so we ran the gauntlet still fighting. Some of us dismounted, wounded more than once, and easy prey for those Cossack bastards. I witnessed many acts of bravery that day as all around me our lads were helping each other off the field all the way until we were out of effective range. I can remember the horror and reality; we had lost over 400 men from the command, there were men walking, still armed with their swords, others leading dying horses still on their feet and many wounded trying to limp, crawl or being helped by their comrades. Looking back, the ground over which we had charged was littered with dead and dying men and their horses. I had not had time to take in the full extent of the obvious 'Butchers Bill' on our return as all my effort and will was aimed at keeping myself in the saddle to be able to make my report to his Lordship. As we got back to where we had first deployed there was Cardigan, he was still mounted but his face was expressionless and not one word was uttered. I can still see the same trooper who a few months ago had received punishment at the wheel of the limber. He was limping from a leg wound, his horse probably dead behind him but what he said still sticks in my memory.

To this day the Captain's words are as clear as they were that night. "Go again Sir, can we?"

This story probably made me stronger and thoughts of revenge promoted my quicker healing. It had certainly given me the determination to find who was responsible for these actions on unarmed civilians had strengthened my resolve to rescue my mother and sisters and return then safe home to the ravaged   south. I had forgotten about uncle and he was keeping well out of my way and would not be left alone in my company. We planned to find information of the regiment who were involved with the transportation of the women mill workers and follow them back to their home counties to avenge this act. The Captain and I agreed these people were guilty of the worst crime that could have been committed against non- combatants and especially women but it was a soul searching moment for us as we remembered what we ourselves had done in West Virginia whilst serving with Mosby. We argued for some time and although I could see what the Captain meant by sentencing them to hang, as this would have been their fate in the British Army. I, since it was my own blood feud, was given the right to decide the fate of these men if ever we were to find them. I got the Captain to see that it would be better to just shoot them down from out of cover and then merely spirit away never to be discovered but here again I'll let you read the story and allow you to form an opinion of your own.

The Captain suggested we travel north the moment I was well enough, and as soon as my mind accepted this I felt better, more so than I had done for several weeks. However as I got stronger over the next few days and I was able to walk outside of the farmhouse onto the porch, things did get clearer. The farms livestock had all been stolen and it's out buildings had been stripped of any timber that was suitable for burning. There was much evidence of campfires close by and everything had been broken down and what was not useable left smashed. Total destruction was everywhere and our farm was not the only one. My convalescence was made all that much easier as I had the opportunity to talk and be in the company of a beautiful young woman. Beth was my younger sister, Roseanne's friend, they had gone to school together and I started to remember things that seemed from another time when our lives were so different. The evenings were times when I knew she would be around and at first I didn't take them to be that special for me. Then one day she was away from the farm visiting her parents and I realised it was her company and the sweet conversations between us that was raising me from out of the dark hole I'd descended into.   A longer convalescence would have definitely resulted with me pouring out my feelings for her, but we were all getting anxious and the longer we waited the more difficult it would be to find my family. Every day we had visitors who told similar stories about the mill workers and the other circumstances just after I had followed the Captain north. The hardships for the civilians got steadily worse. Roseanne had gone with my mother and her older sister to join the girls working in the factory. Things were that bad that in order for them to feed themselves they were forced to seek employment. Beth had been more fortunate in that she was from a family who owned a bigger farm and had slaves and freemen working the land. They had been able to sustain themselves longer but when Sherman's campaign arrived from the west and started its march to the sea it was no longer possible. Our own cavalry and army were now forced to defend, and every yard of ground given up to the enemy was fought over so fiercely and the price paid was so heavy. Not only did our forces suffer under this onslaught but the civilian population were forced to endure every kind of injustice. My uncle had done much to assist our cavalry and had acted as a scout for Wheelers cavalry. They were forced to destroy everything that would be of use to Sherman's forces and after the fall of Atlanta anything which would sustain his army was destroyed so it would be denied to the Union forces.

Much of the population suffered as they were subjected to being robbed not only by the enemy, but their own forces as well. This must have been a very hard time for all those civilians but I couldn't understand why Sherman had thought it necessary to deport women mill workers to the north. These people were no threat to his army and were not combatants. The more we talked on this the worse it became and the Captain said it was nothing else but a War Crime.

I had not thought of our plight in Virginia being as bad in comparison to what these poor civilians had been forced to suffer, but as I regained my strength and we readied ourselves for the journey north my mind started to be affected and I would find myself drifting away into long periods of tormented sleep which could be at any time of day or night. With these came the dreams, some were filled with the horrors of battle and men's faces as they died. Contorted and open mouthed they would haunt my subconscious, their screams soundless but so vivid they would bring me suddenly back to consciousness, when I would be covered in sweat and my heart would be beating so fast it felt as though it would pound out of my chest. Those people who were living with me the Captain and Beth would regularly hear me and would rush to me because my shouting had alarmed them, as it was so loud they were concerned for my safety and state of mind. Was I going crazy? After all the action and campaigning the Captain and I had been through, was it now this loss of my family that would end my days?

At this part in my story I think it would help my reader if they were invited to share my memories and share the dark places in the depths of my troubled mind. In order to be able to transfer some of the horror, mind shattering events and heart stopping action into their own thoughts. Even though it may only be for a little while, but the events leading up to my being wounded will help them understand why it was so important for me to journey to try and settle a score which could only have one outcome. Regardless of whether I would be able to return home with my mother and sisters, this was falling into second place, the leader being this undeniable desire for revenge on everyone that was involved with the abduction and suffering that was bestowed on my kin-folk.

Chapter 3

It was hot, that sort of oppressive heat that saps your energy, and makes even breathing difficult. Sweat was oozing from what seemed every orifice of my body but I was completely absorbed in my task and tried everything I had learned in the past to harmonise with nature and blend into the green wilderness that surrounded me.

I had to supply my mother and sisters with fresh meat as the last harvest had been so poor, and with the failure of this one, we had hardly been able to support ourselves sufficiently to survive the coming months. Next winters hardships and now threats of war with the North would mean we could not simply go on as we were. For the meantime, I had to succeed and bring home a deer so that we could at least, tonight have a good meal and then preserve the rest by smoking it, so it would provide food for the coming hardships that would surely be put on us.

I tried to walk by carefully placing my footfalls on open ground uncluttered by leaf or twigs. In the spaces between dried grasses and browning shrubs, withering away with the drought of that summer. I had been taught by my uncle how to walk with the breeze in my face so that if there should be any animals to my front they would not scent my presence easily, for the passage of air would be blowing my smell away from them. Every step was an effort and I was lifting my leg high so the higher underbrush beneath the red oaks would not make any noise, and as I placed my moccasin boots down again I would only place the edge of my foot then slowly roll the rest of it over until it was firmly set on the ground. In this way, one-step at a time, my progress was painfully slow but without any sound. My uncle had said it was how the Indians did it and was called ghost walking. He had gone on to tell me about how they could do this even at night and could get up close with knife or tomahawk to kill you without you even suspecting there was anyone around.

He was crippled now, and could not do many of the things needed around the farm, so it was down to me to try to take on the chores that he would normally attend to. This was my lot in those days before the war and I didn't think anything about it as I knew that there was no option and if I didn't do it then we'd starve.

He had been in the US cavalry, and had seen much action with some famous Indian fighters and would talk about his adventures sometimes, when after a meal he would settle down to smoke his pipe and raise the jug of corn liquor. He sometimes would startle me with some of the stories, but I could not help feeling he was leaving a lot out, as his face would sometimes set in an expression that was as if he was looking at something in the distance. At these times, his voice became a whisper and I had to go close to him to make out what he was saying. Without warning, he would come back as if he had been somewhere else and his voice would turn back to normal and this would frighten me a little but he would always laugh and joke about it then, but it was obvious something was troubling his mind.

I never knew any more than this as he would not say anymore, but I could remember some of the things he would say from the last time, and some of it became more complete as I began to piece things together.

I was suddenly aware of a slight movement and I could have sworn I heard the snicker of a horse. This was only for a split second and then as I froze and tried to control my breathing it was gone. My heart rate slowed a little and I strained my ears to try to pick up anything that my brain could decipher into something recognisable but there were only the sounds of the forest around me, squirrels squabbling in the treetops and other creatures moving around on their daily routines. Birds were calling and a jay was squawking at something loudly. It was probably me, but then I was under the canopy of the younger regenerated oak saplings and hoped I was out of sight.

The breeze was wafting slowly and hot like the draught of an open oven and right into my face. I knew there were deer in this area and I must try to concentrate on this task and not daydream about Uncle and his painful life.

I slowly moved my position and without a sound raised my head up the deer trail to see if there was anything up ahead. He was there, I could only see the flickering of an ear casting a flash of sunlight but it was the signal I had been waiting for and I knew instantly it was from a white tailed buck. He was unaware of my presence as I had done everything to the letter, and felt proud that uncle would be pleased with me for using all the field skills he had taught me to get myself into this position. My next step was to gain some distance without alerting him, to watch and try to work out my next move. He was probably about 150 yards up the path and was feeding head down but would move from one side of the track to the other and it was at the end of each traverse he would be partially out of sight. This was a benefit in itself as I could probably gain some ground without him running off but he could as easily, just wander off silently into the brush.

There was nothing else I could do, and forgetting some of the techniques and first rules of hunting, I moved. I felt sure he had heard me because in my excitement, my foot stood on a hidden dry branch and the weight of my footstep had caused it to make a sound like a musket shot. I froze again and knew that I could have easily ruined my chances but he came across the track again from left to right. He was looking straight at me and I was shaking with excitement, surely he had seen me and would just keep moving but he was still and then bent down to feed again. My breathing was all over the place and I could not control it but somehow I got the Hawken rifle into my shoulder and rested it on a broken branch protruding out of a small oak just at the right height. It was perfect and allowed me to sight along the barrel at a point of aim halfway between eye and ear lobe.

The Hawken and I were old friends as I had been shooting squirrels with ease with it since I was big enough to stay on my feet from its recoil. Today it was deer meat and not squirrel I was after, and I somehow got my breathing under control and waited for that moment when if you let out your breath slowly there comes a split second when everything freezes and the sight picture is perfectly still. I let the fore sight bead settle on his eye and then moved it a fraction to the left. I was unaware of actually squeezing the trigger and when the muzzle exploded with a flame, it took me completely by surprise. I left my eye sighted along the barrel and did not move my head, just as uncle had told me and through the white smoke, I saw him go down. I waited now for if he was only wounded it would be folly to rush in and prevent him from dying in peace or trying to get up to defend himself.

I waited around ten minutes, all the time praying to the ancient Gods of hunting and any more who may be listening. 'Please be dead, please be dead,' and then carefully after what seemed a lifetime I crept forward using all the cover that was available and listening for any noises that may alert me to movement.

There was no sound and I could now see him as he lay around 150 metres away. He was quite still and I could not help thanking all those that had been obviously listening, for their help. He was a magnificent beast with a set of antlers in around its third year of growth. Every part of him would be used and there was much to do once I got him back to the cabin.

I took out my bowie knife and moved him onto his back to expose his underbelly. I then thanked him for what he was gifting to my family and then gently pulled up on his fur to provide a separation of his skin at a low point between his hind legs. Lifting it upward and placing the knifepoint into the skin, I made an incision about one inch long, and then put both my fingers in to gently touch his intestines.

It was at this moment I heard the voice, so clear and loud that it made me jump and I dropped the knife from my hand. "What a nice animal," it said and that "you made a good shot".

Was I dreaming, but how? Then the realisation came to me of the horse that I had thought I had heard before. I spun around now not knowing what to do, half expecting the owner of that strange voice to shoot me and steal my food that I had worked so hard for and was for my family.

I could not believe my eyes and they must have widened at the same time as my jaw dropped. This must have amused him as he started laughing. I remember this annoyed me and I got to my feet, my head levelling with his mounted legs, but my eyes quickly taking in the spectacle before me. He was dressed in a short grey shell jacket cut to military style, leather reinforced cavalry breeches of light blue, all similar to the illustrations I had seen of US cavalrymen officers from the volunteer regiments. I remembered these being formed to campaign in the Indian wars in Texas in the 50's and when I was still a whippersnapper of a lad. His accoutrements and weapons were also of military style and the only thing missing was the sabre, I knew that was carried by cavalry regiments. His horse was tall, 16 plus hands and was magnificent. A pure black stallion, it stood relaxed under its rider's calming hands and gentle pressure of his legs. He was holding the animal just by these gestures, so gentle but even so very authoritive. The horse was obviously used to these measures as it was so relaxed it merely switched his tail at the troublesome flies.

I could not speak and this obviously amused him further but I heard him say, "That was a shot to be proud of," and went on to ask what the musket was and where it comes from. I now found my voice and told him the Hawken had belonged to my uncle and that he had given it to me now, as he was not able to hunt as he had done before he enlisted to go to Texas with the volunteers. This seemed to interest him and he enquired of my uncle's name. I studied his face and tried to read in it if there was any reason I should not say my uncle's name to this man who carried himself so confidently, and whose charisma began to work on me. He reminded me of all the stories and reports in the gazette about cavalrymen and the brave actions they had fought. This one was a fine example in the flesh and I began to warm to him, and felt as though I could easily answer his questions and more unbelievable, I was eager to give him what he wanted.

He looked at me hard when I told him my uncle was called John and that his family name was the same as mine Schofield. He jumped from the saddle and hitting the ground came to put his arms around me in a powerful grip. I was startled and struggling for breath as he released me and then laughing said, "It's a good thing I was amused by your hunting techniques, I may not have followed."

I was a little annoyed again, but I could not work out how any horsemen could have followed me through such country. How had he controlled the horse and stopped it making any sound? Some questions I put to him and in answer, he merely smiled and asked about my uncle. It proved from the exchange that they both knew each other and he was keen to see him again, after the last time they were together when he told me uncle had saved his life. It was a fascinating tale of savagery and vicious actions while both were serving in the same regiment.

Chapter 4

I finished the field preparation of the deer and he helped me load the carcass onto his horse. We then made our way back to our family cabin. As we approached, I could hear my two sisters arguing about something and as I turned to look at him, he was smiling and saying that, "He hoped there would be an invite for supper."

He could have stayed forever for me as I had been totally taken by him and even then, after so short a time I think, I would have followed him down the barrel of cannon. My emotions and warmest feelings for this man were repeated many times that night as he made his presence known to my uncle, things were magical, and I do not think, I had seen two grown men show so much open affection toward each other. That night after my mother and sisters had finished all the chores, clearing from the gigantic meal the buck had provided, I was allowed to sit in these two men's company. The jug of corn liquor fuelled the talk and my uncle was so happy he had continually smoked his pipe exhausting his months' supply of tobacco. I was amazed by their talk and enthralled by the tales of the actions in Texas. These were short but never the less brutal and savage. As the evening went on into the small hours of the morning, the talk came around to why this meeting had really been important to our visitor. I was starting to call him Captain now as his easy authority and charisma seemed to warrant it. My uncle's respect for this man was obvious but equally the Captain returned this with an easy manner.

He was looking for horses and men for putting together a unit of cavalry, and then volunteering to fight for the South. He was convinced there would be war and his loyalties were firmly grounded with offering his services to some old comrades who definitely would be resigning their commissions with the US cavalry and looking to swear allegiance to Jefferson Davis.

He then talked of his plan to form an out of the ordinary unit that would be the eyes and ears of the army, and provide intelligence of enemy movements, troop strengths and lines of supply and communication. He was convinced the lessons learned from the mistakes and so dearly paid for in Texas and Kansas would not be repeated, and which could be used to advantage in training an elite unit. This would encompass the entire Captain's experience from somewhere he called European fights and all the most recent with another most worthy cavalry, Apache and Cheyenne. He questioned my uncle about other comrades they had both served with and there were a few, which he knew, were still contactable. His next question was if uncle would accompany him to find these men and to persuade them to join him once again.

He went quiet then and looked into the fire but after some time he replied that he was not fit enough to follow his old leader, but that his nephew, namely I could, if his mother permitted, follow his service. I knew he was nearly always in pain from his back and legs and on some occasions when he had been bathing down by the river I had seen the long deep scar on his back and the wasted muscles in his right leg.

I was speechless, and in one thought so eager to please both these men but in the other frightened, I would not be able to do my duty. To make them proud and to prove to my uncle he had given me the best training anyone could have wished for. Training I would be able to use in helping me take on more, but this time, from this man who would demand everything I had to give him and more.

He answered that this was good for him and the next day, if my mother accepted it, then I was to accompany him to contact his other comrades. He then told me about my uncle's injuries and how he had come by them. They were from an action with the Cheyenne when a large war party had cut off a small detail of cavalrymen from their main unit. The action had been swift but savage and they had tried to fight their way through them, but despite each one of them shooting several braves with their pistols, they were still surrounded and outnumbered. The carbines were single shot and once empty, useless to a mounted man, saving for that as a club. This left the sabre. He said that for him it was the last resort and told me of the Cheyenne he had killed who was on top of uncle and cutting out his leg muscles so as when he died and entered the sacred hunting grounds, wouldn't be able to control a horse. He then explained how he was then taken with two arrows and a lance point in the chest. Falling near to where uncle lay bleeding, he went unconscious and not until after he came around was he to learn, that uncle had covered his body with his own. This must have satisfied the remainder of the war party, both troopers were dead and they didn't have time to confirm this before the remainder of the troop came up forcing them to retire. So uncle had saved the Captain by covering his body from view and the fact there was so much blood, it looked likely both were not even worth dismounting for.

The next day I was given my mother's blessing to follow the Captain and it was now understood there would be a war with the North very soon. My uncle had told us where we may find the comrade they both had served with. As it happened, our destination was close to where the Captain would also be able to find horses, for close by there lived a breeder whose bloodline produced some of the finest mounts in the South. He also knew the ex-troopers, and it was probable his allegiances would definitely be for the Confederacy, which was the term, being used to describe the States seceding from the North.

We were to travel to Cobb County near to a town called Kennesaw. It was about two days march at an easy pace. Uncle only had a team of mules and I was given one of these to take, as possibly there may be a chance to make a trade later in which a horse could be found. The Captain advised me on the selection and I ended up with one of the most amiable beasts and the best choice for the purpose. As he said, if I was to join the cavalry unit he was forming then the mule would be useful for carrying equipment, ammunition or supplies. My training started almost immediately we set out, and he was telling me there was noise coming from my saddlebags and the haversack I had across my shoulders. The Yanks will know we're coming all the way in Washington he would say. This was only the beginning and every hour he would show me manoeuvres that would either allow us to travel without sound or allow us to stay hidden in the surrounding vegetation. This would always amaze me, but he would say that people tended to look straight at things and never to see through them. He would stand mounted in the forefront of some scrub trees that were in shadow and then ask me to come along the trail, and then shout when I had seen where he and the horse were visible. Often I was right up on his position, and not more than ten yards from him before I shouted. Then there was the rifle drill and target practice. He would select random targets along the trail, a pinecone or a small rock and get me to fire at them. At first, I could not support the long Hawken rifle well enough to be on target but he would explain that I had to shoot instinctively and bring up the muzzle quickly and when it passed the target, squeeze off the trigger. I could not perfect this, as it was different to settling behind the rifle and waiting until you had a steady shot, then firing, but this was so different. He would show me how his own weapon, a Sharp cavalry carbine could find its target three hundred yards away and he would hit it time after time. I did make some slow progress and for this, I think he was pleased as he promised me a Sharpe as soon as we could get hold of any. On the third day, we reached the small farm in the foothills around Kennesaw, the two small mountains visible in the morning sunrise in the distance. There was a man in the road as we came up, but I was unsure if this was, our contact. He was about the same age as my uncle but from the look of him, was able bodied, not crippled as he was. He stopped what he had been doing and set the wheelbarrow down to stare at the two of us, I mounted on my uncle's mule and himself on that beautiful black horse.

The Captain called out in that sing song voice I was to become so familiar with. "Column of two's, point and rear troopers out." He stared harder now and looked as if had seen a ghost, his face ashen, but his eyes seemed to smile and I could see the tears coming down his cheeks and making tracks through the soil crusted on his face.

"Captain is that you, by all that's holy it couldn't be." Well by this time we were up alongside him, the Captain had leaped from the saddle and was lifting him off his feet. I marvelled again as this was no small a man but he was as though a babe in his arms and could do little but go along with the ride.

Chapter 5

We were soon ushered toward the house, the Captain introducing me as John's nephew. The next few hours were spent again with me listening to the most exciting tales I had ever heard. These were like those I had heard from old books like King Arthur's Knights, round tables, and memories of my father, as he would read me a bedtime story. Only these were real and about action in the desert with Indian warriors, so fierce the pictures in my mind were frightening. Little did I know then that what I was to see with the Captain would pale them into obscurity. We talked through until the late hours and into the morning with the Captain and his old trooper comrade, waiting for the dawn light helped along with alternate sip from the stone liquor jug. His name was Silas and it turned out he was a Sergeant in the volunteer cavalry unit the Captain had led during the Indian wars. Many names were called that night but there were only a few that were left that could muster for active service. Many were, as my uncle, invalided out as unfit and were all suffering from injuries both physical and mentally from those actions of 55-58.

The Captain did not say much about his army career in the British Army, but I knew he was a professional. That night he had mentioned about how he had found himself in the right place at the right time to be able to offer his services in the cavalry on the frontier, and had met a Lt. Stuart, an officer in the newly formed regiment 1st US Cavalry. This regiment was created from the mounted rifles and dragoons. He then went on to describe this officer, and told me that his intention was to travel north to join him and that Silas and I could be part of the plan if we wished. He had come to the Americas from all the European wars, and his trouble going up against the military justice system that would have had him to the gallows if he had not slipped through their clutches. As soon as it was light, Silas took us both outside onto the porch where he had his bow. This resembled the one's I had seen before and knew they were of Indian design and make. He promptly notched an arrow onto the string and drawing it back merely shot it as soon as it was drawn back. I looked at the flight of the shaft but only caught up with it as it struck a wooden target made from a thin slice of a tree branch.

The shaft quivered in the centre of this log about fifty yards distant. The Captain merely commented that Silas had not lost his touch and that the visit to his farm was to ask him if he would train other lads to somewhere close to his own skill level.

The following day, well before daybreak, we were on the road. The country was quiet but everywhere there seemed there was an air of expectancy. This was hard to explain but it was like when there is that calm before a twister comes howling in destroying everything in its path. To bring this home to me the Captain had explained that it would only take Virginia to secede from the Union and it would be all out War. The task for us was to first to see if we could purchase some good horses from this breeder that Silas had told us of.

We had been going for most of the day, but by late afternoon we were opening the outer gate of this ranch with strong split rail fencing, good grazing, and tidy well-maintained barns and outhouses. There were some horses grazing in the nearest pastures, I was impressed at how strong and healthy they looked. The owner must have seen us as he came down the road from the main house buildings. He seemed to recognise Silas and they greeted each other warmly. He introduced the Captain and me as his friends and informed him of our intention to purchase horses with the intention of taking then north to enlist in the Confederate cavalry as soon as they were called for. My childhood friends lived close by in this county and I enquired if he knew them, or could say where they were. He listened intently to all of us and invited us into the house where his wife busied herself to offer us refreshment and coffee.

After a while and talk on many matters, he became annoyed and his good nature seemed to vanish. It was the subject of State rights agitators that made him change and he soon began to tell us of these people doing a great harm to the cause of the new Confederacy, as they seemed to be convinced that the new government in Richmond was out to look after themselves, and the Southern States would be left penniless. The corruption had already started and it was obvious some wealthy planters had done their upmost to disrupt the plans of new government. There were rumours of a new tax system, but this had aggravated the situation even more and strengthened the cause of the agitators. He then started to tell us of the armouries owned by the State and how when they were ordered to prepare to equip newly mustered regiments with good modern or newly modified arms, they had simply ignored the order. Instead, they selected all the oldest and less efficient small arms and simply kept the best weapons safely locked-up inside.

What made this more annoying, were the militia units and State home guard units that had been issued with the best weapons available. European revolvers and rifled muskets, breach loading cavalry carbines and Colt and Remington revolvers. I could see our Captain begin to look more interested as he started to question the rancher in earnest. He was asking whereabouts these armament depots were and if there was any such units of militia close by. We were told then of a unit of slave hunters who operated out of this county and earned their living by hunting down runaway slaves and returning them to their masters for a bounty. The Captain seemed to be in his element and he questioned the rancher even more, asking if he could tell us where these men may be found. We were given full details of the country where these men would patrol regularly and I could feel there was going to be some action shortly as the Captain started to outline a plan in which we were going to relieve these people of the weapons that would better serve the Confederate army.

So with the help of the rancher, whose name escapes me at this time as my memory is not what it was, but I do know he helped us put together a rough sort of plan. I was allowed to sit in on these and I sat almost shock, at the Captain's ability to organise and by questioning the rancher on what to me seemed like every detail of the last place he knew they were, and their area of patrolling to capture runaways. The next morning before daylight, we had already saddled up and were saying our goodbyes to the rancher and his wife when it was still dark. We parted company, and I was leading two horses, both thoroughbreds, whose lineage could be traced back to the original stock the breeder had started with 40 years previously. They were fine animals both geldings and black in colour high to the shoulder and measuring 15-16 hands. The Captain had another mount with him. This was a beautiful stallion of high spirit but in his hands seemed to be peaceful and contented. The mule I had set out from home upon was also with me and brought up the rear of my string. We were going to find these slave hunters and we travelled north along the roads, which were still at this early hour, and we met no other travellers. Silas was also mounted on a fine looking mount, she was a steady well-tempered filly that suited him and looking at them both, you would have sworn they had been together for years.

We had talked about going to find my childhood friends Squirrel, Clem and Joe, who were living and working on a plantation not too far away. Sales of cotton had risen and the planters were making a fortune but the newly formed Richmond government had tried to impose taxes that would provide war funds needed to supply and arm the Confederate forces. This we had learned from the horse breeder and had been met with much protest and mistrust of the new authorities.

The plantation was reached before nightfall and we were able to make contact with my childhood companions. It was explained to the planter what we were going to do, and the Captain enquired if he was prepared to help in any way. This was met by a definite refusal and the owner went on to tell us of his distinct mistrust of the government in Richmond and his opinions that they would be only looking out for themselves.

However, we were invited into the colonial looking plantation house with its fine and elegant reception rooms. Refreshments were served to us all and we drank cooled lemonade from fine glasses while looking around at the rich and expensive looking furniture and decorations.

Chapter 6

Our Captain seemed to get along with the planter, and it was soon agreed that my childhood friends could accompany us on our enlistment into the Confederate forces and he would supply food and a little money for our journey to Virginia. We were soon ushered out of the main house, and only the Captain offered accommodation for the night. We were to be accommodated in one of the barns but even these were fine places compared with what I had been used to back on the farm. Our Captain was soon back the following morning and was enjoying himself by giving us a boots and saddles British army style with a riding boot squarely placed into our backsides. He was now confident we would be able to find these slave hunters and had gained other information of their whereabouts from the planter over dinner that night. Joe had foolishly made a comment about the planter's wife, this greatly annoyed the Captain, and I felt sorry for him as he was knocked to the ground where he received a further barrage of kicks. Silas was then ordered to get him to his feet and it was plain to see both were shaken by the Captain's sudden change of mood. The Captain then explained to us all that he would not tolerate any disrespect of either civilians or their property and so long as we were under his command we would respect his wishes and obey orders. From that morning, we had become his men and even though his treatment of Silas could have been perceived as unjust, Silas and all of us just accepted it. The horses were readied and we were on the road with him leading within fifteen minutes. Silas knew the Captain from before as they were comrades from the early cavalry days, and he did not seem upset at all merely saying we were in the army now and in his regiment.

We travelled along the narrow roads and open country of Georgia between farms and good grazing land. The weather was fresh with cool temperatures in the early hours, but then getting pleasant when the sun came out.

The trees were all in full leaf and everywhere there was that fresh smell of early summer when nature works its magic and you feel so alive, it seemed that this war was only part of our leader's imagination. How stupid that seems now looking back, but we were not to know although I was sure Silas had ideas but was keeping them to himself. It was good to be in company with my childhood friends and Joe who seemed to be enjoying himself. He looked like an Indian warrior with buckskin trousers and shirt, His weapons again could have been easily mistaken as coming from an Indian brave, with five foot flat bow and arrow pouch, tomahawk in his belt and his Hawken rifle slung on a strap across his shoulders. We were the only ones that had weapons apart from the Captain. He was carrying a Sharps carbine attached to a cross belt with a rifle sling attachment. This enabled the carbine to hang on his right side within easy reach. He was also in possession of a Remington revolver in a closed holster on his belt, and I had noticed that on the saddle there was another holster for a Colt .44. He was also in possession of a cavalry sabre but this was stowed carefully on the left side of the saddle, but so securely it did not move.

We found them on the second night as we were travelling along a high road between some trees. The sound of shouting and some argument alerted me as I was in the lead and without the horse string, this being given over to Clem bringing up the rear. It was unnecessary to inform the Captain for he was right up with me in an instant. I knew this was it, and my stomach muscles began to tighten and a bead of sweat ran down my face. He spoke quietly now and I heard him say 'work your way around them, steer yourself around by looking at the campfire and wait for my signal, a shot, then ride into them with your rifle readied.' I set off slowly hoping not to make a sound and trying to remember all the things he had told me in the days after we had travelled to the horse breeders. I was careful not to alarm my horse, and I managed to get hold of my nerves so he would not sense my fear. Using the fire as a marker I slowly made my way all the way into their rear. I was there and my throat was as dry as the desert sands. There was a lump in my throat, but I took the Hawken from around my shoulders and checked the primer cap. All was good and I knew the rifle was properly charged and loaded, so all I had to do was wait.

This was not long, as there was a loud report of a revolver shot shattering the silence of the night. I put heel to the horse and he shot forward as though he knew what we had to do and we flew through the brush and past small trees and were still in that breakneck pace as we burst out into the clearing where they were camped. I only just managed to control the gelding and pull him up. I had the Hawken levelled at the nearest figure that was standing startled by the fire. I was only just aware of the others crashing into the campsite on the other side and saw the orange muzzle flash from the Captains revolver, and the figure by the fire crumpling to the ground. I saw another figure on the edge of my vision and as though in slow motion the Hawken came around to align with my full vision. I was not aware I had pulled the trigger but the rifle bucked in my hands and through the flash and smoke, I saw the figure drop. The Captain swung around and his horse reared onto hind legs. It was like clockwork, and rider and horse were in such harmony there was no doubt of the outcome. He fired at two figures and both went down, one with a spurt of blood from his chest and the second with a large part of his skull flying off followed by a fountain of blood. Joe must have selected the remaining slave hunter as I heard the passage of that shaft, and saw in amazement it had found its target, penetrating the neck and continuing, to end with the arrowhead protruding 6 inches out the other side.

I was shaking with the shock, but he only shouted to check around and see if there were any of them still alive. "Weapons get the weapons," he was saying but I must have been really suffering and I had not stopped shaking. My concentration was gone and he had to grab me to get my full attention. As I was feeling sick this rough treatment caused me to vomit, some of it sticking in my throat making me cough and stagger around retching. He ordered the others to go through the camp and collect everything we could use. He then turned to me and said that this was only the start of it and that it would become easier. When you first kill another human being, it is hard on your conscious and you have to get through it. Thinking back he was merely trying to prepare me in the best way he knew, for there was going to be a lot more battles and situations where I had to react instinctively and without hesitation.

Chapter 7

It was while he was going through this with me the others found them. There were three of them, a woman and a man with a boy around 14 years or so. They were in a bad state and had been beaten, the man having been whipped. He was very weak but despite this, they were shackled together with chains from steel neckbands. The woman was withdrawn and silent, she had probably been raped as her cheap cotton dress was torn and there were wounds on both her knees where the skin had been worn away. Seeing these poor slaves brought me to my senses and the Captain was only too eager for me to care for them. I managed to get the neck chains and collars off and offered them all water from a big canteen. The man could only just swallow and I had to leave him to the woman who soaked a piece of her torn dress and squeezed it into his mouth moistening his lips. The boy was sullen and his fear and mistrust of us was obvious.

The Captain was eager to question them and he was asking the woman if she knew where they had been making for when they were arrested. She was reluctant to say, but after he assured her that he had nothing to do with State home forces she started to tell him about the journey. Our Captain was well informed and he pressed her for information on the underground network of safe houses and sympathisers who helped runaways to escape to freedom in the North. This proved to be ineffective, but she did say that there were many such State Guard units and it had become almost impossible to make it out of Georgia without help. I could not understand what he was after asking about the escape network, but after a while when she was convinced we did not mean them any harm, she become more helpful. The story of their capture and what had become of them since, was not a pretty one. They were to be taken back to the plantation from where they had come. Each one had a brand on their upper arms that signified the location of their owner estate and as they had been troublesome, her man had been beaten and whipped to within an inch of his life. She was made to watch during this ordeal, four men repeatedly raped her, and all the time in sight of her man stretched out but still conscious of his woman's plight.

 This made me feel better as the Captain had said these were scum of the earth and they would continue to do this work rather than enlist in the Confederate forces now being mustered in Virginia for the defence of Richmond, and a probable campaign to attack the Yankee capital. I remember feeling confused and troubled by what had happened. I was 17 years old and until now, my life had been a peaceful one. The Captain had changed all that and together we had just murdered five people. My thoughts were so troubled by this, but as I took in more of the plight these people were in it became clear that they did not deserve treatment such as this. My experience of slaves and plantations was very limited but as the boy and his mother recovered, they were able to tell me of why they had been forced to get away. Her son was to be sold to another planter, who had a reputation of cruel treatment and his overseers were experts at administering it. The whippings, torture and rape were everyday things. The Captain had told us of the cotton prices being at an all-time high and this had caused the plantation owners to boost their production, which made the lives of their workers unbelievably miserable. She went on to say that there was no hope, and their only chance of surviving was to try to run away. She had known of no other successful escapes out of the area and in fact had witnessed the punishment of several who had been caught by the bounty hunters, nearly all of them dying at the hands of their torturers. Some women being separated from the family group to be sold to other plantations to live out a miserable existence until they could not stand it any longer and the journey to the pearly gates stopped their suffering.

I was very withdrawn and although I had taken it all in, there were many unanswered questions. Answers came slowly as I listened to what our leader was saying. I could not see him as a murderer or even a bad person because I was beginning to understand him and what he had been through. The things he must have seen in battle, and the wife, friends and fellow soldiers that were now lost to him. I would have done whatever he told me to do without question but there was another side to this as I knew he was an experienced soldier and leader who knew a lot about everything because he had seen it happen and could tell when it was likely to show itself again. I was pleased with myself when he said I had done well, explaining the very circumstances of our attack on the camp. He told me that what I had done was one of the most effective methods of close quarter battle, and it was my instinctive movements by following my vision around and then squeezing the Hawken's trigger had probably saved all of them from being chased down and hung by State Home Guard forces. It was discovered they had been equipped with good small arms and ammunition. Each man owned two revolvers, either Colt .44's or the Remington. Their rifles were Sharps carbines and almost new, the Captain was convinced they had recently been issued from the State armoury.

This made him angry, as it was becoming known that most cavalrymen going to Virginia for enlisting carried shotguns or old and broken muskets and pistols. He issued these new weapons to all of his perspective troopers and later showed us how to load and service them. What was troubling him now was what we were to do with the slaves but this was soon decided and he ordered me to look at getting the injured slave ready to travel. Joe was pretty good at doctoring for he was experienced and we soon had him bandaged and got him onto a horse. The woman was in much pain but he had made an infusion from willow bark and told her to administer this, as it would ease the pain when swallowed. Clem and Squirrel had been detailed to bury the five men and their horses were added to our string including saddles and equipment we'd taken. We managed to ready everyone before first light and as the sun was coming up, we had been on the road for over an hour. His plan was to deliver these to the next safe house on the underground network but the woman did not know the best route to get us there. She told him that it was only a legend that there was an Underground Railroad with stations and conductors along its route, where runaways could shelter and get help before being passed onto the next safe house. He said that he had seen a poster offering big money for the return of these fugitives, sometimes set at thousands of dollars and she agreed this was how it was and why there were very few successful attempts. The man was getting stronger and with Joe's doctoring was making good progress back to health. He said that he was merely following the North Star at night and during the day hiding in the woods. As we travelled, they all gained strength and began to help in every way the Captain wanted. The man at first did not trust us but the woman assured him we were not slavers and our direction of travel meant we were going away from Georgia.

Chapter 8

The Captain got us together and explained we would soon be going out across the border into North Carolina and then into Virginia. He thought the best way was to go up into the mountains and follow the high ground and ridges not normally frequented by many people until we came into country where we could find the camps of the newly forming Confederate Army of Virginia. The slave boy was becoming friendlier and he would always be around the Captain. He did not seem to mind this and after a few days of hiding during the day and travelling slowly by night they became very close. He must have thought that their only chance was to stick with us and that the woman and the man could possibly find employment around the Capital.

I had come to some agreement with my thoughts and the fact of killing that man was now becoming more justified, if I hadn't been able to stop him from escaping we would have all been on the run now and would have soon been in action with these State troopers. As it was, we stood a chance, as the slave hunters were buried in concealed graves along with all the tools of their trade. Their horses were now with us so there was nothing obvious that may alert our enemies.

On the third day, we came upon a smallholding with barns and a log cabin dwelling. The woman told us this was the house as she was sure as she could be by recognising it from a description given by a misfortunate slave who had been captured and returned to the plantation. There were bedding quilts hung on the porch rail and these and the manner they were placed were a secret code giving anyone who knew the key a signal that this was a safe house. I can remember finding out later in the war from another darkie working on the

Richmond defences that this was true, but so much of a secret that only a few knew about it. However we were not sure at that time, if it would be safe so we watched the house for several hours and only when it was found that there were only three occupants' two women and a man did the Captain consider approaching. It was down to the boy to make contact now and the Captain asked the woman to put him at ease and have him walk him alone toward the house. If there were any problems then we were to ride in and rescue him. It went fine and he was welcomed. I could see him pointing toward the woods where we all were in concealment. There was nothing for it now and we came out of cover and trotted towards the house. The man and the two women were startled and they were suspicious but the slave woman provided them with some information that was obviously some prearranged code, for everything calmed down and we were welcomed into the house. The Captain detailed two of us to hide the horses, feed, and water them in one of the barns.

The network for escaping slaves was not as it was made out to be, and there were many rumours of hundreds of runaways following the railway to freedom, but as we talked with our new friends who were sheltering us, the truth was that it was very much a legend and so far away from reality. They were religious people and probably why they were obsessed with helping and hiding runaways. We learned that it was very unusual for escapees from the more southerly states to reach freedom. Even if they reached the North things were not forced to be easy for them to remain free.

The people in the North were very mistrusting of the runaways and there were slave catchers everywhere just waiting to bring back people to the South where there was still money to be made returning slaves. I listened to this, and it made me wonder if there was any sense to any of this, but the Captain had already put things into perspective and suggested the woman Martha could live and work in Richmond. There was going to be a need for nurses and hospital orderlies, as once it started these places would become a living horror. The man Johan could get employment working as a labourer on the defence lines that would surely be erected around the Capital. This way they would be together and could be relatively secure under the organisation of the military. The Captain had told me later that he knew an engineering officer who he suspected would be around the Capital on the staff who would be definitely involved with the construction work, and it was with a favour in mind he felt he could ask if Johan could be afforded military protection. He then offered to take on the boy Jacob as his own groom as they had become close over the time we had travelled together.

Our friends advised us now on our best route and they explained that all the more direct routes through the Carolinas would be crawling with state militia and slave catchers. Our best plan would be to work our way into the foothills and then to follow the ridge lines in the mountains to work our way North and East before travelling West again to reach one of the cavalry training camps. Our runaways would have the best chance of survival travelling with us and when we reached Virginia they could consider their options again.

Chapter 9

Crossing into North Carolina near a mining town called Copper was where we observed some large logging operation with mules and sleds being used to extract timber from sections of the forest. It was being done with regularity and as we observed from a closer position there were rail tracks over which open wagons pulled by mule teams were being used to carry lumber to a lower location, where there were huge piles of rock and man-made piles of earth. It was around these that the air seemed to be laden with a poisonous thick fog. What remained of the foliage and grass seemed to be burned off and there were little signs of bird or animals. It was a man-made hellhole and I wanted no part of this, but the Captain thought it was the workings of a mine where copper was extracted by furnaces from the mother-load of rock. There would be plenty of fodder for the horses to be had here and he was already planning to relieve these miners of some to our more worthy cause.

That night we left the runaways in good cover high in the trees under the charge of Squirrel and Silas. We then carefully made our way down to the camp area and were immediately alarmed by the noise from the buildings. It was apparent there was no order or sobriety in the place as we saw numerous individuals definitely the worse for drink staggering about between the shacks and storehouses. The drinking houses were doing a good trade, and the sound of men shouting and fighting was unmistakeable. We were in need of provisions for our journey north through the mountains and we were all in agreement that it would be relatively simple to relieve these miners of the provisions we would require.

That night we gathered in the ruined forested area close by the outskirts of town, and there, in the darkness the Captain explained what he wanted from us. The whole thing was again centred on stealth and the ability to gain entry into some barns and stable building near to some large corrals where the mules were kept. It was probable there would be little trouble at that time in the early hours, around three in the morning. The order of things were put into motion and I can remember being detailed along with Joe to enter the barn not far from our hiding place while the other one and the Captain would act as look-outs. He insisted both ends of the street most likely which would be from where we could expect trouble were watched.

With everything in place Joe and I made a stealthy approach as close as we could towards the open, then with each one of us covering the other we made a dash for the shadows under the walls of the building. We stood together in the shadows and listened for any tell-tale sounds we may have been seen. There was no sound, save those of the night, and I gathered some confidence.

The night was hot and I was already covered in sweat but started drawing some inner strength from my companion. He was grinning at me and I could make out his rotten teeth. He knew I was suffering with that emotion of mixed excitement and pure terror. Thankfully I was able to bring everything under control as he motioned for us to make a move toward the big double doors at the far end of the wall.

We made our way silently and with great care and were now standing at the door. It did not resist Joe's persuasion and he swung it open slowly and we slipped inside quickly. We were immediately shrouded in a blanket of pure blackness, but after a few seconds my eyes were able to make out some shapes and objects. There was a space at the far end where the open ends of the barn looked out onto the fenced coral. This allowed us to see a line of food bins against the sides of some stalls. There were horses stabled in some of them, but Joe moved amongst them and I felt myself following his example and we had no trouble soothing them into silence. He pushed me towards the bins and close by I noticed empty sacks and started to fill one of them with oats with a scoop I had found.

Quickly we filled around five sacks each and some others we stuffed with fresh hay. Joe now indicated we stash these by the door and went back for what was left. It was obvious that we could not make the trip carrying them all and would have to make two journeys, so with Joe holding the door I struggled across the open space and into the edge of the trees. I dumped them down and waited for the signal Joe would give before rushing back to the cover of the barn walls. With me now watching Joe made his run laden with his sacks and reached the cover of the trees. It was now my turn to make sure all was well, and then gives Joe the all clear. I was not aware straight away that there was anything wrong but Joe had seen him before I knew anything. Joe was making for the opposite end of the barn nearest the coral and before I could make out what his purpose was, I heard the noise of a drunken voice mumbling and talking and really close to where I was standing. I froze and to this day I still wonder if I would have been capable of putting up any sort of defence had the owner of this voice been capable of attacking me.

I had no time to think about it as with a blur of movement right on the edge of my vision I saw the two of then come swiftly together. It was a scene that often reoccurs as a stage play in my nightmares and one that would be repeated by not only Joe but all of us as we became more and more drawn into the horrors of war. My vision seemed to have cleared and there was a definite difference in the light so I was able to see Joe and this drunk entwined in a death struggle. He had an arm around the man's neck from behind and was holding him in a vice-like grip that was preventing him from breathing. I saw his legs being lifted off the floor and they began to twitch and kick but Joe was lowering him to the floor now and he merely gestured for me to watch the door again. We made it together across the open space without making a sound and we were quickly joined by the Captain. The sacks were gathered up and all four of us made our way back silently towards our hiding place where the runaways and Squirrel were waiting.

Our Captain quickly questioned Joe and he ordered us all to make ready for marching before daybreak. The fodder was loaded on the spare horses and we made our way along a narrow trail that was steadily taking us higher into the hills.   We made good progress but much of the travel was under the cover of darkness. This didn't seem to bother our runaways and they became accustomed to our much regimented, military methods on the march. The Captain would always have us spaced out along an extended single line but with the man and women in the centre. He would have the boy close by himself and held the lead reins of his horse. Strict silence was kept at all times and communication was by signals and a low whistle resembling a bird call he had shown us. In this way we travelled the high country having climbed into the foothills and along ridges. In the dawn's early light he would call us to a halt. We then would go into hiding and he would take one of us off at a time to familiarise ourselves with the coming night's direction of travel. The horses were our main concern now and we had to decide on the safest route for them, not only for their safety but so as not to alarm them in any way causing them to go into panic. This would be done before we settled into the daytime routine of concealing our campfire and organising a 'stag' the Captain's term for a system of people being on continuous watch, changing every three hours. When we came across isolated habitation, either a shack or small farm we would detour around in the small hours of the early morning and then lay-up so as to be able to observe whoever was living there and try and determine their business and way of life. Any suspicious behaviour or actions by the habitants was treated with distrust, and we would avoid putting ourselves any closer than was necessary. We never made ourselves known to anyone on those nights, and during the day the time was spent tending for the horses and talking away the time to use up the hours of idleness. Here again the Captain never failed to show us different method of making our new soldiering life easier. He showed us how to make a small cooking fire called a 'snake hole,' sunk into an earth bank, but with only a small chimney hole made by driving a pointed stake down through the soil roof for the smoke to escape. This was only large enough for a small amount of concentrated vapour to vent skywards and this would more easily disperse itself on the wind. This way if only dry wood was used the fire would not give away our position and to make sure of this we were ordered to go some distance from our camp and look, returning to tell him if there were any tell-tale signs. This he would do with the rest of the campsite and even in the evenings as we were preparing to leave one person, the last to leave would take a leafy branch and sweep over the ground where we had been camped, in order to disperse any signs of disturbance and scattering all human signs of us ever being there.

Our leader was a strange man but I had grown so very fond of him that it was possible my opinion was clouded, as I would not question anything he said or any of his instructions. The others were of the same opinion also and we didn't see any problems so long as he was with us and we were content to have him lead us North, us for the Confederate cavalry and the man, woman and boy hopefully to freedom. Silas and Joe were another two good reasons we stayed undiscovered and Joe was able to feed us with the wild game he would bring down with his flat bow.

It is only after all these years that I have come to question and wonder at his ideas and outlook he had on life. It was as though the only thing that mattered to him then, was us getting to the Army, nothing else was so important and it didn't matter how or who he took along as long as we got to our destination safely and together. I wondered why we had ambushed those slave catchers and why we hadn't joined with the other two regiments being mustered in Georgia at that time, for obviously we would have travelled North together, probably enjoying much support from our home states and not as we were, hiding and living like animals skulking about in the darkness. My memory seems to be cloudy here as it may have been we were all waiting to see what Virginia did; if she seceded then it would be war.

It was only just recently when I have had so much time on my hands that the realisation came to me why he had gone about it in that way. He was a natural teacher and he never stopped relaying the knowledge that he wanted us to learn and all this in order to prepare us for the coming training that was to make us one of the finest scouting cavalry troops either side had ever seen. No one had ever used cavalry in that way before and as the war ground on the importance of this became more recognisable and valued. Our old beloved General must have had so much in common with the Captain that it was almost unreal, telepathic, how they could sense a situation and read just how an enemy would react. They could put themselves and their troopers, even when greatly outnumbered, in the best place to overwhelm and out manoeuvre. This quality was uncanny and no way learned, it wasn't in any books and there weren't many instructors at any military colleges who had the same senses, so to me it was nothing you would be able to learn or pick up naturally. Many things can be taught and learned but this kind of genius coupled with luck had to come from within the leader himself, and without having served with these types of soldiers in campaign and battle I wouldn't have believed any officer could possess such abilities, far in advance of any other officers the North or South had ever known.

His morals were probably founded in fair play and justice, he was from a foreign country where the aristocracy were untouchable and had the law in their own hands. Ordinary citizens who had fallen foul of this system, like himself were not given any chance to have any kind of fair play shown to them for once a person was condemned little mercy would be shown to them. Here the situation was very much the same as before the war, the land owners had enormous power over the country. Once hostilities started there was still this reluctance to comply and pay war taxes to a Confederate government so far away in Richmond. This is why he was so inflamed when we were told of modern weapons being held in State armouries, and not given up to regiments about to muster and march . The trade in catching runaways was always profitable and attracted the scum of society. They were able to play half-heartedly at being patriotic by joining home guard regiments, never leaving the county while others joined their friends and mustered into fighting regiments, that were never issued with these modern weapons, but forced to go into battle with worn out antiques and shotguns.

Things for these rich land owners and many state politicians had gone well for too many years, and they were not going to commit themselves fully to a cause where they may be stripped of all their wealth. Little did they know what was looming in the near future and that the South would be torn apart literally and their wealth would be stripped from beneath them, much of it being stolen by both Northerners and Southerners alike.

We made our way towards the North Carolina border and at Tugaloo we climbed into the foothills up gentle enough ramps. The going was pretty steady and all of us had little problem keeping up with the Captain and meeting his sometimes demanding expectations. Our runaways by this time had very much become part of his little army and he treated them fairly, speaking to them just the same way he did to us, explaining how they should care for their animals and treat them with respect. We would alternate walking for two hours and then riding for a similar period. The path was through wooded areas perched on sometimes knife edge ridges for most of the way so far, but suddenly we would come out of the trees and there you would be as though suspended above the clouds looking down through them to where you occasionally make out further peaks lower down. It was sometimes breath taking but for the

Captain he only saw it as being an advantage over any enemy trying to outmanoeuvre us. There would always be one of us fifty yards in the lead and the same with the tail end, a rider similarly placed following us but keeping their eyes concentrated mostly from where we had just come. For the most part the trail was very narrow, restricting us to travel in single file. The runaways had become just as much a useful part of the Captains patrol as any of us, but we boys and Joe treated them with distrust and couldn't help feeling that we should have left them to their own chances long before we had skirted around Marietta. As I think back after all this time with nothing much better to do but daydream and wonder what it was all for, because we in the South had lost everything and I personally, my own dear family abducted, this abominable even now so bitter it was only like yesterday and the emotion and anger was still very real. I still dwelled upon how easily people changed after the war, their actions coming so casually it was laughable for such an act in the 1860's would have meant a sudden drop on a short rope or a bullet in the head.

In parts, the going was tough but the Captain had schooled us all in the art of allowing the horse to take his own path where possible and only pulling on the lead rein when it became necessary to show them the error of their ways. With the travel being restricted to darkness the progress was slow and dangerous. These trails through the mountains had been used by the Indians and over the last twenty years had been much used by slavers and 'blackbirder's' for transporting their contraband from the North to be sold again all over again, to plantation owners in Georgia. Because of this we were always on the alert as we didn't wish to meet any such men coming in the opposite direction, especially after our last little episode. We had for the most part not had this to worry about but we were about to travel through a gap in the mountains as it would have been really difficult for us to have found another way round it. Silas knew of no other route that would have been possible for the horses, and the Captain knew better than to doubt his word. This meant coming down off the ridge into the pass bottom and this was where there could be more possibility of meeting with someone.

The Captain was very much in a hurry and had told me we were to head for Winchester further north than Richmond itself, as this was south east but probably where we would end up. One morning he had confided in me and Joe that before he came to our farm near Roswell he had had a telegram from his old pal Jeb saying this is where he had to meet him, as the army was training recruits around this area and that much of the town's buildings were going to be used as camp, quarters and a hospital. It was his plan to be able to find the runaways some purpose here as the confederate army was looking to use negro labour for construction of fortifications and that the hospitals would require orderlies and nursing staff, so there was a chance that when everything started in earnest our runaways would be in far less danger of being arrested and sent back to the south with the 'blackbirder's' The boy was a different matter and for some reason I could never fathom he seemed to teach him in nearly every subject he knew about. This was endless, but the boy was intelligent and soaked up his masters preaching. He was already a good groom and would attend to the needs of the horses every day feeding and watering them and telling him if there was a problem with sore back or if they were likely to throw a shoe. Luckily between us we were able to take care of them and we reached the gap with all of them in fine condition.

Chapter 10

I can look back now with affection in remembering those early days, we had travelled through the mountains and were now having to negotiate a gap, split by lower ground forcing us to descend steep ground and into the valley bottom. Here there was much evidence of human habitation with waggon rutted dirt roads following a river with fords and a bridge. There were some log cabins forming a small town clustered around the river crossing and the Captain was not happy about there being no other way to continue our journey onto higher ground on the other side without going close to this settlement.

Silas had told us of this wagon road that had been cut through the mountains in the 40's and 50's all the way from Georgia into Kentucky and Virginia being built on the route of an old Indian trail, used for hunting and following migrating herds of game and buffaloes. We had been able to stay alongside it for most of the journey as the Captain had navigated our route using his British Army issue compass. He would sometimes take me up onto high ground while the others were resting and explain what he was doing. He would say that in order to plan the order of march it was necessary to find a target point, a peak or prominent feature in the distance and measure the angle shown on the compass dial. This he called the bearing and when this was known the angle of our travel was fixed by keeping the compass needle pointing to the north and our order of march on the same bearing he had plotted along the instruments sight line He would explain, when we returned to lower ground, that it was important to pick another prominent point along the same bearing, it could be a rock or large tree anything distinctive and then keeping the needle on north follow the line of the plotted bearing to the feature he had selected. Once at this point then pick another feature on the same bearing and travel to that until it was necessary to plot another bearing from higher ground. In this way we were able to travel roughly in a north easterly direction which he estimated would eventually bring us close to the North Carolina and Virginia border. I soaked up this training like a sponge with water, and if I'd of known then how much I'd need this knowledge to be able to keep most of us that got back alive together, then maybe it would have panicked me, as it would be a lot of responsibility for a lad not yet even 18 years old. This route was made longer by his concern not to meet or be seen by anyone. Silas had made it clear that there were many dangerous wild animals in these high areas including bears, mountain lions, bobcats and poisonous snakes. Another reason was that these routes were often targeted by bands of robbers and outlaws, which if we had come across them would have resulted in a deadly combat situation, one we would be better to avoid. Travel by night meant that all our cooking fires were lit during daylight when they could be less easily seen as long as the smoke was controlled.

Sometimes we had to retrace our steps because we would end up on some cliff edge or crag and forward movement was impossible along our chosen bearing. Here we would have to go back and stop for the night waiting for daylight to take another sighting with the compass. This was frustrating, and would cause some friction among the lads but the Captain would hold us all together in a way which would settle everyone and restore morale as though nothing had happened. He had this ability to inspire confidence because you could never recognise from his manner or facial expressions that he was ever concerned or worried about our position or whereabouts. I can remember once when I got the idea he may have been at a loss about the course of our next action, but this was soon forgotten when he led us out of the tree line to exactly the position he had plotted. I had to admit that when we ended up overlooking the river and small cluster of buildings around the river crossings it did cause some worry. He was quiet, for a while and went off with Silas. We watched them talking, both showing it was serious.

When they returned the Captain explained that we were in the heart of moonshine country and that the men engaged in this were not going to like a band of horsemen accompanied by black runaways moving through their territory. It would be taken as a threat and there would be a fight, no doubt on it, if we should be discovered.

The place was called Big Lick and had been named because the minerals in the ground around the river contained salts that were irresistible to wild animals, and caused them to take water there regularly. This however didn't help us but it must have gave him an idea and he again went off with Joe leaving us hidden on a cliff top but out of sight from all those below. When they returned he didn't say anything, but Silas told me before nightfall that we would be moving out and descending into the valley under cover of darkness. It transpired they had discovered a game trail that was away from the habituated areas and one that animals were using to reach a watering place seldom frequented by humans.

There was a moon that night and we set out as soon as it was dark enough. This was worrying but if we had waited around till the moon was high it would have been worse. I was detailed to take the lead and walking my horse I made my way down the slope from the crag, down towards the floor of the valley and the wagon road. It was slow going and I was covered in sweat as soon as I was told to move out. The horse was a sensible, steady mount and seemed to have learned as much as me over the last few weeks. As a matter of habit, possibly to calm my nerves, I tried to comfort him but this was hardly necessary because he seemed to know what we were about.

Finally after one and a half hours with frequent stops, in which the others caught up, I arrived in a stand of hickory trees. I was to signal the others by sending out an owl hoot, but only after I was completely satisfied that there was no danger or chance of being seen by any of the inhabitants. I can still remember waiting in the darkness, listening for any sound that was human but finding difficulty to settle my nerves and remain properly alert. Every nerve in my body felt as though it was going to be snapped by strain and worry. The muscles in my legs were vibrating causing my knees to jump about out of control. I tried to control my breathing as I knew from Silas that this was the key to maintaining calm. After a few minutes of struggling to get my senses fully in tune I was aware of a noise like the movement of something disturbing the dry fallen leaves somewhere over on my left. My mind was racing now, and my heart was beating faster. I could feel the bile coming up into my throat and it was a struggle to stop myself from gagging. Without issuing a sound I managed to clear my throat and my attention and hearing was again focused.

I could feel a slight breeze on my face so this I knew was in my favour and any smell that was coming from the horse and me was being blown away from whatever was making the noise.

Suddenly there he was a white-tailed buck not twenty yards from us and he was completely unaware he wasn't alone. I let him go without giving my position away and after waiting a few more minutes I was ready to give the all clear signal. Being there in the all-enveloping blackness and seeing the animal go by without knowing we were there had boosted my confidence, if I could get the drop on an animal like that then I was well capable of protecting my friends, and could be relied upon to lead them into safety.

The Captain was there as if he had been right behind me all the time. I had only just lowered my hand from my lips as I gave the signal so could not believe it as there he was silently laughing at me. "Well done lad," was his first words then, "Bet you need to change your pants, eh?"

 I couldn't believe how he could have known about the deer but thinking back I must have known in my subconscious that he was overlooking my every move, teaching me, and then giving me the responsibility of doing it. It made me feel confident as I felt that I was learning everything in the way he wanted things doing.

We skirted around the settlement using the game trail and came to the river. The water here didn't look that deep but then it was a pure guess. I must have known what was going to happen next as it only took a nod from him. I gave the horses reins to Joe and entered the freezing water. It was taking my breath away, but I managed to carefully, without causing too much noise to make some progress. I looked back at one stage and could make them all out crouching by the horses and watching my every step. What a target we could have made at this point but it was very dark under the trees and my progress was by feel alone.

It was with relief when I hauled myself out on the opposite bank but now I had to make sure we were alone and that there was no danger, even dogs could be our downfall.

I listened intently now, dripping wet and starting to cool more rapidly. The shivering started again but this time I was ready. After several agonising minutes I was confident there was no one watching and made the owl hoot again to get them to follow me. I now drew my revolver, I was so proud of this weapon, it was so good looking and seemed to be so well balanced in my hand I felt invincible. Little did I know then that this was so far removed from reality.

They seemed to take an age to cross and fortunately much of the noise caused by contact with rocks and floating logs was being smothered by the sound of the current. Finally we were all together on the far bank. It was not long before the Captain was in the lead, this time taking the point and with me bringing up the rear. We made careful progress and managed to find a likely looking spur that appeared to be climbing away in the right direction and that would lead us into higher ground, out of the valley and away from danger. By morning we were looking down on the settlement from a safe vantage point. There were no definite path only game trails and the Captain and I took a bearing on another peak in the distance to measure the angle of travel and then descended to where the rest were waiting. We were to press on in daylight for a few hours to try and get clear of the moonshiners.

Joe, Silas and the Captain held a briefing that afternoon when we considered we had got far enough from danger. The outcome was that we would be trying to get to Staunton and if we used the wagon road as a marker, we could travel under cover, running parallel to it while actually not being on it.

I knew he had received instructions from 'JEB' Stuart himself exactly what he was to do and where he was to report to.

The plan was to shadow a plank road which had been laid down in the 50's, but which was in pretty good repair as it was linking a town called Bristol to Staunton where the Virginia railroad was linked to Richmond. We travelled cautiously alongside the road avoiding contact with any other users, for we obviously didn't want to be associated with 'black birding' and as we were in the company of what many would class as contraband, things may have got hard to explain and make a fight inevitable. We journeyed for several days, travelling when it was possible by night and then scouting through the day and planning our next leg of the journey. Joe suggested he should be allowed to talk to a farmer and try and get some idea of how far we had to go. The following morning he got his chance as we saw a small farm house not far off our route. The Captain sent Clem and me to the far side of some cultivated fields while Squirrel, Joe and Silas took up positions facing the front of the property.

We were told to settle into a comfortable but well concealed position and then observe everything we could about the farm and its occupants.

After two hours it was safe to assume that there were only two people living in the dwelling. There were some cattle in the pastures grazing and we saw a cow closer to the house. There were a few buildings, a good sized barn and some other out-buildings. The cow must have alerted the farmer as she was bellowing to be relieved of her milk, and being considerate for her welfare the farmer showed himself and ushered her into the shed. The woman then appeared and she was observed entering the chicken coup and several minutes later coming back carrying an egg basket.

The Captain must have told Joe to move out of concealment, and we watched as he rode up to the front of the house. The woman was the first person to speak to him and everything must have gone well as she called for her husband and he came to talk with Joe. We watched for several anxious minutes but there was no reason for concern and Joe continued on as though he was taking to the road again. We all made our way, out of sight of the house to meet up with Joe. The Captain led us off the road into a grove of trees where we would not be noticed by any passers-by. It turned out we were not far away from Staunton and could be there the next day. We spent a peaceful night, it was warm so there was little need for a big fire but the Captain allowed us to make coffee, and we all sat down to enjoy a talk this time with a few less worries.

Chapter 11

It must have looked strange and when I come to look back I sometimes have to smile. The Captain had no concerns at all about being in the same company as these Negroes but for us it was a little strange. Not all people from the South owned slaves for it was mainly the large estates and farms that used them for cotton harvesting. Our feelings towards them were slightly different because we didn't class them as complete equals. That is not to say that I was in agreement with the inhuman treatment that many slave holders subjected their workers to. However here we all were in the same company, sharing our food our water and coffee with these runaways. The boy Jacob was now almost inseparable from the Captain and I thought it was probable that he would take him with us to be his groom and servant. The man's wounds from the whipping had almost healed now thanks to the woman and her potions and poultices. She would tend his back by applying these whenever there was an opportunity. I had noticed that on many of these occasions the Captain would be close by watching. He would talk to the woman about what she was using and they would spend some time in discussion.

I was curious and when the next chance arose to bring the subject up I asked the Captain how it was that the man's wounds had healed so quickly because when I first saw the extent of the horrible mess that the lash had made, I was in doubt if ever the skin would heal?

He had this skill of continually surprising me, and on this occasion it was no different. It seemed when he was wounded in the Crimean war and was first taken to a military hospital there was not much hope of him ever coming out of it alive. Cholera, infection, filth from overcrowding and contaminated water supplies was taking a much bigger toll than the enemy. Coffins could not be made quickly enough for the dead and the conditions in the men's wards were horrific. Then he told me of the nurse, well a head nurse as it happened coming out from England. She was such a fine nurse and organiser that she made the British Medical officers do something about the conditions. Soon things did improve and more soldiers were recovering. Officers were a little better situated as some of the wives came daily to tend them and do what they could. His wife was one of them and she was much respected by the wounded men and orderlies in the wards.

Then he went on to say that there was another woman, a Jamaican who also came out as a nurse but soon organised her own smaller hospital. This is where he went when he had sufficiently recovered and as time went on most wounded officers were looked after in this woman's hospital wards. She would use alternative medicines and the medical officers would not even recognise her for the obvious good results that her doctoring was having. Soon the officers had made her building into a little club where they could relax and socialise.

I now began to realise that this was the reason he didn't think of black people the way we thought, for this lady had saved his life using strange natural herbs and potions from unthinkable sources while in the hospitals the surgeons would just blunder through. Their attitude was that it was acceptable the wounded had a very low life expectancy. Butchers, he called them and whenever we had action he would always talk of our lads who we had lost as belonging on 'The Butchers Bill'

It was during the next day around dusk we became more aware of the increase in traffic and people on the road coming from the buildings dotted all along its route. These were the places of business for suttler's, wagon smiths and wheel rights and this made sense as this county was affluent from commerce and produce. We couldn't be far away from the town and by the time it was getting dark there was the town ahead lit from what the Captain said must be gas lights.

That night our leader gathered us together, and in a secluded glade amongst the trees we took stock of what we had. Weapons were checked and he made sure they cleaned and in working order. Ammunition for both revolvers and carbines were counted and shared equally among us. I still had the Hawken rifle wrapped in a thin blanket across the back of my saddle under the bedroll. The horses were well cared for, the ones we took from the State Guards and our own we'd brought from Georgia all served us faithfully. We had been able to feed them well but their shoes were in need of some attention and this was one of the first concerns we had, to get them to a blacksmith or farrier soon. Everyone was in good health including the Negro's who had become part of our band and were in many ways helpful in sharing the many different duties that were required to allow us to travel without drawing attention to ourselves. It was mid-morning as we entered the town, there were many people about and everyone seemed occupied and engaged about their own business. The buildings were fine looking with columned entrances and porches over the sidewalks, all connected so a person could walk along in the shade and look into all the big windows of the shops, stores, offices, hotel and bank buildings.

We must have looked a strange bunch; all mounted and leading spare horses, each rider with side arms and carrying a carbine alongside the saddle. We were receiving some long glances from some people now and this was not unexpected, as we were in the company of the three Negro's all of whom were mounted on good looking horses.

The Captain was making for the telegraph office and he dismounted in front of the building and stepped up onto the sidewalk giving the horses reins to me. "Wait here and stay together," he said and I looked around at the others thinking to myself we must look like a band of outlaws. You could not have blamed any of these townspeople for thinking that way for we had not properly washed or shaved in weeks and our clothes were dirty and torn. The Negroes were attracting so much attention now it was getting annoying as people would stand and stare or walk up for a closer inspection, glancing from them to us and back again. I was happy when the Captain came out but he was accompanied by a man who looked like he might be an employee of the cable company. They parted and the Captain thanked him for his help. He took the reins from me and leapt up in one movement from the sidewalk. "We will go to the train depot and wait there," but he was already ahead of us and we had to hurry to catch up.

The train depot was a fine sight with track arranged into several sidings each one holding box-cars and flatbed rolling stock. There was a locomotive at the head of a saloon car, passenger train ready for leaving and I can remember being in awe at the sight of this giant. This was the first time the Negro's would have seen a train and I can still see the look on their faces and the boys open mouths as they gaped at the locomotive and the smoke from the huge stack, and steam being blown out near those massive driving wheels. The Captain was interested in where the train was going and he had attracted the attention of the guard. "It's bound for Richmond and will be back day after tomorrow," he shouted. This had decided our fate for the next couple of nights, and the Captain was already leading off toward some open ground where he then indicated we were to set-up camp. Everyone then became occupied with organising the site; horses watered, and rubbed down, saddles removed and our equipment stacked into some semblance of order. We were all accustomed to this routine as it had become so practiced over the last month we were soon finished. He then got us together to explain that he had sent a telegram to Army headquarters at Richmond and requested that an escort be despatched to authorise train passage to enable us to be enlisted in Confederate States Cavalry, The Army of North Virginia and the 1st. Virginia Regiment.

There was a cavalry regiment already being trained at Camp Robinson at that moment and we would be joining its ranks.

He talked then to the negroes and explained that if it was agreed with them he would take the boy as a groom and have him put on the roster as such, in order for him to be officially part of the regiment. The man he could find him work that provided shelter and regular meals as he would be working with the labour crews engaged in the construction of the Richmond defences. The Captain knew an Engineering officer friend of his whom he thought would be stationed at the Capital and be connected with this work. He was therefore in an excellent position to be able to arrange this work for the Negro. The woman he would try and arrange a place for in one of the hospitals that were being built in various locations in the city and within the defensive perimeter. This would enable them to both be together in the shanty town where the labourers were accommodated, and as they would be working for the Army, this could afford them some protection from the 'blackbirder's' who were still operating kidnapping Negroes and returning with them to the Southern States where they would sell them for money. This seemed acceptable to them and the man and woman thanked the Captain. The woman went down on her knees in front of him and was crying and blessing him for all his kindness. This seemed to embarrass him and he told her to stop. We had noticed the location of a livery yard when we entered the town and the Captain detailed Clem and Squirrel to lead all the horses up to the big barn and coral where they were looked after by the business owner, a very friendly jovial little man who was also asking a lot of questions. These fell on deaf ears as the boys were reluctant to talk because the Captain had instructed them to keep everyone guessing, but if pressed, then say we were horse buyers for the Army and that we were returning to the lines at Richmond

We waited till dark and then lit a cooking fire. The Captain and Joe had been into the town and purchased fresh supplies of bacon, flour, salt, lard, baking soda, buttermilk, beans and coffee. The Negro woman made the flour and milk into a dough mixture and added small, cut up bacon pieces. These she laid onto a wooden board which I had found at the rear of one of the freshly constructed buildings. The board was then placed at an angle on the edge of the fire where it would bake slowly. We had a fry pan and placed bacon and beans on the fire to start cooking. We hadn't eaten a decent meal in weeks so it didn't take long to gulp down the greasy plateful, soaking up the gravy from the side of the plates with the biscuits until they were wiped clean and spotless. It was the best meal I could remember and those biscuits were better than my mother's.

We had time on our hands and the Captain was keen to find out what the situation was with the secession and if any other States had broken away from the Union to join the Confederacy. We were allowed to go into the town in pairs but the Negroes were never left alone and there would be always two of us with them back at the campsite. I could not believe the General appearance of wealth in everyone we came into contact with. People's cloths were of good quality and there were no dirty looking children running around. We were the exception as our clothing was pretty much in rags. The Captain had given each of us money to buy pants and shirts as he said that there was a good chance we would be issued with boots from the Army. I bought a good quality pair of riding breeches that were not tight but fitted well and were reinforced on the inside and seat. The shirt was of similar colour, dark grey and when I changed into them I felt like I was back home on Christmas morning, not that I had ever received presents as fine as this.

Next on the list was the bath house and we were all ordered to take one before we boarded the train for Richmond. The Negroes were also thought about and their cleanliness was improved by the woman being provided with a large copper in which she heated water. We had also acquired washing bowls, one for them and one for us, and with these she made sure the boy, her husband and herself were cleaned and refreshed. The Captain had also purchased new clothes for them all from another store that dealt in providing working attire. I can remember the look on their faces when he gave them to her.

The following day, around noon the train from Richmond arrived. We watched from a distance and looked at each of the passengers they got down out of the saloon cars and coaches. There were fine ladies in hats and dresses accompanied by gentlemen, some ordinary looking passengers and then a soldier.

The soldier was all dressed in a parade dress uniform with a black wide hat complete with ostrich feather cockade. The boots were of fine looking leather and were tight fitting over his cavalry riding trousers. His jacket was short and open up to the top two buttons. This was completed by yellow silk facings, braids and high collar where his badges of rank were visible. He was a Lieutenant in the 1st Virginia cavalry and the sash around his waist indicated he was on the regimental staff. The Captain's mood changed a little and I thought for a second I saw him smile but there wasn't enough time to ponder as he marched off towards where the young officer was standing looking about him and searching the people's faces about him for any signs of recognition. The Captain had managed to stay reasonably dressed and he was still wearing the bits and pieces of the military style dress he had been wearing when we first met. He marched up to the youngster and barked at him, "Lieutenant don't you know how to present yourself to a superior officer?" Well, this just about floored me but the boy swung round at once his boots making a loud slap as they came together 'to attention', his left arm slapped his leg and his right shot out and bent at the elbow to allow his open palm, fingers extended to come to rest at the side of his splendid hat plume in 'the salute'

"Sir, I am Lieutenant Barclay of the Staff of General Johnsons and have been ordered to escort you and your party to the cavalry training depot at Camp Ashby."

Our Captain was silent but he had walked towards the officer and was now standing so close it looked at first as though he was going to embrace him. When he spoke it was so much of a shock that it made all of us watching jump, almost out of our skins. He bellowed at him like they were one mile apart and I saw the boy flinch at the sudden loudness of the Captains voice. "Why are you flinching boy?"

A little lower this time but still loud enough to have attracted a crowd of people who were now looking at them both wondering what was happening.

"I hope you are not alongside me when we face a squadron of regular Yankee cavalry." were his next words, and I thought I saw the boy as though he was about to break down into a jabbering wreck but all at once the Captain started to laugh and slapped the lad around the shoulders.

The blow knocked him off balance, and we were trying not to laugh as he was bellowing again but at us this time. "Take the lad across the tracks to our camp I will join you presently."

He did join us about a half hour later; he'd been to obtain a bottle of whisky and produced seven shot glasses.

He handed a glass to each of us Silas, Joe, Squirrel, Clem, me and the young officer and one for himself. He poured the whiskey into the glasses and made us stand in line. The officer came to attention and as he stiffened the Captain voiced "To the regiment and Col JEB Stuart," and with that he raised his glass and emptied the contents in one easy swallow. We copied the gesture and I can still think of how that liquid burned my throat and caused me to cough. He shouted for us to remain still and then poured himself another shot and raised it again but this time he shouted. "The Queen," and with this the measure again disappeared. For me this was good as I hadn't wanted another chance at burning my throat away, but the others were looking down at their empty glasses. It would seem we had not been good enough to drink to his Queen.

"That's enough," he said and swung the bottle which still had a little left in it onto a pile of cut cord wood where it smashed into pieces. He bid us to throw our glasses after it and the cord wood pile again received a barrage of the 6 empty glasses. We got to talk to the young officer and at first he seemed as though he thought of us as low-life but when Silas talked to him of his service on the frontier, he started to listen and look on us as experienced horsemen who would make worthy recruits for his regiment. There was an air of mystery around our Captain and anyone that didn't know him was hard pressed to get to know him. The young officer was no exception and the Captain kept him at a distinct distance. He must have been informed by his superiors in Richmond of whom he was to meet, but at no time while we were waiting to board the train did he address the Captain by name, either personally or to us. I learned later while in conversation with him that his authority was from Governor Letcher and General Johnson himself. We had been supplied with warrants for passage by train in order for us to be taken directly to

Richmond where we would be enlisted in the regiment and our leader would receive a CSA commission.

Chapter 12

The train was due to leave early the next day, so we spent a peaceful night on our own as the two officers went into town to take up accommodation in the best hotel in town.

Early the following morning they both suddenly appeared. I was still shaking the sleep from my head as the two of them started hollering and shouting for the horses to be brought from the livery yard, the equipment to be taken to the third box-car in line and all of our animals to be bedded down in the one in front. Squirrel and Clem were to stay with the horses and keep them calm on the journey; the Negroes would be with us in the same car as Joe and I, while the officers were seated in the saloon car, next in line.

The young Lieutenant could not quite understand why we were in company with these people, as he called them. He was obviously from a rich family who would be the owners of a large estate somewhere in Virginia, the breadbasket of the Shenandoah Valley. They would be slave owners themselves, and how they treated their Negros workers would show in the young man's attitude towards these three, who had been in our company for many weeks.

His thoughts on this were surprisingly liberal for he didn't show any loathing or bad feelings towards them, which was probably a good thing for him as the Captain would have definitely thrown him out of the car as it was moving had he shown any resentment.

The journey was pleasant and we travelled through rich country with many prosperous looking farms. Passing through Rockfish Gap, Charlottesville, Gordonsville and then to a junction on the Fredericksburg & Baltimore line where we had to wait while another train was shunted into a siding in order that we could proceed.

We were soon at the rail depot, and all hell seemed to be waiting for us. The two officers seemed as though they were not the same people, the Captain was hard to recognise as he shouted and balled rushing from one car to another. The horses and the equipment were unloaded and we set about putting their saddles on and loading the spare horses with the other equipment. The Captain now seemed to be addressing Joe much more and it was to him he passed on all his instructions, when you come to think of it Joe was the obvious choice as Silas was a loner and responsibility would not sit too comfortably with him. The Captain's choice for Sergeant had been decided and this is what Joe soon became, by ballot on the first day of enlistment.

The next thing that was to be organised, was our enlistment, and we soon learned we would be sworn-in at Camp Robinson later that day. This left the Negroes, but even this was organised as the young officer had some time ago disappeared and we only just realised we had company when he came along our line as we were standing to horse, with another fine looking gentlemen officer.

This time he was a Major of engineers and as the Captain and he exchanged greetings Joe had gathered the three Negroes to within speaking distance. There was nothing to fear and the Major spoke to them about their immediate future. The man was to accompany him to the construction camp where he would be working on the city's defences. He was to be part of a skilled party of workers who used timber to bolster up the huge piles of earth and make them stable and solid enough to withstand both explosions and any other movements. This was a better and more technical job, and as such was awarded more respect and fairer treatment from the engineers. A wagon and four horses pulled up, and the Major had the man say his goodbyes to his family then quickly step up into the open wagon back for the ride out to the workers shanty town. The woman was next for an ambulance was to take her to the hospital where she would be working as an orderly. We watched as she hugged the boy and started to cry but this only embarrassed Jacob and it looked as though he was glad when the transport bearing both his parents away had disappeared.

I can remember feeling sorry for them but I know they all survived the war, and the boy was with us for a long time, but on this I'll not say too much as you'll be finding out exactly what happened later. The Captain had been ordered to report to Head Quarters that day and he was insistent that we knew exactly what was to happen. Joe would lead us out of Richmond along the Brooke Road toward the rail tracks we had just travelled along. We were to follow the rail when we reached the point where the road crossed and then turn north and proceed to Ashby and our camp which was to be our home for the next few weeks. The name had been changed from Robinson and it was now being converted for cavalry training. Already under training was the Amelia Light Dragoons and we would be adding our names to their muster roll. That day we travelled around nineteen miles to a converted racecourse on the south of the little town. Here we were met by training staff that had been given prior warning of our arrival. Amelia light Company were billeted in some converted stables and other ex-racecourse buildings on the east side, away from the rest of the camp. There were also large areas of canvas where other troops seemed to be in abundance. The strict instructions were not to wander away from our allotted area. The other boys in the company had been there for two days and were all looking very tired, but showed us a good cooking line where we were able to get a good enough meal of stew pork and some hard biscuit.

They informed us that the training was hard but that they had progressed a little and were not shouted at so much now. Our mealtime was cut short by a smart looking Sergeant who made it plain we were to accompany him to report to the actual camp Commanding Officer Colonel Richard S. Ewell, and the officer in charge of training a Captain T. Rowland. They were seated at a table in the open and we were brought up to them and ordered to assume a position of attention, this meant you would have to stiffen yourself up and not look at the officer's face who might be talking to you at the time.

He knew we were recruits from Georgia and had come north with an ex US cavalry officer who would soon be commissioned in the regiment. It seemed we were famous already as he went on to say we would be joining the Amelia Light troop for training but would be singled out for other duties as couriers and scouts attached to Headquarters Staff of Colonel JEB Stuart.

We were then requested to take The Flag Pledge, which involved being in the same stiff position but with the right hand raised in the air, palm open facing the flag of the regiment and the newly formed Confederacy. We all recited the oath of allegiance together and I remember feeling proud that we now belonged to the Cavalry. The date was 25th May 1861; our names were taken by a Captain, then each of us given a sheet of paper having a space at the bottom to put our signatures. This was the allegiance in writing and as we each stated our name we signed the entry in the muster roll record book. We only just had enough time to report to the quartermaster who wanted to record all the property and equipment each new trooper had brought with him. A value was put on everything and this was again recorded. My horse was valued at $80, which surprised me as he hadn't even seen it. It turned out that I was wrong here as it seemed while we were eating and gossiping the quartermaster's were rooting around our horses. True they were fine animals and we loved and respected them. The Sergeant was now hurrying us to saddle - up and form ranks with the rest of the company. We ran for the horses and threw the saddles on them. The rest of the boys were drawn up into a mounted line, and I admired how they looked for it was pretty straight and everyone looked very much a cavalryman. We were pushed into the line at the far end and the Sergeant was shouting for us to control the horses. We were used to this and didn't embarrass the company with any poor show of horseman ship. The Captain now rode down the line and he picked on every trooper for something. I had my Hawken rifle wrapped in a blanket on my bedroll tied on the saddle. This interested him and more so because we were all in possession of Sharps cavalry carbines, complete with rifle sling hanging from the left shoulder with the weapon ready for use on the right. He started to question us on the holstered revolver and military issue belts displaying Georgia State seal buckle. As we all had these, Joe answered him respectfully, that we were issued these weapons from the State Armoury when our leader had requested weapons since we were about to join a regiment of cavalry. It seemed we were armed as well as any regular troop but he was still eager to find out what the Hawken's capabilities and my own in shooting it were. I was ordered to report at the end of the drill session with rifle, powder and balls.

On the 30th. May another company arrived into camp, these were The Rockingham Cavalry but we were not to have much to do with these boys as our training kept us pretty much isolated. However we did met them again whilst we were at Ashland but I'll tell you about that once I've finished explaining about the training.

There were about ninety men and horses together on the training ground and the Captain and his two Sergeants repeatedly went over drill after drill. We would be drawn into line and stood to attention standing at the horses head and holding the reins. Then we would mount from a standing position, swinging up into saddle in one movement, but if anyone failed to achieve this to their satisfaction the drill would be repeated over again until the whole troop were perfect. Next would come the numbering off, column of two's, then fours, riding round and round in circles. This was very tiring and dull as it seemed senseless. The next drills were more exciting and they would involve squadron attacks and other formations used to engage both mounted and dismounted enemy formations. We would practice fighting on foot having to deploy in fours with carbines while the fifth trooper held the reins of the horses.

This went on for five hours, and I was relieved when the Sergeants ordered us to retire the horses and stable then in the barns and other ex-racecourse buildings. I had only enough time to unsaddle and then had to rush after the Sergeant carrying the Hawken. He took me to an area of ground that was being used by the infantry for shooting practice. The training Captain was there with another more junior officer and he told me that I was to shoot at a wooden barrel one hundred yards away down the range. I went through the loading procedure and cocked the action. "Proceed," was the order given so I raised the rifle to my shoulder and took sight along the barrel. This was not a difficult shot as I had hunted squirrel back home. The target came still for an instant and I squeezed the trigger. The rifle bucked but I remained looking down the barrel at the target. No one could see if I had been successful and so the officer sent the Sergeant down range to check the target. They were all looking on expectantly and when he raised his arm to signal a hit they seemed surprised as though I had done something impossible. The Sergeant was then ordered to place an empty whiskey bottle on top of the wooden barrel. I had already re-loaded and was standing waiting with the rifle uncocked.

"Hit that," the officer said, so I again put the rifle into my shoulder and sighted down its barrel. This was more like it and I waited till the muzzle was still and lined up with the bottle. Just before it was due to start moving again I squeezed the trigger. The powder smoke clouded my vision so I didn't see the bottle but the Lieutenant was shouting "He's smashed it."

The Captain was extremely pleased and he wanted to know at what range I could expect to achieve 'hits' with using the same size targets.

I had to think now, as I hadn't done this for some time. I trusted the rifle and knew it would reach out to three hundred yards as uncle had shown me more than once.

It was not the same model as the long rifles used in the frontier day as this had a shorter heavier barrel. It also had two triggers the rear one for setting the front one so it would be very sensitive. The calibre was 0.50 inch and it was all in good condition as I kept it clean and well oiled. I was nervous now, and although I wanted to say three hundred yards I didn't and came to an agreement with myself at two hundred and fifty yards.

The Captain was amazed and whether or not he believed me I don't know, but he instructed the Sergeant to put a whiskey jug up at the range I had said. I was worried now as it was a long way away but I suddenly remembered Uncle showing me how to steady the rifle by placing it between the forks of two crossed sticks, lashed together with their bases planted firmly in the ground. I stammered out a request to the Captain for permission to 'fall-out' in order to cut two from a bush growing nearby. He was fascinated, as on my return he observed closely as I tied a length of hide thong around them both, and then opened them to form a vee shape. I sat down behind the newly fashioned rifle rest and placed the stock in the vee and looked down the barrel at the target. I could make out the jug, it was sandy yellow in colour and when I tried the front blade front sight to it there was not much room or space for wobbling on target. It had to be quick, I set the rear trigger and offered the rifle into my shoulder, and I came up from underneath the barrel and kept the muzzle moving slowly onto the jug. Just as it reached the top part of the barrel I applied my forefinger, ever so gently to the front trigger. It fired, raising a cloud of white powder smoke to mask my vision but I kept my eyes down the barrel. The Lieutenant was jumping up and down shouting "A hit, another hit".

The Captain was overjoyed, and congratulated me on my marksmanship. He was eager for me to become a sharpshooter and to train other troopers in this art. He then said that there was an English officer, a Captain

Stanley Robinson who would be specialising in training scouts and small units of troopers in reconnaissance and sharpshooting. He continued to say he was expected the following morning, and if I should like to volunteer he would make this known to the officer on his arrival. I couldn't believe my own ears, the excitement must have shown all over my face but I didn't care. Here was the chance for us all to be together again. "Please Sir; I would like to volunteer all the troopers from Georgia that I enlisted with." He assured me that so long as it was acceptable with the commanding officer and that the English officer was in agreement, and then it would be granted.

We spent a comfortable night in the company of the rest of our troop who we were sharing a building with. We had been given fresh straw and by using saddle blankets and our own bed rolls were able to make ourselves comfortable. The next morning we were roused at four by the training Sergeants. The horses were saddled and what equipment we had was secured in the most soldierly fashion. We mounted and there was now a dash for the exercise field where we jostled around until the line was formed in the same order as we'd been given the previous day. The training Captain now came to our front and addressed us.

He said this was the day when we would be practicing squadron attacks, and that there was another troop parading close by and at a given signal they would advance to contact with our troop. These men were the troop I told you about, who had come in on the 30th May, and although we were both stationed here we'd not seen them much, so didn't know anything about them. I was wishing that we would be up against the troop which had just come in, the day before, 22nd June.

They all looked like they were handy lads and like a few of us had been issued with Sharp's cavalry carbines, but they all had the cavalry sabre and looked proud as if you had been given a brand new set of Sunday church clothes. We were to learn these were the Washington Mounted Rifles and soon, both our troops would both be assigned in Col. JEB Stuarts Regiment.

We were expected to defend this position with its buildings, stables and sheds. With this said, he turned his horse and left the ground, I had only just realised that there was now another horseman mounted on a pure black horse over to our right. He trotted over to us and immediately I saw it was our English Captain. He quickly organised half the troop to dismount and with every fifth man acting as a horse holder, he detailed dismounted troopers to find cover around the perimeter of the exercise field. The rest of us were to conceal ourselves, mounted, but within easy charging distance of our comrade's. When he gave the order to charge we were to form quickly into a solid arrowhead formation and follow him.

Suddenly there was the sound of horses galloping and shouts and yells coming to us over the hoof beats. It was strangely exciting and I can remember feeling so alive and in a way I'd not ever felt before. The boys came up out of cover and forced the horsemen to veer away from their firing positions. No one had loaded weapons and it was probably a good thing as I believe somebody would have been shot in the enthusiasm our boys were showing for whipping these pretend enemy cavalry.

Chapter 13

The Captain must have had other ideas as he now led us out of hiding at the gallop. Our horses were in good condition and very fit and they were enjoying this as much as we were. We rode after the Captain as he was shouting for us to form an arrowhead formation. This was achieved just before we hit them and it took them completely off balance. They scattered before us, some of them dropping the reins and becoming badly seated. This looked funny and we were cheering and shouting insults at them but unfortunately our manoeuvre had caused some of their lads to hit the ground rather hard.

He wasn't finished, and turned us back into those who were still left in some kind order. We hit em again but not in as tight a formation as the first charge. Horses were rearing on hind leg; riders were being thrown over their horses heads as they were driven back into our firing line. Some thought better of it and in ones and two's made off, out of the field. We were just calming down when the training Captain came onto the field; he was smiling and greeted our officer with a raised hat. He congratulated the Captain for achieving a decisive victory and they both laughed and shook hands.

For the unfortunate losers they were rewarded with extra drill sessions and picket duties around the town which according to the company orders should have been ours. Over the next few days we were again put through our paces. Sometimes we would be with the other company and it began to look as though we were getting better. The parade by squadrons was good to be a part of, and it had the same effect on all of the men as it made you so proud and made up for all those other drills which seemed unnecessary. At least the Captain was not shouting at us as much. I couldn't see what value some of the endless drills were to have on our fighting capabilities, but the Captain was skilled at demonstrating and he wanted us to copy his movements exactly. He was not easily pleased. There were occasions when he would inspect us. This was with the troop drawn up into a straight line with the training Sergeants as flankers on either end; they would straighten us by numbers, these being first voiced by every trooper calling his out, 1, 2, 3, and so on, down the line. So you would get "No. 3, move forward," or back as the case demanded. It was on one of these parades when he told us we would be training with our commanding officer Col. JEB Stuart as he was due to meet us soon, We could expect more drill, sabre practice and squadron exercises.

I can remember this was to be the start of a little more training which had a different, definitely a more useful reason for practicing it. They had one trooper standing out on foot in the middle of the exercise area and he would then have two mounted troopers ride down at a gallop leading an empty horse. The dismounted rider was to reach up around the galloping horse's neck and vault upwards using the momentum to swing himself into the saddle. From there he was to bring the horse under control and halt, with the reins held and both boots in the stirrups.

This was not easy and we practiced it over and over again until he was satisfied.

It was a strange atmosphere in the camp, and although we were almost continually kept at daily training there were occasions of off-duty time, these were pleasant interludes when much time was spent idling away the hours, talking, sleeping or writing home. I had not heard from mother or the two girls since we had left Georgia. This wasn't a surprise as we were never in one place for long, and had been continually trying not to draw any attention to ourselves.

It was on one of these days of blissful rest that we were informed of the news that the war was definite. The State of Virginia had seceded on the 23rd May and this seemed to reinforce the threats of war. Fort Sumter had been attacked and had surrendered to Confederate forces on the 13th April, about the same time we were all hiding up in the mountains, but it seemed as though things didn't get started in real earnest until Lincoln had apparently requested thousands to join the US Army on longer engagement terms; as the first were for only 3 months. We were so full of confidence, this was of no consequence as we all felt one of our boys was equal to ten Yankee's. It would be foolish to continue thinking like this as it was a lesson we all had in store for us.

However on the 2nd June war was started in earnest. A Yankee army of 3000 troops under McClellan had begun an advance toward Philippi and later in the month his forces were approaching Centreville with more than 30,000. It didn't end there, as a few days later our Captain told us that a force of our infantry had been caught napping and been forced to run before the Yanks. The News Papers were having a great time calling it 'The Philippi Races.' What a disgrace, even if they had been badly placed and surprised by a much superior force. If there had been a cavalry picket with them there would have been no surprise and possibly some more Blue Bellies could have been accounted for. Our reason for being in the Forces of the Confederacy seemed justified with everyone being unanimous in the belief our cause was, in every aspect right, and it was for us to do our duty and fight united, standing together to end the injustices and tyranny these Yankees were going to force on us.

The situation seemed to get worse and a few weeks later we heard that on the 15th June, Jo Johnson had retreated from Harpers Ferry and pulled back towards Winchester.

On the 17th another engagement where our boys were in a hot action was at Scary Creek. This was a brave defence of the river crossing in the Kanawha Valley which was let down by being followed by a General retreat. Oh! What we would have given to have been with those gunners, and placed right to ride down on those attacking Bluecoats. Our Captain could not contain himself, as he was both angry and sad that this strategic and vital position had been given up without a cavalry fight. For us it was frustrating as our morale was high and to a man we were itching to get to grips with the Bluecoats. Our training was coming to an end, as you can only mount and dismount, draw sabre and ride around changing from column of two's, then to four's over and over, till you're sick to the back teeth with it all. We had been practicing with our leader some different manoeuvres which were a pleasant change to the drill, the training staff appeared to be obsessed with. He would have us jumping fences in line and then in column. Some of the Amelia troop had been issued sabres before they arrived, and for these boys it was great fun to slash down with the sabre onto corn sacks mounted on poles at the exact height of a standing infantryman. They took delight in this and it was good to watch this troop and the other company go through their sabre attack drills. For us who hadn't been issued with sabres, or any other weapons, come to that, it seemed less effective than just shooting the Colt revolver into them.

Our Captain however was insistent that the blades of the sabres were kept sharp and he would have inspections carried out at the most inconvenient times, like early mornings before breakfast or in the evening when you were trying to relax after a hard days boring, repeated drill.

He was very good at explaining why these drills were so important and often changed the opinion of the most ardent complainer. He would explain that the Yankee great coat or foul weather cavalry cape would stop a dull blade and make the effort of slashing down at the enemy rider's body a waste of energy. A dull blade would do little, probably not even capable of wounding and the other rider would be immediately given the advantage. He would go on to say that after several days of rain and damp conditions the sabre had to be continually cleaned, the edge maintained with sharpening stone, and kept rust free. If there was an engagement where the sabre was going to be used then it was better to select your man early and maintain your attack line. When the distance closed you are not to change positions but go for that same enemy rider giving him the point of the blade and not the backhand slash.

We were never to meet our beloved Colonel while we were at Camp Ashland, but the Captain had told us he was to be commissioned to command the cavalry. We were to be part of a regiment and would be enrolled as a troop alongside the Washington Mounted Rifles. The regiment would be one of the largest in the Army having 12 companies. On the 2nd July we were ordered to depart for Winchester.

We travelled by way off Fredericksburg and then Warrenton, arriving at Winchester in the early morning off the 9th July. It was not long before we were ordered to make our way to Camp Jeff Davis located near Bunker Hill and we got there at around noon on that same morning. Everyone was exhausted. Just after we got there, both our troop and Washington Mounted rifles were assigned 1st. Virginia cavalry regiment. Our troop was lettered "G" Amelia Light Dragoons and our comrades were "L" 1st. Washington Mounted rifles We again were detailed an area in which to camp and this time we were in good company as the total cavalry numbered at around 350 men. There were no tents for us and we had to make shelters and provide for the horses as best we could. The officers were under canvas and our Captain did what he could for us in providing occasional little luxuries like coffee and flour, which his servant Jacob had managed to find, or more likely stolen. We didn't mind though, and it was good to be close to our officer, as before they had been billeted in the old racecourse hotel. We had two Captains as our company officer was Captain S.S Weisiger. We didn't know much about him, as he'd been absent, recovering from an accidental wound while we were at Camp Ashland but it was rumoured he was now fit for duty and was expected to re-join us at any time.

The boys from the company had elected a Lieutenant Irwin and so we didn't have another Lieutenant as was customary, because of our English Captain being appointed by Stewart himself and having the blessing of the Governor in Richmond. This in itself was also not customary, as the troopers would elect their officers and non-commissioned troop leaders by process of ballot. This didn't seem to bother the troop as the Captain was so respected and well thought of by everyone. More than once he had defused situations of insubordination and absenteeism by skilfully administering his own style of justice.

This was swift and final, but there were never any repercussions and the offender was always put firmly back on the road to being a good cavalryman even though his face was probably a mess of bruises and his eyes closed over for a few days. The men respected this, and even when the Captain was out matched the discipline would still take place. I can remember this actually happening, but the guilty trooper would still be forced to stand toe to toe with the Captain and fight it out. The Captain was no easy mark and by the time they were both battered and bruised and totally exhausted, both men would usually have developed a deep respect for one another. It was funny, as on morning inspection, all of us mounted for parade in companies. The officers would ride slowly down the ranks and it was at this point you would see the Captain's face, black and blue with swelling around his eyes. You'd know straight away what had happened the night before as there would be a trooper in the line whose face was even worse. This justice was his way of gaining the respect of the men and I think that any trooper who knew him would not hesitate to follow him in a charge down the barrel of a cannon. This was something that was proved on many battlefields.

Our Sergeant Joe had been given three stripes to sew on his newly issued shell Jacket. These uniforms had been issued a few days ago and consisted of grey shell jackets with loose fitted matching trousers. All the facings were black, these already unpopular as we preferred the yellow ones, standard on other units jackets. Not all the troopers had been issued with this uniform. This caused some arguments but seemed to quieten down when Sharpe's cavalry carbines were issued. Off course our little troop of Georgians already had these weapons; in fact ours were more modern, courtesy of the Georgia

State Guards. However the problem was with the colour and quality of the uniform being issued to the Washington boy's. It turned out these were from the State Penitentiary and originally intended for prison inmates. The Washington troopers refused to wear these, and stated they would rather continue to wear their ragged clothing than to put on those dull yellow clothes. Thankfully when the officer Capt. Jones had the carbines given out it took their mind off the insult of the prison clothes. Revolvers were in short supply but a few Colts were issued to selected troopers, again from the Mounted Rifle's.

Chapter 14

It seemed that our little troop of Georgia recruits had gained some reputation. The quality of the marksmanship had reached the ears of our Colonel and one day we were all summoned to his headquarters, a small farm house not far from our camp area. He was an imposing man, who had a fine athletic stature but the most unforgettable part of his features was the eyes. They were the most piercing that I have ever seen. He was capable of looking right into your soul or that's how it seemed that day. He wanted to see us shoot because he was of the opinion a troop of cavalry sharpshooters would be extremely effective against enemy gun crews. He motioned for a Lieutenant who was standing to attention just to one side of his desk. My attention was directed toward him and I immediately recognised the face as it belonged to the young staff officer who had met us at Staunton. He doubled away and a few moments later he re-entered carrying a new looking rifle. "This my boys is the British Whitworth rifle, and I've been reliably informed by your company officer that in the right hands it is well capable of hitting a target at over 400 yards." He was looking right at me and although it unnerved me I wasn't going to let an opportunity slip away that could help us stay with our officer. Joe was our non-commissioned officer and he must have been keen to show his superiority as he took the weapon from the Lieutenant. I couldn't wait to hold the weapon, but Joe seemed like he was mesmerised by it and kept stroking it and turning it over in his big hands.

Our Colonel broke the spell however by inquiring, "Well do you think you can get to grips with it." It looked like no one was going to answer so I replied, "yes Sir, I think it's well capable of that sort of shooting, and if the Captain says it will, I'll have a try."

This seemed to excite the Colonel and his ruddy complex seemed to glow making his reddish beard and side whiskers look like they were on fire. He looked up at me now and instantly got to his feet shouting, "Follow Me, and we'll see what we've got eh!"

There was an open area that hadn't been occupied yet for camping and the Colonel told the young Lieutenant to pace out 100 yards, then 200 and finally 300. I was completely unfamiliar with the musket but it wasn't hard for me to figure out. I was given a cartridge pouch with paper wrapped charges and bullets. I split the wrapper and poured the charge down the muzzle then rammed the Minnie ball down on top of it. I then applied the percussion cap onto the primer and closed the hammer to safe position.

The Lieutenant had by this time placed a target out at 100 yards; it was an empty whisky bottle. I was nervous now because I had never fired this rifle before and I was completely in the dark as to its capabilities. The officers had gathered around and their number had increased. I now noticed our Captain and Lieutenant Irwin were also watching. This made me even more anxious but I was determined to prove myself, and hopefully get recognition for our little troop. Our Colonel now indicated I fire down the range at the bottle. I f I was to have any success at the longer range it would require the use of a rifle rest. I asked permission to fire from a sitting position with the rifle rested on part of a broken fence rail, just at the right height.

The Colonel agreed, and I sat behind the weapon and sighted down the barrel. The rifle was fitted with adjustable sliding blade rear sights which were calibrated from 100 out to 1200yards. These were sophisticated and the Captain saw that I was struggling to fathom out what these were for. He requested permission to instruct me in the use of the sights and as the Colonel accepted he came up behind me and explained the sliding contraption he called a vernier. "It's for when the wind is blowing across you either from right to left or vice versa," he added that, "you will not need it today as it's very still." I put the weapon into my shoulder, cocked the hammer, and squinted through the sight. I controlled my breathing and slowly let out my breath until it was almost gone, then I gently inhaled and the sight picture before me froze just long enough for the front ball and post sight to align. At this moment I squeezed the trigger. Immediately I was blinded by the muzzle flash and the smoke but the Captain was saying, "Good lad, it's a hit."

The Colonel now wanted me to fire at the 300 yard target and there was an empty barrel set up about the same size as a man's head would have been at that distance. I reloaded and put a primer cap on the nipple.

I cocked the weapon and squinted again down the realigned sights, set this time at 300yards. Again it was a simple matter of controlling my breathing and as I slowly exhaled the front bead started to stabilise in line with the blade. It was now or never, and I applied pressure on the trigger ever so slowly. You never really know when it is going to fire and I can remember uncle saying that if it's a surprise then you've done everything right, so long as it's a hit. The rifle bucked in my shoulder, it was a viscous kick and as I couldn't see anything of the target it was a relief when the Captain shouted, "You've done it again, well done lad."

The next few minutes were taken up in fast negotiations between the Colonel and our Captain. Joe, our Sergeant was asked to demonstrate his shooting and afterwards all of our Georgia Company in turn proved their marksmanship. The results were impressive and the Colonel was further convinced his plan to have mounted sharpshooters was going to work. The Colonel and all the staff officers must have been really pleased, as the next day six LeMatt revolvers were issued to us and we were even treated to a shooting demonstration from our Colonel.

This was to be a break in the training routine but we soon started again with the squadron training. Drills were repeated, where we were required to draw the sabre standing, trotting and then at the gallop. Nearly all of our squadron had now been issued with these weapons and it was a daily routine where the regiment would be thrown over and over again at a split rail fence. Every time we turned and galloped back the rail height had been increased and we would have to clear it with the sabre at the ready in attack position.

These drills were not only for the trooper. The troop officers and staff also, were put under pressure. Many times we would witness the sharp torrent of words from our Colonel, not thankfully directed at us, but at company Lieutenants and Captains. They did not like being singled out and put to shame in front of their troops. Some of these were gentlemen farmers and estate owner's sons from Virginia and were not used to any sort of discipline. When I think back to those days I can recollect there were certain officers who simply disappeared after a particularly bad, heated argument, but others would be reduced to the ranks, there and then. They were given the choice, either buckle down to our Captain's direct ways or ride away never to be heard of again. Although there were some content to be simply told what to do and not have any responsibility.

We just thought it was real funny to see these upstarts, who had never done any work in their lives, always had everything done for them and would never have had to make a decision, apart from deciding how best they could next amuse themselves. These moments were a good source of laughs, seeing these rich boys brought down to earth was often enjoyed for many days.

Our Captain was the exception and the Colonel would use him to demonstrate manoeuvres and tactics, I doubt there was much between them in skills or tactical manoeuvres, and reading the manual written by J. Lucius Davis would not teach anything that these two didn't already know.

One day in particular comes easily back to me it was one of those days just before we were to receive orders to Advance in support of Beauregard at Bull Run.

The Colonel was in fine order that morning resplendid in his grey uniform coat with high stock, displaying his Colonel's insignia, yellow silk braids and facings. He looked every inch the cavalier, sabre on the left side, high leather boots with sparkling spurs and a fine black broad brimmed hat complete with ostrich feather.

Our Captain was equally dressed as I knew he had been fitted with a new uniform from one of the best military tailors in Richmond. He had gone out of his way to pester the quartermaster service and with the backing of the Colonel they were successful in getting our whole troop issued with fine quality confederate grey kepis. We were so proud of these; they had leather chin straps and were fitted with a neck shade cloth which could be rolled up when not required. The officers were now on parade and we were numbered off to form a squadron in column of fours. With the Captain in our lead we followed the Colonel at a smart trot. I was excited as this was an active patrol, as there was every likelihood we would meet the enemy, if not in force then at least a picket. We had probably gone around 3 miles when one of our outriders came in on a lathered horse. This man was to be our future Commanding Officer but at this moment he was just like me or you, a private in our other troop the Washington Mounted Rifles.

There was much conversation and our Captain was ordered up to the head of the column. Just after he had reined in between the Colonel's aid and the scout the Colonel shot off leaving the others to catch up as fast as they could.

We waited in sets of four's, my nerves were on edge and Joe had to calm me down with something like, "We haven't even started yet," going on, "Don't let us down, just keep your head and watch me."

It wasn't long before they came back. "The Colonel's face was beaming with joy, his eyes all sparkling and quickly looking us up and down. "Gentlemen we are about to see how much you have learned." To be followed by. "I am about to show you your enemy and we'll advance to contact at the gallop. We looked at each other for a second but there was little time as the Captain was shouting "Column of fours, at the gallop, forward."

The ground sped past at an alarming pace, we flashed through a small wooded hillside and breaking out he was drawing his sabre. "There to your front is the Yankee."

We could make out a skirmish line of enemy infantry just coming up a slope. Their heads and fixed bayonets were now plain, at around 1000yards away. Suddenly there was an officer on horseback and there seemed to be some confusion, then a marching column in ranks were visible on the left. They were being drilled into firing lines of two men deep. I was worried now, this was real and not a bit like the training drills. Joe was talking in his usual calm voice and though I couldn't take in what he was saying his voice calmed me, and I knew immediately what the next order would be. "Squadron halt, into line by troops, officer's front and centre." He was now swinging the sabre around in a circular motion, while as if by magic we formed line around 200 men long. "Squadron, Charge." I was taken completely by surprise as the next order was to move to the left and away from the enemy line. Still pretty much in line we turned, how we managed to keep from riding over each other I don't know, but the horses seemed to know what to do better than us riders. This manoeuvre had been practiced only two days ago but the spacing had to be wide enough to allow the horses on either side, from not colliding with you. The other problem was, as it had been raining quite heavy the ground was wet making the soil heavy. A galloping horse needs space to make a turn, but we had achieved this by not bunching from the offset. The sudden change in direction however does mean that the cavalrymen on the extreme right of the formation were out closer to the enemy firing line. Miraculously there were no casualties, but a 12 pounder gun had raced up on the infantry flank, unlimbered and gone into battery position. As if by magic there appeared a cloud of smoke at its muzzle; followed immediately by the scream of the shot which had gone high but was over our position before we had swung to the left.

"Captain Robinson, take your sharpshooter detail and make them count on that batteries gunner." I was aware of the Captain shouting the order and we Georgians broke away and sped after tour leader. There was sporadic musket fire now, and I could hear ball whistling harmlessly passed over our heads. My horse was enjoying itself and when I looked down I could see his tongue rolling and those big eyes opening wide showing white circles around those sparkling black pupils, like he was laughing.

We were following the Captain towards a clump of dead trees several of which had fallen to the ground and would make an ideal firing position. We reined in behind him and he shouted for Clem to hold the horses. We had only enough time to snatch the rifles from their leather cases on the back of the saddles.

We were ready to fire as the Captain had instructed we load and should take 60 rounds and cartridges before we were ordered out on patrol. I quickly got down behind a fallen tree, worked the hammer back and checked primer cap and set sights for 500 yards. The Captain had estimated the distance and he quickly went down the firing position making sure we were all set at that range. I could see we were being fired on now by a line of skirmishers, but the Captain said they won't be around long as the Colonel would flank them and bring the squadron charging down. If the Yankee's were not sharp enough he would catch them still drawn up in line and would cut them to pieces. Just take your time and pick your targets. I sighted down the barrel through the ladder sights with the extended blade now set to 500yards. I picked out a Lieutenant, busy shouting orders to the crew and fixed him in my sight picture. "Aim for their bodies, centre of their chests," adding "If your shot is high it takes him in the neck, or if low, it'll still do some damage even if it hits him in the legs." I waited with my aim steady; he had stopped moving around and was now looking up towards where he had seen us stop. Our horses were in cover a little way off in a fold in the ground. "Fire, at will." I squeezed off the round, the rifle bucked into my shoulder but I had it firmly tucked in. The smoke rose from the five rifled muskets, 2 Whitworth and 3 Enfield's.

The wind whisked the smoke away quickly, and I saw all the gun crew go down. One was wounded and started to crawl, but he only moved a yard before he went down again and was very still. The Captain didn't have to tell us to reload and I was ready just behind Joe. "Shoot at the end of the line." The Captain was shouting. We again gave them a volley and again witnessed more of them falling. "Another volley," he was saying, and we again sighted down on the Yanks. "Pick the officers," the Captain was shouting and I was lining up on the mounted officer who had come up behind the skirmishers. He must not have known about effective ranges but we'll never know, as when I squeezed the trigger and tried to see where my shot had gone there was his empty horse, running off.

We were immediately surrounded by the Colonel and his staff, and he was shouting orders for us to mount and join the column of fours again. We were now being shot at, but the distance was over 400 yards and the Yankees were just wasting ammunition. "Now gentlemen that was your enemy," "they always shoot high or overestimate distances." We will trot away now. "Column of fours, squadron will trot." "Forward."

The next day 18th July we were ordered to advance in support of Gen. Beauregard.

We were on the move again and it felt good to get away from all that humdrum routine of camp life. There was a lot of sickness in the camps and although we didn't visit other troops the threat of becoming infected was always on your mind. The sick and hospitalised troops were to be evacuated and I thanked the gods we had not been detailed for the escort duty.

Being holed-up in bivouac, was not pleasant as the weather had been very wet. We had managed to build shelters out of branches and bits and pieces of canvas and so had managed for the most time, to stay fairly comfortable. When we were not on exercise or training we would get picket duties or more senseless drills. Cleaning kit for parades and reviews, didn't relieve the off duty boredom. Some would have liked to be back there but for me it was heaven to be on active duty again and especially with this officer.

He had told me many times before about some place called England where they must all talk funny but for us it sometimes made it hard for the lads to understand him. Most of the troop was getting used to him now after this past 2 months. I myself had grown to respect him, not only for his knowledge but also for the way he had of just being one of us, the easy manner with which he could explain and demonstrate, showing the way he wanted things done. His ideas were so different in many ways and were not what we were used to. Most of us had led simple lives, but this was now war and it had hit most of us but in different ways, some were still full of bravado and bragged continually about how the Yankees would soon be beaten. I couldn't help feeling that this was just brave talk from frightened men. I felt we had been very fortunate to have been given the opportunity to train under our officers. The Majority of the regiments commanders and troop leaders were experienced men, having come from the US Army. This effectively was what would keep many of us alive through the war and what made you trust their judgement. It became easy to warm toward them and why they were so popular within the company.

Little things like tending to the horses first, so when on the march you could be sure they were going to be fit, with regular feed and watering. Some of us were natural horsemen as we'd been brought up around horses and learned to ride from an early age, but there was a need to ensure that our horses were kept in a state of continual good health. With this in mind, the Captain schooled each troop member in the style of riding that would be easiest on the horse over long marches and that would not cause sore back from sitting too deep in the saddle or having a tendency to slouch or move to be heavy on one side. He was so attentive to ensure provisions were enough for the horses in our troop, his constant ranting and arguments with quartermaster staff made him very unpopular but his temper and overwhelming, authoritive manner got results. This paid dividends, as our mounts were fine animals from our home counties and could be relied on when we needed to get somewhere, or out of it, in a hurry. We had trained every day to jump them over obstacles and each day was harder. He would have us practice manoeuvres where some would be the attackers and the others the unfortunates. He would show us cut-off tactics where any retreating enemy could be effectively bottled-up and taken prisoner. I knew we were getting better, as by this time I could pretty much read his thoughts, so could see he was pleased with our progress this far.

It took us 36 hours to reach Manassas and save for small amounts of time when we stopped to rest the horses we were continually on the march. In two days and a night we had time for only one hurried meal. We must have looked a sight that morning, the 21st. July. We were wet, tired, and hungry but there was little time to reflect on this and our two troops were divided the next morning Sunday 22nd July 1861. Half of "L" was lucky as they were ordered up to support some infantry very early on. We unfortunately, were for hours drawn up behind some of our artillery and ordered to remain mounted in column of fours. This was a bad position and matters were made worse as we were under the command Maj. Swan. Our role was to remain in reserve to be able to act as a cavalry screen to protect the army should things go completely wrong. The problem being we were being subjected to enemy fire from their guns who were engaged in an artillery duel with our boys. Fortunately the Captain came to our rescue and he organised scouting patrols to scour the battlefield and report on any enemy activities that looked likely to flank our infantry or come up undetected on the guns. The bulk of the regiment numbering around 300 sabres had been distributed along the length of Bull Run; where they were to watch the crossing points between Mitchell's and Ball's fords. The Captain had explained we were to maintain contact between our own companies in reserve under Maj. Swann and the Colonel's command. We flew all over the field in small numbers of two's or three's watching for any opportunity that could be forced, or a mistake by the Blue Bellies that we could take advantage of. The Colonel was with us on several rides, often being fired on or having to dodge parties of skirmishers. This was bad cavalry country and the Yanks had the advantage as their positions were nearly always surrounded by woodland.

Then there was an attack by the enemy on Jackson's position, it was when two Yankee batteries were ordered across the Warrenton Turnpike and came hurtling down the Sudley Road. The smaller of the two batteries unlimber, and come into battery within easy musket range of the Henry House, atop the high ground opposite Jackson's artillery, formed up in front of his firing lines. The larger battery flew further down the road and came into battery south of the house; both batteries engaged Jackson's position merely 300 yards away. The Captain had observed the manoeuvre as we were well placed near the position. We made for the house which was occupied by civilians, but making our apologies, broke out glass from the upstairs windows and upended beds to get mattresses to use for firing positions. We started to fire on the enemy gunners and some of their horses were shot. I couldn't condone this and always fired at the artillery officers first and then the non-commissioned gun commanders.

We didn't have long as these boys were not too happy about losing some of their friends. The nearest gun was being levered around to bear on our position. Joe, Clem and I got off another volley just as the gun layer sighted down the barrel. We ran down the stairs and raced for the horses. Squirrel was there already mounted and he led the mounts around for us to jump in the saddles and spur away.

The sound of shot striking the building caused us to look around and we saw some civilians coming out of the building carrying out an elderly woman who looked like she had been badly injured.

The artillery duel was hot and heavy, Old Beauregard himself had a narrow escape when a shell exploded near him killing his horse and blowing the heel off his boot. Poor horse!

The Yanks then started to reinforce their positions on the hill and there was another two Yankee regiments moved into the line to support the guns. The next thing we knew was that our 33rd. Virginia on the left of Jackson's line were engaged in a hot firefight with them. Funny, as one of these outfits was wearing grey uniform, confusing really but it happened more than once that day. Our boys were still dressed in civilian clothes but it didn't seem to affect their fighting prowess as they sent the Yanks running back to the road.

We galloped towards where the Colonel was sat astride the Manassas-Sudley road, with about two and a half companies, roughly south west of our 33rd. Virginia. He was standing in the stirrups trying to make out who these grey clad infantry were as we galloped up. "Captain Robinson what do you make of those men coming across the road there?" "They are from Heintzelmans division Sir," The Captain shouted, "We saw them deploy." The Colonel would not have it to be and he called for an advance in their direction. As we closed on them a standard bearer came across our path, It was a Yankee regiment and the Colonel was only just finished attempting to turn them back thinking they were panicked Confederates.

He was angry now and called the charge. We were not prepared and only a few of us got the correct order it was so confusing that we had very few men engaged in the action. The Loudon Light Horse "H" company had galloped into the enemy with only 33 men and some of "D" company managed to join us. I was caught up in the wild charge being hemmed in between the Captain, his man servant Jacob, Joe and the rest of the sharpshooter's. We jumped over a split rail fence into a hail of musketry. They were still in disciplined fighting lines and were able to account for a lot of horses and around eight or nine officers and men.

We put them into thick cover on the wooded sides of the hill. I was aware of firing my pistol but couldn't recall if my shooting had accounted for any of the New Yorker's. We were immediately recalled and trotted away down the road to our starting position astride the road. The battle see-sawed all day, backwards and forwards across the Manassas-Sudley road, but around 16:00 hrs. There was a change of fortune.

The battered remains of Sherman's brigade and what was left of some others who had been engaged earlier started to pull back towards the Warrenton Turnpike. Reinforcements came up in the form of some South Carolina troops and these were engaged immediately with Yankee's freshly moved onto Chinn Ridge. We could see there were fresh reserves arrived close to where we were positioned. These were from Colonel Elzey's brigade. We joined with this and flanked the advance toward the Manassas – Sudley road. We were now in the company of Colonel Early's brigade and we moved forward with our regiment covering the flank, our small battery hurling shot and shell towards the enemy line. We were stalled for a few minutes as the infantry of Howards thin line exchanged volley for volley with our lads. In the end it was too much for them and they started out towards the turnpike. Things were going badly for the Yanks now and it was turning into a panicky rout.

We were ordered forward to harass the retreating Bluecoats. They had drawn up a battalion of regulars on the junction of the turnpike and the Manassas-Sudley road. They gave a good account of themselves but didn't want to have their position turned and so when this became likely, they turned and retreated in orderly fashion. However the Majority of the Yanks were not made of the same stuff. We were again chasing the New Yorkers that we had bumped earlier and some of the lads had scores to settle. Horses and comrades killed were avenged that afternoon. They attempted to form up into firing companies and achieved this a few times. It was soon obvious where our duty lay, and together we all crashed into their line. Several men fell as they got off a ragged volley and as we broke through them a number of horses went down. We came at 'em again now from behind and they were losing their nerve. You could see there was a definite break in their disciplined ranks and a swell of men broke and started to run away from us. We couldn't help ourselves now and we turned on them, cutting them down as they tried to look over their shoulders at us. Some were still in small disciplined squads and these took aim and fired into us. If they had all been as determined we would have lost more men that afternoon. Our Captains were frantically trying to stop us and as the recall was accomplished, we quickly regrouped close to our lines. As it was this sudden surge of movement by enemy troops triggered a panic for real. The whole enemy line was moving; resembling an army of ants as they bulge out when on the move. This was so infectious there was no stopping it. We were again turned around and were sent back again to harass the fleeing Yankees. We were suddenly alongside our own two troops "G" and those of "L". They had been held in reserve all day, apart from some being used as couriers and scouts. I laughed at some of them I recognised and made a joke of their bad luck but they were with Maj. Swan and he didn't look as though he wanted to share in our little victory. We were off again at the gallop; the

Captain's swinging their sabres and many of our lads, completely drunk with battle fever were following their example. I was merely using the LeMatt and couldn't help counting the shots as I cocked it again and again until it was empty. Suddenly there was a Yankee on horseback right in front of me. He had seen how we were despatching his comrades but instead of running away he was coming towards me. It was then that I panicked as I had an empty revolver in my hand but the LeMatt has a shotgun charge also and I remembered just in time to change the hammer position so as it would fire off the load of buck shot. He was up to me fast, his line was perfect and I could see his sabre drawn back ready, and as we passed within inches I fired into his chest. The sabre was already on its way towards me, it had possibly lost some of its momentum but the blade struck me on the top of my right shoulder. We were past each other now, and I caught a glimpse of him falling out of the saddle to be swallowed up by a press of men and galloping horses. His blade had cut me and I was bleeding. There was blood running down the inside of my shell jacket and it was making the revolver still in my hand, sticky with my blood. I had not lost any feeling and was able to holster the revolver. All I could think of was would I be able to defend myself. Just then Clem came up behind me and saw immediately that I was hurt. We galloped over to a clump of trees and were about to dismount when a group of Yankees from the same regiment we had just ridden over came out of cover. Clem unholstered his revolver but there was no need for any further action as these boys were finished. They threw down their muskets and I can remember seeing these were a mix of Minnie rifles and muskets, old weapons and not worth us picking them up. I dismounted and took my new issue Colt in my left hand and covered them while Clem put a makeshift bandage around the wound. It was not that deep but it would have probably continued into my neck had it not lost some of the force originally intended. There were now more cavalry units coming up and were detailed to shepherd the Yankee's back behind our lines.

We continued until nightfall and there were now many more Yankee prisoners to escort back to our lines. I used to hate doing this as I would start to think of what I would do should one or more of 'em decide to have a go at me. Would I be able to shoot 'em down? The Captain had taken the worry away for me as he had organised a party to pick up enemy weapons and ammunition. The whole route of their retreating army was littered with equipment, guns and small arms. We were not interested in rifles as we were well equipped and had the Enfield's or Whitworth also, but revolvers were the sought after prize. Boots and shirts, belts, haversacks, blankets, ammunition, pouches, primer cap boxes and canteens were everywhere and so we reequipped ourselves with everything we needed including clothing. This was like Christmas morning at a rich auntie's house; everything they had thrown away was gratefully accepted. However it was folly to wear an enemy jacket or coat as it would make you an easy target for our own men, who would look at the colour of your clothing first and not who you were. Exactly what had happened earlier today.

Chapter 15

Our Captain led us away that night and we camped far enough away from the many wounded that were still lying there out on the battlefield. He was again in a talkative mood, the first time since before we had mustered into the regiment. His servant Jacob was with him and as far as I had seen was never very far away from his side. He kept the Captain's clothes, weapons and horses in fine condition and took great pride in keeping his master looking his best regardless of the weather or enemy action. I looked at him that night and it was the first time I had noticed he was in uniform with boots, trousers, jacket and forage cap. He was walking behind the Captain and when I called out to him he came across and greeted us. We were always a close knit, little unit of sharpshooters and tended to keep ourselves to ourselves most of the time. This was the first opportunity we had been given to talk with our Captain. The other Captains did not tend to mix with the ordinary ranks in off duty periods but our officer was an exception. His first words were full of praise for our professionalism. In today's action we had not only served as efficient sharpshooters but had conducted ourselves with honour and bravery throughout all the cavalry actions. He went on to say that this had been noticed by the Colonel and that he had commended us to the General.

This made us very proud, but he was not finished and enquired how my wound was. I couldn't think of how he had known about this incident, but he did. "You must use this as an example," he said, and then went on about not being preoccupied by shooting a pistol. How the Hell he had found out about this I still don't know to this day.

"The LeMatt requires more concentration than any other revolver and you were lucky to have come out of your dream in time to change over the hammer position."

"I want you to be more confident with all weapons and in particular the sabre."

I still was carrying the Hawken short rifle and it occurred to me perhaps he would allow me to give it to the boy. I asked him and he immediately said that it would not go down too well with the other men or indeed the officers. However I then noticed the boy was wearing a pistol belt with cartridge pouch and holster. This was brand new issue Yankee equipment and was complete with a .44 calibre Colt. On leaving he mentioned we could go through some shooting training with the lad when we were forced to camp for the winter and with that he turned on his heel and walked into the night, followed closely by the boy.

The Bluecoats did not stop at their bases around Centreville but kept on; many acting independently or in small groups reached Washington in 'Quick Time.' We even heard of some running all the way back up north into Philadelphia and New York. I often wondered if the New York boys we had that run-in with ever got paid, as that's all those prisoners we took were on about. The fact they were not given the proper uniform and they hadn't been paid in months. Best laugh was their three month engagement term was up that day. What a shame!

We were in such high spirits and although we were not engaged in any enemy contacts for a while, there was always the picket duty and the reconnaissance patrols. We got a chance to be with the Captain again and for a few days we were on patrol with him and his man servant. Conversation was always centred on the battle and he would explain how things went badly for the enemy and how we could have done better. He would always ask our opinions and from these returns we would learn lessons which would give us an edge in the conflicts to come. He told us what the 'Butchers Bill' was, and that our forces had suffered 1,982 losses. In this there were 13 captured, but this was not counting all the horses and these losses were to be more serious than their riders as the war dragged on. It was also his opinion that the battle had been fought with troops commanded by too many civilians and not enough experienced officers. We had been lucky as I said before, but the Yankees had suffered from the inefficiency of McDowell, his inability to be able to see the whole picture and the slowness of his advance. He also criticised Beauregard for his insufficient control of the actions on Henry Hill, if he had been more forceful and hadn't left so much organisation at regimental level, things may have run better. We discussed Johnson's clever escape from Winchester and how he had evaded Powell's forces, but the crowning glory had to be the use of the railroad to deliver men and equipment to the battlefield. We didn't benefit from this, but I'd rather have travelled mounted on my horse, together with my company, than have had to sit twiddling my thumbs in a box-car.

The wounded were being shipped by ambulances to Manassas Junction to board trains either on the Manassas Gap Railroad, or the Orange & Alexandria Railroad. These special hospital trains would be added to the supply trains running to Strasburg in The Shenandoah Valley, or farther south west to Gordonsville where the Virginia Central Railroad connected to Staunton and Richmond. This railway transport could have been better utilised but owing to bad management from Johnson's appointed railroad supervisors, a lot of mistakes and hardships were created, many of which could have been avoided had they been properly supervised.

A lot of poor lads would end up in the Richmond hospitals, and I wondered if the Negro woman we came through the mountains with was now serving with the hospital orderlies. She knew a lot about healing and the use of plants and herbs for dressing wounds so I felt sure she would be a great help to our wounded lads.

We covered every crossing point along Bull Run and watched from every hill for blue coated cavalry. Within the next few days we would be advancing with General Jackson to set up a base at Centreville. Beauregard was sent south on other duties and Johnson had been promoted. Jackson was to remain in the Valley while we stayed with Johnson's army and moved to Centreville. Every day we pushed forward until we were looking down onto Washington's church spires and the sprawling mass of buildings. Jacksons words come back to me now as he was said to have shouted, "Give me 5000 fresh troops and I'll be in Washington tomorrow." Whether he did or not I'll leave up to you but sitting on my gelding on top of either Mason or Munson hill's the Yankee Capital is within spitting distance.

There were further promotions and if I remember rightly our Colonel was also promoted around that time. Johnson must have thought there was a need for more cavalry units and so we learned we were to be brigaded with the 1st, 2nd, 4th, and 6th Virginia, also the 1st North Carolina and the Jeff Davis Legion. Our beloved JEB would be Brigadier General of Cavalry in the Provisional

Army of the Confederate States. I would be still me and Joe was still our Sergeant.

We were always kept busy, and as the weather was starting to get colder by the day it was essential that foraging parties had to be sent out regularly to try and provide for our boys, these as you can imagine had to be escorted. This was down to us and although it was not all that exciting it was better than being on picket or camp guard duty. Our headquarters were around Fairfax and the camp had been named by the General himself Qiu Vive. These little things amused him, just like his love of singing and entertaining the ladies. He was a show off but we didn't mind as reviews were always popular and sometimes you'd benefit from some civilian family presenting you with a delicious food parcel. One day comes back to me pretty clearly now. It was on one of them famous scouting details that we came across a little hamlet named Lewinsberg. It was pretty much centred on a cross roads that received attention from both our patrols and those of the enemy. We had worked our way around the few buildings and had come across an enemy cavalry camp, holding about a half troop. The Captain sent me back to where we happened to be sharing a bivouac with some of JEB's junior staff. I reported to a staff Captain who detailed a Lieutenant to come back with me. It was the same officer who had been with us since that day at Staunton, when we boarded the train. The Captain showed him the enemy pickets and he must have thought it was worth reporting because he trotted off towards headquarters for orders. Leaving us to simply melt away back to our camp, safe and concealed in some woods well away from the hamlet.

The next thing we hear is a challenge and the sound of real commotion from one of our pickets. A trooper from our outpost nearest the hamlet has come in with a message for our Brigadier; this has been left with them by a civilian who had been tasked with its delivery but had been sent by a Yankee officer from the cavalry camp.

Needless to say, I am detailed to deliver the message to Headquarters. I report to the Captain on duty and explain I have a message for our commander and that it has come via a civilian in Lewinsburg.

I am ordered to follow him to the Brigadiers office where the adjutant officer allows me to deliver the note. I am ushered into the room where sitting behind his desk is JEB Stuart. He recognises me as soon as I attempt to march up to the table in my awkward, but best soldierly fashion. I manage to control my legs and arms and give him the right arm in the correct salute befitting of such a brilliant leader. He smiles at my obvious nervousness and listens to my tale of how we had come across the enemy and the delivery of the note by a civilian.

He took the note and laughed out loud while still reading it. "He wants me to go to dinner with him in Washington this Saturday night."

"What do you say to that sharpshooter?" I couldn't believe the words that came from my mouth as I was listening to myself say "I would ride in there with the squadron Sir and deliver an answer in person."

He roared with laughter, his face beaming making his beard go even redder but his eyes were sparkling like the stars in the sky on a summer's night. "You're right lad," he said and then shouted for the adjutant to summon Captain Irwin of 'G' troop.

I was to wait for the troop to form up and I amused myself watching some of them panicking to find their kit and get it all on the horse before the Sergeant came back again. They were soon in an open square formation in a clear area and sat mounted waiting for The Brigadier. He rode into the centre and whirled his mount around. "Gentlemen we are tasked to deliver a message to another misguided soul who has decided to serve the Yankee's." "This officer I knew at West Point has invited me to dine with him at the Williard's Hotel in Washington on this Saturday night." "However I consider this extremely rude not to have included you all, and so you will be invited by my invitation to deliver the apologies." "Mr Irwin the troop will march on me." The Captain shouted out. "Troop, by column of fours," "Sergeants lead out."

I joined the column in the rear but our Brigadier sent a galloper to bring me up with his staff. I was to direct them immediately by the safest route to rendezvous with our Captain and the rest of my sharpshooters. We made contact with Silas one of our party and perhaps the strangest character I have ever met in my entire life, past and present.

He still wore the buckskin shirt that he had when we all left Georgia, but he had gratefully accepted the Confederate cap and the cavalry trousers. His weapons were the same as ours as we all had benefitted from the Georgia State Guards, the night we relieved them of their duty. The only difference regarding weaponry was even though we both still carried a Hawken short barrelled rifle, in addition he had the Indian flat bow and a quiver of arrows. The Brigadier was intrigued with him as he was not even visible until he had moved out of cover. If he had not wished for you to see him then you would have simply ridden passed his position and you would not even of known there was anyone there.

You could make out the enemy pickets and hear the hum of men in conversation perhaps 5o yards away.

Chapter 16

The Captain had now come up in a hurry and looked embarrassed that Silas had been drawn into a conversation with the Brigadier. He made some apologies for the unusual appearance of one of his men and went on to recommend Silas to be promoted Chief of Scouts. "We are not on the Frontier now Captain." He said but was laughing behind that mass of side burns and whiskers.

"Trooper Silas can you take out those pickets yonder?"

"I want you and the lad to go around and take care of them all, and then fire a single pistol shot when you have achieved it." He then went on to relay his orders to the two Captains that they should have the troop mounted to surround the camp keeping within short range. There were four pickets, two were static, together nearest the road and then the other two were mobile, patrolling the far perimeter.

I had had little to do with Silas, and even though we had been together for months he was not the sort of man you could get close to. He was an old comrade of the Captain's, from their Indian fighting days and was tolerated for that reason but he would always prefer his own company and would eat and sleep away from the rest of us. I now had to kill these men without a weapon. It was obvious that Silas would use the bow and so that left me with a lump in my stomach again that was fast coming up into my throat. I asked him in whisper what he intended and after he had drawn us away to a safe position where we could see the first pickets, he took the tomahawk out of his belt and handed it to me. He whispered and indicated that I take the one nearest on the right while he shot the other with the bow. I looked toward the enemy picket, but when I turned around Silas was nowhere to be seen. There were no sounds at all save the noise of men talking in the camp. I got my senses together and decided on what I was going to do. I made my way as quietly as I could, using all my hunting skills and every piece of field craft I had ever learned. He was around five paces from me now but I had planned my approach carefully. I had spotted every dead branch or leaf litter on the ground that would give me away should I tread upon it. The soldier was three feet away from me now sitting on a fallen tree and tending to a coffee pot on a small fire just to his front. His attention would be diverted from my approach and so, as if I hadn't known I was going to do it, I launched myself forward with the tomahawk raised above my head in the strike position. He suddenly turned in my direction and the blow that had been aimed for the back of his head now came down to crunch into the man's skull above his ear. I felt the blade smash through the bone but he was still alive hunched over on all fours at the side of the fire. I swung the weapon down again this time into the small of his neck at the base of the skull.

I was shaking, but felt Silas pulling me away. He said we had to go for the other two who were mounted and patrolling around the far perimeter. I don't know how I managed to do it but we were now there, in a position to see where the pickets were. We had observed their patrolling pattern and there was an overlap as they passed each other on every circuit. Silas indicated we would take them at this point. He would take the one farthest away leaving the other for me. I moved out silently before him this time, and I was determined not to let the Brigadier and our two Captains down. I was crawling toward a bush which I had selected because it was on the side of the path the rider would take. If my timing was right, then I could reach up as he rode passed and put the tomahawk into his head. I risked a look out of cover and on the balls of my feet I inched my head up so that I could see where the rider was. As if by magic or thanks to the gods that must have taken a liking to me, he was just in the right position. They had passed and were again riding away from each other. I jumped up and grabbed him by his rifle sling. He came towards me easily and as he continued to fall I swung the tomahawk at his head. He made a stifled shout but the blade was nearly there and before he could struggle it was buried in his head. He was still, and I couldn't help looking down at the terrible wound where his brains and splintered bone could be seen. I was just collecting my senses when I heard it. It was the noise of the passage of a turkey feathered arrow, and as I looked up it was just appearing on the other side of the rider's neck, having gone clean through. The next noise I heard was the crack of Silas's revolver. If it hadn't have been for his quick thinking the enemy camp may have been alerted too soon.

They were there now, rushing out of cover twenty yards away, the rebel yell echoing through the trees and making that eerie sound. Most had drawn the sabre and were racing into the enemy at the gallop. It was over in a few minutes and the Brigadier was looking around at the blue coats that had been killed in the action and those who were now prisoners. His old friend was not present but there was a good chance he was one of the few who had broken through our screen and ridden off at a great pace. There were only three riders, so I have often wondered if the Brigadier's dinner host was there at all or back in Washington getting ready for an off-duty weekend. Our troop managed to ransack the Yankee camp and we all came away with something, either food, items of clothing, boots or small arms. We laughed as we mounted and trotted away from the scene pushing the prisoners ahead with the point of the sabre when needed. We had four men slightly wounded in the action but they were still able to ride.

I was looking at Silas and he was stuffing a large piece of cooked ham into his mouth as we marched. The remainder he had dropped into his kepi and it opened like a sack with the weight. These kepis were able to take most joints of cooked meat, especially hams, chickens, ducks and goose and then could be placed back on your head and secured with the chin strap.

I have some pleasant memories of that summer, as when it did stop raining it made the air so crisp and clean. Everything was green and fresh with an abundance of wild flowers in the open glades in the woods. It was so easy to forget the war and what we were doing all this way from home. I had finally received a letter from mother; it had been months since I had written to them from camp Jeff Davis. The mail had caught up with us now though, and all of us had received letters from family or a special girl. The news was not good, as things were not going well with the farm. Mother could not keep the home going and uncle was unable to help as he had joined some militia and was away for long periods. How he had managed to be accepted with his injuries I'll never know. The girls were well, and Beth was helping them with food and a little money now and again when she could but times were hard and money was tight. The blockade was tightening around the main sea ports so cotton could not be sold as freely. When a blockade runner did get through, Beth's family were able to sell some of their cotton or tobacco but they were not able to dock very often. Mother told me she and the girls were going to find work in Roswell, at the mill. It had been awarded a contract to manufacture Army uniforms and tents so were in need of workers. I didn't know what I felt but if they could support themselves from earning wages then it couldn't be that bad.

The next day I found the time to reply to mother's letter. They seemed to be giving us a few off duty days and these were welcomed with open arms. The war seemed it had been stalled. Cavalry were busy in the valley being engaged to destroy bridges and railroad rolling stock. A new rail line was being built from Manassas to Centreville to bring up supplies and troops to keep Johnsons army fed and supplied. I wonder what it was like for those Negro's working to drive that line through the difficult terrain. Funny how in periods of inactivity your mind often starts thinking to all manner of things, which are less important and don't immediately concern you. However I did think about what had happened to Jacob, the Captains man servants' father. I wondered if he had been able to be together with his wife in the shanty town around the Richmond defence line. There must have been plenty of wounded now after the recent battles so she would be needed as a nursing orderly. There was also the sickness; it would spread through a regiment so quickly. Meat was a problem and we were being supplied with plenty of it, but it was very often spoiled by the time it got to us. This would give you the 'trot's' and if you didn't get over it, this would render you weak and unfit for active duty. We were lucky here as there was good water but it wasn't always to be the case and there were often hospital camps where typhoid had decimated the whole strength. Measles and Mumps were common and infectious it would make us stay away and try not to be involved in any duty that may take us even near the place.

I started to spend a little bit more time with Silas, as since the action at Lewinsburg there seemed to be a change in his attitude towards me. I was interested in learning how to shoot the flat bow and he took great pleasure in training me and some of the boys in the company, in its use. I was impressed with his skill; I had seen it before in Georgia and when we were on the march over the mountains. This was something that had to be done instinctively, similar to when you're in a close quarter contact with the enemy. The rifle can be used in a similar fashion if it is aligned with your line of sight. It's hard to explain if you've never fired at anyone but imagine if you are looking at someone, but your rifle is aligned in the other direction. You are not likely to survive this, so let's just say that whatever you are looking at needs to be covered by your weapon. If your head moves then it is followed by your rifle. The bow is like that and you would never hit anything if you were looking down the arrow and aligning its head on your target. The strange answer to success is to look at your target and the arrow will automatically be aligned if you are holding it properly. So you don't aim, you just make sure the arrow is going to follow exactly where you are looking. It takes practice, but after a few days we were all managing to hit man sized targets at fifty yards.

There were other pastimes that kept us in good spirits at this camp, one of these was hunting. Our Captain was a keen hunter and we would go off into the woods and shoot game. The Negro boy Jacob would be with him and I was allowed to instruct him in shooting the Hawken short rifle. He learned quickly and became a very reasonable shot. We all were very partial to squirrel and often shot these with these rifles that only Silas and I still owned. The thing about hunting squirrel was that you always went into the trees in a group of three or four men. They would watch you, but the secret is to have one member of the hunting party remain hidden while the rest walk away. They must not be able to count as always they would come down out of the tree canopy when they thought it was safe. This was their mistake, as they could now be shot as they travelled down the trunk of the tree. This way there was a back stop for the bullet and you'd not shoot your fellow trooper by mistake. The meat we shot was a pleasant change from what the cooks usually gave us and sometimes we would cook venison steaks on our own campfire. The Captain had the use of a tent and there were many of us that had been given these. There was so much captured equipment after Bull Run that while we were here things were made very comfortable. We, as a scout unit were not always that lucky, and had to make shelters out of more natural materials. Our favourite being the frame shelter made from small tree poles and then covered with a network of branches. Finally these would be layered with earth holding any grass or other vegetation that would be likely to stay living and continue to grow naturally. This shelter would blend in to its surroundings and when it was lined inside with dry, dead leaves to a good depth, it could provide the best comfortable night's sleep you'd had for weeks.

The best days laugh was when Joe made a wager on whose horse would win a race between our Captain's mount and another trooper from "L" troop. Some of you may have guessed already, and yes! It was the very same trooper who we would serve alongside later in the war. Only then he would be our Colonel. Our trooper had been a favourite of the Brigadier, ever since Bull Run. We had been used most of that day, since the early hours on courier duty. Flying all over the battlefield with messages and taking orders to commanders who were often in the thickest of fire fights. Later that day we were relieved of this duty, so as to act as skirmishers and sharpshooters but some of the "L" company boys were in the saddle for over twenty hours. This trooper Mosby was one of them and had rightly so, been commended and recognised by our leader JEB Stuart.

Only the previous day we had watched these two race out of camp having swapped horses. The Brigadier on the trooper's horse and Mosby on the recent, fine mount the Brigadier had been given by a high society, widow woman from Richmond. This lady was often the centre of some scandal involving a married officer. However if the Captain knew I had been talking of this to anybody I'd have been on camp guard duty for a month.

Mosby told us afterwards that they had ridden out through our pickets and swung out across a field, then another and then cut a road several miles from camp. He turned out onto the road at great speed, and had not even looked around when Mosby tried to give a warning about there being an enemy picket in the woods further along. He didn't even raise an eyebrow, and Mosby had to use all the horsemanship he ever learned to keep up with him. The horses were evenly matched but Mosby's may just have had the edge. He then told us that they were flying headlong into two enemy pickets on foot at the side of the road. As they came up on them they were joined by another two. All that the Brigadier said was that they'll not be expecting anyone from this direction and urged Mosby's mount on. They would be raised in the stirrups now allowing the horses to move without the press of a human body bearing down on their backs. He said he was bent forward along the Brigadier's horse's neck and his mane was whipping into his eyes and half blinding him. When they burst through the picket line Mosby said that all he could think of was the pain of bullets striking his backside. Luckily the Yanks were shooting high but he described how you could hear those Minnie balls whining over his head. They put rowels to the horses now and they opened up even more. There was no word from the Brigadier but he said you could see the wild look in his eyes. Minutes later they both jumped through our boy's picket line and upset them. There was much cursing and swearing but the two had reined in on skidding horses and the Brigadier was jumping to the ground well before the horse had stopped. The winner was Mosby by merely a nose but never-the less a winner and poor old Joe was, like our Brigadier the loser.

Chapter 17

The weather had been kind to us, which enabled the horses to be looked after really well. Our troop had managed to build shelters for them. These were simple but managed to keep our remounts, and horses that were at rest, off duty sheltered from the occasional wet and cold that was coming in every few days. As December grew older and Christmas approached it became more important we should not have to rely on the supply from Quartermaster or Commissary departments. All our Captains had expressed their concerns about the failing of supplies, and as we were constantly in contact with the enemy it was important to operational efficiency that we could maintain our mounts in the best possible condition.

This, coupled with the obvious signs that the winter was to take a hold soon must have brought the situation to the attention of the Corps Commanders and henceforth to the Army Command. I can remember the mission was to escort some foragers into the country around the town of Dranesville. This was to be a combined effort and we were to screen wagons and a force of infantry to allow them to collect whatever they could from farms west of the town. The area was only twenty miles from Washington so we would be making sure they wouldn't be bothered by active enemy patrols.

There were constant contacts with enemy pickets and scouts, but we had not lost any men or horses for some days. The Yankees were not as country wise as us and you could normally get up close without alerting them. We came to the conclusion that if we left them alone and just kept them under observation it was better than have them try and retaliate in larger numbers than we could muster. So after a few weeks we stopped shooting them from cover and simply reported their positions to the Captain. It was on one of these days when I was with Joe and Silas and patrolling around, off the roads in the vicinity, we saw a Yankee half troop. They were trotting down the road as if they owned it, and obviously thought there was no need to bother putting out flankers. Silas was disgusted, and was in favour of laying an ambush and knocking a few down, then galloping off. Joe put this out of his mind and I was sent back to inform the Captain what we had seen while the rest of them shadowed the Yankees. The Captain seemed to be more involved these days with staff meetings and would be most likely at Head Quarters, the charming little farmhouse which our Brigadier was using situated between Centreville and Fairfax Courthouse. I drove my gelding on at such a pace we were soon approaching the picket lines. There is a daily challenge which if not answered correctly will produce a hail of Minnie balls. I had no problems as we were well known but not liked by the infantry, had this been at night then it would have been different. On reining-in outside the cottage garden I pressed forward in my best military attitude. The adjutant was seated at his desk in the outer room which was the brigade office.

I was ushered in to see the Brigadier; he was sitting on the couch in front of lovely fire writing. I threw up the smartest salute of my army career and blurted out what we had run into. He looked amused and watched my nervous twitching, but as I started to relax I became aware we were not alone. My Captain and some other staff officers were stood around a large map spread over the table. "Well sharpshooter, can you please show the gentlemen where these people were." I stumbled toward the table watching my Captain as he attempted to calm me down with a friendly smile. I drew out the movement of the enemy and gave them an opinion on their destination. They were on the Leesburg – Washington Pike and riding in that direction they could have only been going to Dranesville.

I was dismissed and allowed to ride back to the rest of the patrol. This was the dangerous part as if I'd been bumped by an enemy patrol that had fresher horses than mine, and then I would have been killed.

I found them again nearer to the town and we looked down on the buildings from a wooded hillside. There was a cavalry patrol headed in our direction, so we simply faded away into the green background and made our way back to our own lines. The next day we were roused out of our sleep by the Captain, he was with Captain Jones and the fresh faced Lieutenant Barclay who had now joined as an aid on the regimental staff. Our company was paraded with a half troop of "L" company and some of the 4th Virginia, close to one hundred and fifty troopers. We were numbered off and it went without saying the first set of 'fours', was us.

We made good progress and were soon close to the area where we would be able to observe the town. The infantry, mustered around one thousand six hundred men, had marched before us and they had been followed by the train of six wagons. We were also with a two gun battery of twelve pounder guns. The Brigadier had split us up and while our troop was in the van, our other troopers were a little further behind us with the guns, We could not help noticing as we looked down that morning into the town, the large numbers of enemy troops. There were cavalry and infantry patrols all around and they had expelled a small picket of our boys who had been forced to beat a hasty retreat and were now with us, being questioned by our officers. The

Brigadier sent "L" troop to ride back towards the wagons and to draw them away to the west. They were to get them into a defensive position and then return to us bringing the infantry with them as fast as they could march. It soon became evident that the Yankees were out to gather forage the same as we were but far outnumbered our force. Very soon the main body came into view; they had already been alerted and were now in a fighting formation and manoeuvring westward to take our wagons as part of the prize. I still wonder how he managed to bring us down on that Yankee line. The Captain came galloping down between us as we were deployed in cover in the trees. He told us to form into two diagonal lines meeting in the front where the Brigadier was to be. The guns were tucked in behind us as close as was possible without giving their position away to the enemy line. They were advancing now with flags and officers riding about them and we could see their mouths opening and shutting as the orders were passed down their line. Our infantry had appeared to our left and the Captains and the Brigadier had left us with Lieutenant Barclay. We watched with interest as the infantry deployed, they were not as many as the Yanks and it looked to me as though we were outnumbered around four to one. The Yankee battery now opened up with shot and shell at around two thousand yards. Our Captain came up now, and told us to hold as the infantry deployed and moved in attack formation across the open ground. It was hard to watch those lads, never been in action before in their lives most of them and they were taking casualties. Gaps started to appear in their ranks as canister and round shot rained down from the Yanks two guns. The Sergeants were fighting to hold them together and plug-up the gaps. We were getting anxious now as we were ordered to stay hidden and not to move till the infantry were up to within three hundred paces. It was hard to just sit there and I turned away and picked a line where I thought we would have to charge. He must have seen what I was doing as he came and pointed to their right flank. We will trot slowly away in a minute and work our way around into clear ground. When we have enough space between the woods we will charge their right flank in an arrow shaped formation with the guns in close behind us. When they see us coming they will be fully engaged with our infantry and won't even see the guns. They will try and manoeuvre so as to be able to receive cavalry, but we will open our formation and swing behind them to ride down their line.

He had only just finished explaining when it happened. Our Brigadier was suddenly there at the edge of the trees and they were all shouting to advance at the trot following the officers. We worked our way through the cover between, and in and out of the trees until we were opposite some open ground. The guns were slower and we waited in line for them to tuck in behind us. Here we were ordered "Forward, at the trot." and as soon as the pace started to open naturally, and we were in a reasonably straight line. The order to charge was heard.

The ground flashed passed, it was enough to stop you breathing, my heart was pounding and I was straining to clear my revolver from my waist belt, closed holster. Not many of us had drawn the sabre as the Brigadier was not completely in approval of the weapon, much the same opinion as the Captain in that these were not as efficient as the revolver. We had two revolvers and all of our little sharpshooter section had been working on attaching another pistol holster to the front saddle.

I had been in such a state; the order to draw weapons was completely missed by my deaf ears. Thinking back, had I been near to Joe he would have made sure I was ready. Joe was well over to my right and I had become separated from our little Georgia Company. I started to panic as I noticed the enemy had seen us and their line was changing shape, maybe five hundred yards away. Suddenly the order to open ranks and turn right came down the line. By the time we were in column of two's racing towards the blue bellies the guns had unlimbered and come into battery five hundred yards from them. Suddenly the guns crashed out almost in unison and I saw a great swathe of humanity who moments before had been firing away towards us, were now a broken bloody mass on the ground.

We were curving around their right flank now, but keeping far enough away from the canister and round shot being alternately thrown into their ranks. I levelled the revolver and started firing into any Yankee that appeared to be a threat. Our revolvers were taking a toll now and we were flying down their rear killing anyone who made himself obvious.

My revolver was empty, and I pulled the other from my belt having replaced the empty one back in its place. This was the LeMatt and I had practiced to be able to fire the shotgun charge first before having to change over the hammer position so as to be able to fire the cylinder loads. I was completely in control now, as my nerves were like steel and the killing again began. Our lads were falling now and I knew the infantry had lost many of their number. They sounded to be locked in a volley for volley, deadly exchange but I couldn't see anything. On a battlefield the gun smoke is like a cloud and after the volleys it hangs in the air often obscuring your view of the enemy.

We had been recalled and had now to take up the single shot carbine. The Captain took us back down the line firing as he went, and we did the same, only this time with just one single shot available. I was beginning to shake now with the fury of battle. It is hard to explain to anyone who's not experienced it before, but you are so aware of everything and feel as though nothing can harm you. Fear hasn't time to enter your brain, not yet anyway but it will catch up. You even start to laugh out loud as enemy fire whizzes close past your head or tugs at your clothing.

The enemy infantry were engaged front and rear for a while and with our battery on their flank they were taking a lot of casualties. However there were blue belly cavalry all around us now as we came out from behind them. Our chance to draw the sabre was fast approaching and again we turned with the Brigadier at the head we crashed into the enemy. They had not realised we had guns so close and those gunners must have been good for they waited until we came out from between them and regrouped. They had stalled but it was too late for a lot of them as our battery gave them canister and grape at a rapid rate of fire.

The enemy battery had now realised what was happening on their left, and started to drop shells and round shot in amongst our guns. A shell exploded close to where the battery horses stood and one was killed outright. This gave us the opportunity to draw away and in column of four's we trotted back up towards the tree line. The gunners withdrew in orderly fashion and they made a splendid show galloping after us, the horse's manes blown out straight with the wind of their passage. Their battery which had been engaged with our infantry was now chasing us and the shells and round shot started dropping amongst the trees. We had given the infantry a chance to disengage, and after two hours of fighting they had severely mauled the Yankees. As we gathered ourselves in the trees and began looking about us for lost comrades who hadn't been seen through the fighting, the Captain came through our ranks. He was pointing to where the Brigadier was still below us on the field where our battery had taken a hit from a Yankee shell just as we were withdrawing. He was on foot working around a dead battery horse. "Looks like he's removing the harness," the Captain said. "We'd better ride down and bring him off." There was no need really, as by the time we had drawn level with him he was swinging up into the saddle clutching the entire horse harness from the dead animal. "These are in short supply, never leave these behind."

We were ordered to form on the wagons now and with us acting as a screen and some companies of infantry forming a rear-guard, the command regrouped. The Yankees were severely shocked and we had given them a bloody nose. However we had lost a lot of lads and many we were forced to leave to the good nature of the enemy. We must have persuaded them it was not worth pursuing us as we left them to the town and trotted away but without any forage.

We moved around six miles and two gallopers were sent back to army headquarters to ask the General for help. They arrived before dawn and we were ordered back towards the village later that morning. I couldn't believe that we were again going into that position. However when we stopped to reconnoitre they had already left, not even bothering to bury our dead.

When we returned our Captain formed us into troops and indicated he wanted to talk to us. The action with the enemy line had gone well, and when we were told a couple of days later by some residents of the area, that the Yankees had wagon loads of wounded in ambulances pass through the town and that burial parties were busy the remainder of the day. It was obvious that they had lost many more than we had. Our officers were pleased with how we had conducted ourselves and wanted to press home awareness of the most effective weapons for use in a cavalry contact. We were all convinced that the answer was to be able to carry more revolvers and especially the Remington which had a removable cylinder that if you had more than one, could be preloaded and stored in a cartridge pouch ready to replace an empty one.

Chapter 18

Christmas 1861 came and went; it was a happy and jovial atmosphere in the cavalry camp. Our Brigadier had his wife visit him with the children and they could be seen often, running around through the trees in between the puzzled pickets and camp guards. JEB would be chasing them, laughing loudly much to the amusement of everyone around. His family took up residence very close to where we were later in the New Year, but the Captain told me it didn't work out as it was hardly convenient for him to have the time to visit them. However, owing to the wintery conditions and the impossible state of the roads we were often allowed some off duty hours. It was strange when I come to think back as there was always singing and a banjo playing in and around Headquarters. If you could sing then JEB would want you to perform as he loved to have entertainment as often as possible. He could be often heard singing and laughing even when there was nobody else in his company.

The weather did get warmer, and as we hadn't seen much snow the roads started to dry a little. This we all knew was an obvious sign there would be action very soon. We had had batteries on the river opposite Washington, and they exchanged fire with each other for weeks. Our patrols had kept constant watch on the crossing points and observed the steady build-up of troops and guns. Contacts with enemy patrols were commonplace. By February we had pulled back to Centreville and our Headquarters were there by early March. The army was again back at Manassas as all our supply trains and Quartermaster and Commissary stores were stockpiled there. It was fortunate that there were some rail facilities still intact as a great deal of railway property had been destroyed by both armies. Fortunately the Confederate army still had some use of the track and wagons of the Virginia Central R.R. the withdrawal started around the middle of March but it was badly managed through constant bickering from railway officials, total waste of resources, rolling stock and facilities on the Orange & Alexandria and total mishandling of both. Neglect resulted where if some hard-line military organisation had been applied from the beginning many disasters could have been avoided.

There was now an obvious build-up of enemy troops and naval vessels capable of mounting a seaborne assault on the Peninsula which would likely smother McGruder's twelve thousand man command around Yorktown.

We were all pulled back to Richmond and as usual the cavalry were kept active with fighting patrols and picket duties to screen the army's movements. We didn't stop but were ordered to reinforce the Yorktown defences. Then the end of the month saw McClellan's army landed at Fort Munroe on the seaboard of the Peninsula. By 4th April he was drawn up in front of our positions around the Yorktown defences. For a whole month we dilly dallied around trying to put on a show of force that would give the impression we had a far superior force than what we actually had. The strategic position of the defence lines had become dangerous with the James and York rivers being now open to Yankee gunboats. Unavoidable after the *Virginia* was scuttled owing to her being too deep hulled to penetrate further upstream to be of any further use.

Our Captain had told me about this Yankee General McClellan. He said he had met him when in the Crimean War when he had visited the British lines. He was working on a design for a new cavalry saddle but his main interests were in siege warfare and this reflected in his character. He meant that the Yankee was not a warrior, was very mistrusting and of a timid personality. This was evident by his painfully slow movements in those early days of May. When his army finally drew up around Yorktown, Johnson had already pulled us out.

We left in the night of the 3rd May and McClellan was so slow it took him another day to realise we had already withdrawn. Pity about our large guns as these had to be abandoned, but the artillery boys stayed at their posts and kept up a barrage until early morning, when they slipped away with some of us guiding them.

We were engaged in some hard fights as we were tasked with the rear-guard of the army and to slow the advance of McClellan's troops. There was a defensive position at a place called Fort Magruder near Williamsburg on the James River. The retreat was slow and the battalions were constantly being held up along the route. This made it easy for a force of Yankee cavalry to catch up and deploy to attack us as we prepared to offer some protection. We were together with the 4th Virginia and a new regiment to the Brigade, the 3rd Virginia. There were also some attachments to Pelham's Battery, joining as we came through Richmond, The Floyd County Militia. Our units stood alone on the 4th May against cavalry and horse artillery.

The area around the defences is heavily wooded and we watched as they deployed. I was sent back to report to the Brigadier and he directed another squadron to come up. There was a sharp action on the Telegraph Road, when our company had come up in support of Colonel Wickham's 4th Regiment. They were heavily engaged with a larger force and were being so pressured in the centre that as we arrived the Colonel and his troop were in fierce combat. I rushed in with the revolver and took the pressure off him but he received a sabre wound. The standard bearer was killed in front of me but I was still not close enough to be able to offer any help. A force of cavalry then broke through and threatened to cut off the 1st Virginia but we rode down onto the beach and around, but this attracted the attention of gunboats on the river. They fired away at us but all they achieved was to make us laugh at them. On the 5th when Pelham's Horse Artillery were back to support us, the next day we started to manoeuvre more aggressively. The enemy had to make their approach through the densely wooded areas and this gave us an advantage as they couldn't form without exposing themselves to concentrated artillery fire. We attacked them in small numbers as they attempted to break out. The enemy had sent up reinforcements on the 5th and the woods were full of them. We had now gained so much experience of working with the guns we were able to give them support close-up to the tree line. They raced up to within two hundred yards of them, wheeled around and unlimbered. They came into battery and immediately started to hurl shells and round shot into the trees. The enemy must not have been able to withstand this as our gunner's poured volley after volley into their ranks, alternating between round, shell and canister shot. The Floyd County Militia with them made a fine account of themselves, bravely facing the enemy fire from that range. We offered them support by dismounting and with householders taking the mounts we engaged on foot. Again we used the British rifled muskets to good effect.

Our Captain was selecting targets as he passed amongst us; indicating officers, non-commissioned and section leaders. The infantry now came up and they volleyed into the enemy with such accuracy that it caused their fire to fade. The day was won, we had lost some good men and horses, a standard and many officers killed and wounded. The Yankees had lost more however as we were now the proud owners of some artillery and horses and had even taken one of their cavalry flags. There was now a threat of being out manoeuvred on Eltham's Landing and there was another sharp action where the Yankees were again hurled back to the river from where they had come from.

We gain the Richmond defences without much further hardship.

It was a relief to return to camp life for a while and get ourselves and the horses rested. We watched throughout the remainder of the month, McClellan's army of 100,000 men, as they moved into positions astride the Chickahominy River, just a few miles from Richmond's lines. At night we saw his lines marked by the soldier's campfires and wondered what next was in store for us.

There was much talk between us of trying to find the Negros we had brought with us across the mountains. The Captain's servant Jacob was a good lad and he had actually been with us on some of the picket duties. Silas had instructed him in many things and he had proved himself to be a very reasonable shot. It was decided that we appoint a spokesman to ask permission to visit the construction camps in order to track down the whereabouts of the boy's parents. As always that spokesman was me, and I was soon presented with an opportunity to ask our leader. He listened to me and when I finished he didn't say anything for some time. He then told me he could find out the next day but he warned there had been many movements of labour gangs and that he could have been sent to work at any of depots on the Virginia Central R.R where they had extended the rail sidings and constructed passing points to prevent train hold-ups.

The next day the Captain had some news for me. Johan had been fortunate and with his trade knowledge of carpentry he had risen up to a better position than that of a labourer. In fact he had been given a position of trust, in charge of a gang who specialised in reinforcing defensive breast-works and excavations for heavy artillery. The Captain had told the boy he would take him to see his parents and we were keen to come along as this would be a change of scene from the sprawling cavalry camps that seemed to be becoming more overcrowded daily. The boy's mother Martha had a paid job as a ward nurse at the huge facility at Chimborazo Hill that was soon to be the largest hospital in the City. We set off that morning and made our way on foot through the streets. It was unreal as there were people everywhere. Rich ladies and fine looking gentlemen travelling in carriages alongside poor women dragging children dressed in rags. Men obviously intent on crimes lurked on every street corner waiting to pounce on the unwary. I was hoping one of them would try it on us but we made our destination without any incidents. The Captain had told the boy to lose the side-arm revolver from his belt, but he still looked every inch the soldier in his grey uniform complete with kepi.

We were told by a guard to enter an office building on the other side of the entrance gates and the Captain told us to wait for him as he made enquiries. When he returned he led us off through a maze of alleyways until we were outside of a building which had a sign saying it was the Virginia Hospital Wing. He again made us wait outside and disappeared through a side office door. We waited for some time and I was beginning to feel uncomfortable as we were attracting attention from some guards who probably thought we were deserters. Our leader eventually returned and behind him was the boy's mother. It was a touching scene as they both clung to one another. The woman was crying and thanking the Captain between sobs, but after a while things settled a little and we gathered around them to greet the Negro woman. She was telling us there was much sickness and infection from putrefied wounds and amputations. There was this smell that seemed to hang about you, in the air so you couldn't get away from it. She smiled at our obvious discomfort and nodded. It was very hard to keep the wards clean and care for the wounded. Sometimes the hospital ward budget would be exhausted so there wasn't enough clean bedding or bandages. This meant urgent appeals had to be sent out to the rich ladies of the city, to donate sheets, linen for bandages and old clothing to enable the wounded to be kept comfortable. We persuaded her to walk away a little distance where the air was a little cleaner. The boy pressed her for news of his father and she excitedly informed us that Johan was doing very well. They had a shack near to where the defences were being constructed and he would meet her from work every day. She was working twelve hour shifts at the moment, as they had wounded from all the actions in the valley, Bull Run, and now the ones from Williamsburg. I thought it would only get worse.

We were going to have to leave her as she was frantically being called by a doctor. The Captain left her with the news we would be visiting the defences now, and going to find their shack. She was trying to say goodbye while at the same moment giving us directions to the shanty town. They broke away as we pulled the boy with us; he was trying to prevent himself from breaking down and did a good job. We tried to assure him we would come back again but it's only now when I think about it, that it may have been tempting fate.

We went to the Engineering Headquarters located near the inner defence works, and enquired in the company office for the Major of Engineers who was the Captain's friend. He was supervising some emplacements on the outer howitzer battery. When the Captain led us over to him he was absorbed in some construction drawings spread out across a table. He walked up behind him and called out his name. The Major spun around and our leader sprang to attention and saluted him in the best display of military etiquette I had ever witnessed. They warmly greeted each other and the Captain pressed him for information on the Negro Johan, who we were searching for. We found out he was not far from where we were. As there was not a lot of time it was important we find him as quickly as possible as our leave of absence would be soon expired.

We came across him working with a group of labourers and carpenters shoring –up some trenches and gun pits. He wasn't sure at first, as this Negro boy was in Confederate grey, but as he ran to him, he dropped the axe and picked him up, swinging him around. They were both trying to outtalk each other and it was comical watching them as neither of them could finish a sentence. They settled down and after Johan found out his son had visited his mother he almost lost control. We all greeted him and he couldn't thank us all enough. I don't think he understood about his son wearing the army uniform though. We left them alone and wandered around the fortifications. There were huge cannons and some short barrelled howitzers. Everywhere there was an air of confidence and looking at these preparations you couldn't help being taken up with the same opinion, as the professionalism was unmistakeable.

The Gods of war had obviously not been appeased because we didn't have to wait that long as Johnson attacked Casey's division in their front line nearest to us, on the 31st of May. We were not engaged as the ground where the battle took place was an evil hell-hole of wet ground and deep mud, nowhere suitable for cavalry. As it was, the conditions on the battlefield were horrific. During the day our Captain had been with the Brigadier and the Generals with their staff. The next day he was with us and ordered us to mount and patrol around the area to screen the infantry as they disengaged and started to clear the battlefield and bury the dead. He told us of the terrible conditions in which the two opposing infantry forces had to battle. The mud was so deep in places that the fallen wounded could not lift themselves to breath, and they drowned. A lot of shells fired from artillery would render almost harmless as thick mud can absorb the force of shrapnel. It was difficult for the guns to give close support as they were hampered also by the bad ground and ended up being bogged down. Longstreet's boys had struggled all day in the flooded swamps but in the end Casey's division was forced back. He explained we had suffered badly and Johnson himself was wounded, he wasn't alone as our army lost over a third of its strength and later we were to learn it was around seven thousand men. The enemy left us a few thousand rifles, Springfield's and some British Enfield's also. The top prize was the cannon they left for us, ten pieces of modern artillery.

The Captain thought we would be under the command of General Lee now after this battle, which was being named Seven Pines. The situation in the field didn't look that bright. The Captain was of the opinion that Richmond couldn't withstand a siege as this McClellan was an expert in sitting around waiting for big guns and starvation to do his job for him. We were surrounded by three separate Yankee armies. One consisting of three smaller armies in the Valley was being whipped by Jackson. He was so successful the Yanks were convinced he'd soon be knocking on their doors in Washington, and had pulled out troops from McClellan's command to cover the threat. We had just danced with the second, McDowell's army at Fredericksburg and the third was the siege master himself, McClellan's stretching from supply bases on the Pamunkey and York River, to lines along the north bank of the Chickahominy and east curling around toward Fredericksburg. What was important now if Lee was going to involve Jackson on the west flank of their army would be to gain information about his exact position and how far his flank extended.

We now knew what was going to happen to us after sitting around in camp for weeks with only localised patrol duties of to keep us amused.

Chapter 19

The Captain had told us we were to scout along a line parallel with the James River, with White Oak swamp to our north. Joe, our Sergeant had not given us any more information, so not one of us in the troop was aware of any other details. This is the way he wanted it. I wonder now looking back if he had some plan in his mind, knowing him he'd have looked at all the possibilities but the very fact was, that he was a lucky officer and because of this and his experience as a cavalryman most of us might be still alive at the end of the war. This route had been scouted before and was familiar ground to some of us when we had acted in recent rear-guard actions in May. Our leader himself had to take evasive action and detour into cover on the beach to avoid cannon fire from US gunboats on the river. However, more information was needed, so we were ordered to travel to Charles City Courthouse passing Buckland Plantation, around 25 miles east of Richmond. From here, we were to turn north for around a further 12 miles towards the Chickahominy River. Our objective here was to find a favourable crossing point as it was known the bridge at Forge Mill had been destroyed when our lads had been ordered to give up ground for new defensive positions closer to Richmond. We were all now told of our mission and each one of the troop realised the importance of our task and how, if we got back with the intelligence, how vital it would be, to our almost besieged army. We had with us some troopers who were local to this country so would give us the advantage by acting as guides and able to offer information on farms and landowners as to where their allegiances might be. I can remember looking down on the river and it seemed full of river craft, Yankee transports and gunboats were often threatingly close to our hiding places as we slowly made our way east. There was an air of doubt about the men, many thinking this was suicide.

This did not alter the fact we were honoured to be chosen as the Captain had handpicked every one of us. He had selected good horsemen owning fine animals that could endure the march in difficult conditions and bad cavalry terrain. Today was no different; we had been riding for hours on this scouting mission for Brigade travelling carefully through what was now enemy held territory. That first night there was almost a full moon allowing us to penetrate further; probing along in the moonlight with cloth wrapped around the horses hooves. During the day, we rested up but there was always a picket out to the front and flankers posted to give us warning of any enemy activity. Although it was difficult country the narrow singe track roads were very often the only route through this very wet bottomland with marshes, all covered by areas of dense woodland. It was as if he had thought of everything and I enjoyed the times he got us together in a group, briefings he called them, when he would explain things and ask if there were any suggestions or ideas. Sometimes there were stupid sessions when some of the younger troopers would say things but he would smile and then go on to say what he wanted and then explain why. He was good at this, making people listen and soon we learned that listening to what he said was the best way of coming out of this and hopefully being able to return home all in one piece.

Home seemed like a dream, mother and my two sisters were faded into the mists of memory and I could not remember their faces, only their voices came to me regularly, especially when on the move in column, single file, staring at the troopers back to your front, dreaming and not paying much attention to anything in particular. I had received two letters from them and knew they were working in the mills and were managing to support themselves. Uncle had been drafted as the new draft bill had been drawn up in April and all able bodied men up to 45 years were being taken. I don't know how he could class himself as abled bodied unless he'd been exaggerating his injuries and getting me to do his work for him all these years.

I only hoped it would all end soon and we would be going home, as I missed my family so much and worried deeply how they were managing. He had warned us of this loss of concentration and after the four months, we had been soldering with him it was only his insistence of training, self-discipline and following his orders and routines that was to save us from near annihilation. Every mile of route had to be covered sometimes three times, doubling back and then going into concealment, waiting until the road was clear and then reporting to the Captain, but it was essential we saw the enemy before he saw us. We had come through some marshy ground and were now close to the river. They were right about Forge Bridge it had been burned down to the pilings so we turned NW up the river to Sycamore Springs, the ford to the Christian family farm. The son of the family was also with the brigade and a Lieutenant with the regiment back in cavalry lines in Richmond.

We were able to cross although it was not easy as the flood waters were rising rapidly, and I thought there would be a great chance we could be cut off once on the other bank. The Captain assured us that all would be well, that we would go further north to Talleysville and then to a place called Tunstalls Station on the York River railroad, where he was certain there were supply depots. We would then take up positions, record troop, and supply movements. The troop carefully, without being observed made further progress, crossed the railroad and passed undetected, past forage parties, much wagon traffic and cavalry pickets on the roads. We reached a busy road junction with branches leading from it to all compass points. North was the Pamunkey River and a Major supply point for the US forces around Richmond. North east alongside railway towards White House and west towards the Totopotomoy Creek and south west alongside the rail tracks toward US lines astride the Chickahominy. This was where we were divided, the Captain taking the larger part of the patrol north east to a point on the river called Garlics landing.

 It was from action this night and its horrors, which even now return regularly to me after all these years, still vivid, so very real, wakening me from sleep by the sound of my own screaming. These images would leave me fighting for breath, wet through with sweat from living it again, those pictures trapped inside my head, impossible for the mind to let go and forget, so they have now became part of my life forever. I had killed men in action and in hand to hand combat over these few months but it was as if things were catching up on me.

We were shadowing a road, much used to military traffic for we had watched enemy cavalry, sometimes in troop strength gallop along through the heavy going surface mud. In places, it was bad with the road ankle deep in mud. It had rained a lot for months and everything was so damp, but the air was humid with remorseless heat draining your energy and making it hard to concentrate on anything other than thirst and sleep. The Captain had ordered me and two other troopers to stay in concealment and watch the cross road where it was close to Tunstalls Station. He had explained the importance of gathering intelligence and then reporting it back to Brigade where hopefully it would aid our struggling army to gain some advantage. Our leader had taken the rest of the patrol of twenty men further east on the river where he was convinced the Yankees had a depot filled with ordinance and provisions, which our poor lads needed so badly.

Clem, Squirrel and I were watching from a vantage point in the woods, holding our horses and smoothing their noses gently talking to them. They were exceptional thoroughbreds from back home as we had brought them with us when we enlisted, presents from the wealthy landowner we had all worked for. They were good steady well-tempered animals and the training with the Captain had turned us all into what he told us was one the finest cavalry units in the world but not as good as the 11th Hussars, his old regiment. Sometimes on a quiet night when he was doing his rounds before we turned – in, he would tell us about them, as they were famous from battles both past and more recent, like Waterloo and the Crimea where he said he fought Russians, whoever they were. "Cossacks," he would say, "now there's an enemy."

As I remember this night was an exception as the horses were unbelievably skittish and were becoming more difficult for us to quieten. I had Clem lead them back about 20 yards to a thicket of dogwoods and stay with them until I give the whippoorwill birdcall for him to come back. It was at this time that the road below us was filled with wagons, seemingly heavily laden as the horses were blowing hard as they reached the top of the slight gradient about level with our hiding place. It was our job to count the wagons and we had been doing this for a half hour, this was a considerable amount of ordinance and it confirmed the Captains hunch, there was a depot further along the road, the one we had been searching for.

We were looking down in amusement as the rearmost wagon in the column slowed to a halt. The driver and his guard on the front seat could be heard cursing and putting the whip to the horses trying to get some more motion through the mud before the slope in the road. It was no use as the rear left wheel was in a poor condition and as we watched, crumpled under the weight tipping the wagon bed at a crazy angle. Almost immediately an officer appeared and stopping the wagon in front ordered some men to unload another wheel and levers and then run back to assist the broken down last wagon. The weight of the load was too much to allow the wagon bed to be raised in order to prop it to be able to change the wheel. The officer was going mental at this stage and was cursing and shouting for the wagoner to start unloading the contents.

For us this was an added bonus, as it would enable us to see exactly what this wagon train was carrying and this would certainly put us in the Captain's good books, maybe enough to get lighter duties and off from picket or flanker duties. The Yankees could now be seen clearly, as the moon was out from behind a cloud and lighting up the scene below, maybe it would rain tomorrow and we could wash our clothes and get fresh water for the mounts. There was box after box coming down off the wagon bed now and these looked like rifle ammunition. Kegs added to this, which could only be powder for artillery.

Suddenly the air was filled with the whining of bullets as they passed close by. I had just had time to upholster my LeMatt, 9 shot revolvers; it, like my Captain was from England and just as efficient. I have talked to you before about it, how it shoots a charge of buckshot from a grapeshot barrel and then has a cylinder taking nine, .35 bullets firing down the pistols other main barrel. You never load a full cylinder to capacity and I used to keep a rolled up Yankee dollar inside, so when I was killed the new owner of my revolver would have money to pay the 'ferryman' when I was buried.

For what happened next, I still believe the revolver is the only reason I am still here and the newspaper man is writing this down for you to read. I turned from the road and glanced to shout a command to Squirrel but at that moment, his head seemed to explode as a Minnie ball hit him. I was running now up towards the dog wood thicket and hoping for all things to help me and that Clem would be there with the horses. Suddenly he was in front of me, mounted and leading the other two mounts. "Squirrel's dead, head up for the higher ground." I did not have the words out of my mouth when the shots started coming in on us again. I reached for the bridle and grabbed the reins. Vaulting into the McClellan saddle I felt the passage of that bullet, it had missed me by inches but as I was soon to learn it had done its job only too well.

We put spurs to the mounts and flew over the ground but there was a fallen log to our front and behind this several Yankee riflemen. I still can feel the violent motion of my faithful gelding as he tore up the distance to that rifle position. I just had time to hold on as he lifted from the ground and seemed to sail over those heads and as if by magic, I pulled the trigger of the big

158

revolver discharging the buckshot load. His face exploded in a cloud of spray and brains and then I heard Clem emptying his weapon at them.

I can still see those faces as we closed on them in that mad charge firing into their faces as we held onto the reins seeing the bullets from our revolvers stopping them firing at us, and silencing them forever. In an instant, it was over but I had felt the gelding falter and he was now slowing and his limbs shivering. Suddenly he was going down and instinctively I swung my leg out of the stirrup swinging myself to the ground. I glanced around in those same seconds and spotted Clem; he was obviously hit and slumped over in the saddle. We had made around a hundred yards from the ambush, my horse was dying but I had to see whether I could help my friend Clem. There was nothing I could do for him as he was shot in the lungs and blood was spluttering from his mouth as he tried to talk to me. I lifted him down and laid him on the ground. He died there after a few minutes and it upset me as we had been through some hard campaigning together with the Captain and before this, we had been childhood playmates and had been inseparable.

Putting all this out of my mind, or trying to, the survival instincts and training were taking over. I realised what he had been trying to say was for me to leave him, but it had not sunk in. Now I had to get away. I could hear shouts of command from the road and knew they would be organising a fighting patrol, which would not be too happy when they saw what our revolvers had done to their friends. I went to my poor faithful gelding he was not dead and I was going through the motions of taking equipment from the saddle. The sabre was useless as they were seldom used but I could not leave him like that. Tears were coming fast now but I knew what I had to do for him. Taking the scabbard and tossing it away, I plunged the blade into his throat and opened his artery. Luckily, he had not been looking at me, he stopped struggling, and hopefully he bled-out without much stress. I was crying now but I'd done my best to ease his suffering, as to fire a bullet would of alerted them to my position. I collected all the ammunition and both our rifles, we were issued with Whitworth, English rifled muskets and most of our patrol could hit a Yankees head at 300 yards and had proved it at longer ranges targeting officers and Yankee gun crews. So leaving my friend and my horse to the ferryman and hoping I'd meet them again if that was what was down for me, I led Squirrels horse and mounted on Clem's I made my way silently away from that scene, that same one that still keeps me from sleep.

Chapter 20

We were lucky that night as the moon was hidden making it black as Hades, but it was not long before it started to rain. It was soft at first and this refreshed me but before long, it had soaked me to the skin. I had been sweating with the heat of battle and my loss but now I was cooling rapidly and could not believe it when I started to shiver. Thinking about it now I realise it was delayed shock from the action but this did not help matters, as I was worried that I was going down with fever and not be able to make the rendezvous with the Captain.

He had showed us on his map where he would leave another out-rider who would wait for us until the following morning. This was further to the east beyond the road junction heading North for Garlics landing. It was getting a little lighter now but the rain was still coming down hard. I knew I would have to keep going if I was to ever get home. The horse was very much leading us out of the scrub-wet woodland on his own and following the natural course of some dry ground, which would lead us away from that bottomland up onto relative safety away from the marshes. I must have dozed off, just after I had put an oilskin horse slicker over my shoulders. This must have helped, as my body, temperature had come up a little and I had stopped shaking so badly. The horse must have woke me as it was snickering and jerking around, bringing me to my senses but the violent thrust of a cavalry Sharp's carbine shoved into the small of my back broke me out in a sweat again. "What the hell you got that Yankee slicker on for, hell I could off blown you into Sunday."

Well, I could have kissed him, it was Joe, our patrol Sergeant and I was glad he had waited in the rain to lead us to where the Captain was. Joe was telling me he would probably be relying on my report and any information we had been able to gather to decide on his next move.

Our Captain had halted the patrol around an area of dry ground, north of the road and only a few miles from the creek. They were sheltering from the rain in a wooded draw, which was almost hidden, from any casual glances but had still not allowed any fires for cooking or coffee and everyone was bad tempered and chilled to the bone from the nights patrolling. I reported what I had seen and told him of the running battle, the loss of Clem and Squirrel and the count of wagons on the road and their probable contents. He was pleased and told me to tend to my horse and look to my weapons and equipment. We were to move out very soon and I was to take one of the rested horses. There was then another one of our little briefings and he started it off by informing the patrol of the losses from my night's action. Everyone was saddened from the news as they were both popular, but he added we were going to try to work our way through the enemy patrols and so it would be very likely we would be getting an opportunity to put things straight.

The Captain was an expert in this covert reconnaissance work, and he put out flankers and point riders then another picket to follow up in our rear. We picked our way slowly through the woods down to lower ground. Crossing of open ground was avoided where we could, but the horses were hungry and we were all in a poor condition, miserable after the night action. The road was the easiest route to follow and we were forced to use it, as progress through the white and pin oaks was infuriatingly slow. The orders were to make a hasty approach to a point two miles further east where we were to cross the Totopotomoy Creek. Then try to get provisioned from any of the farms along the road toward Hanover Courthouse. The horses were badly in need of rest and watering but we were all worried about what the locals would think and if they would sympathise with our cause. The two troopers with us from this county had assured the Captain we would be welcomed at a farm just to the east of the creek

To split us up may have been an idea but the Captain did not want to reduce our effectiveness as a fighting unit. The progress along the route was unbelievably slow with many stops and hold ups in the line. Eventually we got to the river and turned to our left keeping hidden from the bank by using every bit of cover available, often dismounted and trying to keep the horses quiet. Each side of the road was lined with dense forestry that made flanking movements almost impossible so we had to rely on point and rear riders.

We had obviously come to the crossing as the point riders had come in and were in conversation with the Captain. It was not long before he came walking back down the column to me. What he had to say did not exactly thrill me for he wanted me to pick six men and stay where we were hidden to act as a rear-guard. We were to wait for daylight the next day and then come on in to the farm, or if we heard gunfire then to come to the sound of it. He wasted no time and after the lone point trooper had given the clear signal they were all gone leaving us to our defence.

I quickly dispersed the men to good observation and firing places. We were in good defensive positions at both sides of the road that followed a steep sided ravine. It was a perfect defensive position and any enemy attackers coming down to the bridge had to come past us. We settled in to wait it out. It was still mid-afternoon and the humidity had raised again making it sticky and energy sapping just to walk about. We cared for the horses as much as we could and then relaxed into the routine he had trained us for. Stag duty he called it and it was a system of one out of two men resting for two hours while the other kept watch, and then rotating. This way there was always a good many eyes watching for the enemy who could not be too far away.

It was getting dark when we heard them, by the sound of it, they were probably at half troop strength and we were only seven men. I knew I could rely on the rest of lads, as we were all well trained and confident with our weapons.

I got down in cover and raised the Whitworth to my shoulder, I was with another two good lads and had no doubts they would not shirk their duties but would stand with me until I gave the order to pull-out. The Yankees were around 600 yards away now but they were backlit and I could see the leader was a typical strutting peacock of an officer, recognisable from the large feather in his hat. We almost simultaneously selected our own targets and I had not had to give any orders.

I picked the officer and sighted through the ladder rear site of the rifled musket on his arrogant head, the range was around four hundred yards. "On my command fire." I then placed the aiming point on the centre of his forehead just under the hat brim. "Fire" and the flash from priming caps rose followed by muzzle blast and grey smoke.

The sight picture had gone for a second but I moved around trying to see through the smoke and if I could get some idea of the results. The officer was falling from the saddle my bullet must have fallen off; others were down, off their horses and sprawled out in the road. There was confusion now and panic had taken over, I knew this would be short lived but we were all too occupied with reloading to enjoy any small success. They would come again, probably led by a Lieutenant or Sergeant and they would not be too happy.

We were ready again and I was pleased with everyone, as without having to give orders every man had done his duty, aimed, fired as one, and was now ready again. It was all down to our training from the Captain and I couldn't help being proud of what he had done for us and what we'd achieved but we were going to need every bit of this professionalism to get us away from this.

It was rapid fire drill now as they were coming on firing their pistols, which at that range were as much use as peashooters. It would not be long but we'd managed to get off another aimed volley and I could see we had accounted for at least a dozen.

"Pistols now lads." and we were waiting for the range to close before taking them on again with the Le Matts. It was total confusion, but I knew we were taking them down and that we were not losing anyone yet. I fired the buck shot charge and then the chambers. When these were empty, I then grabbed the second pistol. These pistols were taking a terrible toll of these Yankees as we all picked our targets and made every shot count. We had now four pistols each, two carried in special buckets around the saddle so as when in a mounted engagement we could quickly keep up a barrage of fire without any delays or having to revert to use of sabres. Here we were in dismounted defence but still in possession of our revolvers having removed them from the horses before we got into position.

I had fired my third pistol off and was starting to feel that rising lump in your gut as it grows and starts to swell up, coming into your throat. You always get an unbelievably dry throat and mouth as the adrenalin pumps round your brain but if you cannot control the rising swelling then it would be all over because your panic would take over and you would forget everything. Not all the drill and combat training in the world would help you then. So fighting this back stopped me realising, at the time, something had altered. They had stalled, horses were stampeding in panic, some were rider less others throwing riders, and across the sunken lane to our front the dead and dying were piling up around our position. They were obviously leaderless now and most of them had ridden back out of pistol range, so it was now or never.

Our horses were still saddled and secured in line, ready for us to mount up. As we approached them, they seemed to know we were in trouble and that need for haste was paramount. Into the saddle and away still clutching the Whitworth's and only just managing to thrust them into the modified rifle sleeves and the empty revolvers into their buckets around the saddle pommel. We all had several shots left in our fourth revolvers and it proved fortunate for us, as we would soon be in trouble again. We flew across the bridge, the hooves of our horses sounding like cannon fire on the old wooden timbers. On up the road at full stretch toward where we were hoping the Captain would be at the farm he mentioned.

It was with relief to make out our patrol at full gallop, at the 'charge' as the Captain, controlling his mount with his knees alone had drawn sabre in one hand and a revolver in the other, was leading them down to rescue us. We all gave out a ragged rebel yell as we almost collided, turned and raced after our comrades. We crossed over the bridge at breakneck speed, the bridge timbers echoing to the impact of our horses and were soon up with them and then into the enemy horsemen. They had reorganised and were being led by a burly Sergeant who was shouting insults and bullying them on. They looked young and did not appear too happy to be there that day. Our Captain in classic cavalry drill reversed his sabre and lunged at the enemy Sergeant with such force he was unable to avoid the point. It took him in the throat, and I can to this day, still often hear his scream as it plunged out the other side. We were through them in an instant as they were in poor order, breaking up, and fleeing for their lives. I had emptied my last revolver and was again shaking as the adrenalin rush starts to ease. Sadly we had lost five men in the action but must have accounted for around fifty enemy, our little rear-guard alone having shot down probably a good twenty. We were laughing and slapping each other on the back and whooping and hollering around. This was to be short lived, as the Captain brought us back to earth with a severe bump. "Recall and follow me." He was turning his mount towards the water again. We flew after him and were going at a fast pace for almost an hour. He finally eased the pace and we got ourselves into some order as he led us into the cover of some big oak trees where he gave the 'dismount'. "Weapons and pickets out on foot form a perimeter and go into defence." He then detailed horse minders to tend to the horses while the Majority of us started to reload weapons and organise for another defence. We were close to another cross roads as our point troopers had come in and shown the Captain exactly where we had ended up. It was discovered we had been in action with the fifth US cavalry as our scouts had discovered their camp not a mile from the creek. Our position was roughly about three miles from Hanover Court house where there was a detachment of the same cavalry regiment and some teamsters, supply and foraging units.

Further defence never became necessary and after a much-needed rest while the horses were fed and watered from the provisions the patrol had been given from the farm. Our main concern was reloading our revolver chambers with the nonstandard ammunition. This was the .35 round not issued from Quartermasters re-supplies. This meant us having to cast bullets and involved melting down lead then pouring this into our bullet moulds. The Captain allowed one small fire between five men but any fire that gave out smoke would result in the owners of it being the target of his explosive temper. On completion we again mounted and slowly with flankers and rear-guard and point troopers out, made slow but steady progress. The terrain around our position was all dense forestry and it was proving hard to reconnoitre. We adopted the same techniques of slow movement with regular stops to listen and then only progressing if all was clear. Several times, we had to negotiate the heavily wooded sides of the road to hide the horses from view. This proved successful and we were steadily marching further east.

We were close to Winston Farm, Ashland Station being four miles to the south, coming across the highest ground from Hanover Courthouse and by keeping off the roads when it was practical and avoiding any contacts with the Yankees we were able to head towards where we could pass between any bivouac's or outposts along the Virginia Central R.R. Then back into our own territory. We watched their fires by night and from doing this, the Captain was able to lead us through without contact, between their picket lines and patrols and around in a circuitous route back across the Richmond Fredericksburg and Potomac Rail lines and finally home to the regiment and our lines around Richmond.

Before the rain started to fall.

Chapter 21

We were welcomed back in the early morning of 8th day, having ridden out east along the James River on the morning of the 1st June 1862. At the end of our mission, the 'butcher's bill' was at seven troopers dead but had brought back all the horses except my own sad loss of the gelding. I had not time to dwell on this as a Corporal in the 1st regiment had just informed me, the Captain wished to see me. I couldn't help feeling concerned as normally, if he had something to say he would come straight out with it, there and then. Therefore, it was troubling me as I reported to the Captain's tent. I presented myself from outside and was told to enter immediately.

To my surprise, our commanding officer, the Major was present; he and our Captain were sitting around a camp table cluttered with maps. I saluted and was told to relax, this putting me a little more at ease. I was however not allowed this luxury for long as the Major asked if I thought I had acted responsibly at the creek. This astounded me but I was more surprised by his next words. "You, by your actions at the bridge have probably jeopardised future operations in this area." "Furthermore, it may have caused the enemy to realise where weaknesses are on his northern flanks and so encourage him to move more troops in and develop new outposts." I could not believe what I was hearing, as I had been confident I had done everything to protect the Captain and the troop from being whipped, out at the farm. It was then the Captain spoke out for the first time and his words seemed to calm the atmosphere and my distress. The sweat was pouring down my face and throat but I heard him say the Brigadier was not altogether concerned. He had just heard from a scout, that Mosby's men had also been at the bridge. The Federals had not defended the ravine with infantry but had strengthened the 5th US with another squadron. It turned out that unbeknown to us, Mosby had observed the action at the bridge and had stayed hidden in the area whilst sending a galloper back with intelligence on any new troop movements. The Brigadier apparently had considered the fact we had almost been caught, a good reason the Yankees would think it was highly unlikely we'd try the same thing again. Little did any of us know then, we would in fact soon be put at this mission again but on a bigger scale and from the opposite line of march, North East instead of North West. I was then made to swear what information, directly or indirectly, I had heard was to be on pain of death, not to be repeated. The Major then told me that on reflection he had considered my actions were the only means left at my disposal to ensure the patrol was unmolested, further resulting in our escape back across the railroad lines. Once again, I was indebted to my Captain but found it hard to take what could only be an insult from this arrogant West Point officer.

That night and through the following day, there was much off duty socialising with good comrades and a little corn liquor drinking. We had been fortunate and had been able to provide the General staff with much intelligence. We were just a small detachment of scouts but had proven our worth with the Brigadier and given our Captain, something we'd hope he would be proud of. For each trooper had done his duty and in doing so had protected his fellow horsemen, as this is what soldiering is about, looking after one another as a unit. Something else that he had said had become reality.

The Brigadier reported to Divisional staff and apparently, although we were all in complete ignorance, the intelligence that we had gathered was to be used in the planning of another lightening raid on supply depots and communication lines. Planned to be carried out as a prelude of an advance to engage the Yankee army threatening to encircle us.

There seemed to be a few Colt and Remington revolvers available and I considered being equipped with one would certainly cancel the need to cast your own bullets. The Captain was sure to be leading us out soon so I decided to trade two of my LeMatt's that were in poor shape for Remington's. Therefore, I now carried two of these new revolvers and had several spare cylinders to go with them. Having these, it meant you could preload in advance and by carrying them in special belt pouches they could replace fired, empty ones more easily than having to use the reloading lever for individual chambers. These were good looking revolvers and a bit lighter and not as brutal to use. The Le Matt was becoming more and more difficult to reload and there were mechanical weaknesses in the reload lever system that often put them out of action leaving only the buckshot barrel able to be fired. The last patrol had brought it home to us, the realisation that if we were prevented from lighting fires to melt lead for balls, then we could be in real danger of carrying useless weapons into battle. With these new revolvers, we could at least resupply from issued revolver ammunition. However, I was to miss the terrible efficiency of this combination in the LeMatt and if I had known how much of a difference it would make not to have them, I would have possibly gone and tried to get the old ones back.

On the 11th we resupplied with what we needed a small amount of coffee, corn poke, hard tack, some meat to cook up and horse feed. The Captain had ordered us to be on immediate standby to march at a moment's notice with feed, water, 3 days meat rations and 60 rounds carbine ammunition. Early on the morning of the 12^{th,} we were roused with the call 'boots and saddles' ready to mount in ten minutes. We were soon mounted and ready to ride, rations packed and pouches full with carbine ammunition. The entire troop, now the proud owners of these fine breech loading Sharps carbines, all courtesy of the Federal, Yankee government. These were 1859 models sporting a 22-inch barrel.

We were again part of a larger force but our orders were not even known to our regimental officers. Only the Brigadier knew what we were about and he wasn't going to disclose this until we were well clear of any northern scouts or spies watching the Richmond lines. We mustered 1200 sabres consisting of selected troopers from 1st, 4th and 9th Virginia in company with others from the Jeff Davis Legion and 2 horse batteries. There were no orders then, but it looked by the direction we were taking we would be going to join Jackson Army. Brigadier Stuart led us out on a daring manoeuvre to get information and find a position where it would be possible for our army to come upon the enemy. In a place he would not know about and certainly one where he would not want us to be. Having had a little prior knowledge of the country ahead and probably because the Captain was so efficient in bringing back intelligence, we were on our own again but at troop strength. The Major and Colonel and himself had gone over in detail what was going to hopefully happen, and he was in possession of the big picture, but for it to be successful was going to be down to us as our mission was an important cog in a bigger machine. To scout for an expedition to ride around McClellan's army and to bring back information of enemy dispositions, strengths and weaknesses and details of supply depots and lines of communication

Thinking back, the column must have made a splendid sight that morning as we made our way through the infantry lines around the Richmond defences. Column of fours the individual companies being led by their officers, colour bearers, buglers and troop Gideon's. The officers looked every bit the shining example and our Captain in particular was only shadowed narrowly by our commander Stuart himself. Jeers and catcalls came up to us from the toiling infantry and black labourers digging rifle pits. One fellow cheekily shouting across to ask where we were off. The Captain answered sharply "To Hell where the birds still sing." Our officers were Colonel Fitzhugh Lee, commanding our 1st regiment, Colonel W.H.R Rooney Lee, Fitzhugh's cousin, commanding the 9th regiment and Lieutenant Colonel William Martin commanding battalion strength Jeff Davis Legion. There were also the guns, two batteries, which were led by Lieutenant James Breathed. Colonel William Wickham being wounded and still recovering had his 4th regiment divided between the 1st and the 9th. Another South Carolina company 'Boykin Rangers' was used to reinforce Martins battalion. The 4th regiment comp. 'E' would be acting as scouts and had riding in their company Mosby, our Brigadiers pet scout, who had only just returned with his report. As we were about to clear the outer defences we broke into song giving the infantry their entertainment for the day. It was the ballad 'Kathleen Mavourneen' this, being prompted by Stuart himself in a reply to officers asking how long we were to be away. "It may be for years and it may be forever," I thought this might be a bit of a bad omen. Fortunately, *Dixieland* took over and I heard afterwards it could still be heard long after we had gone out of sight along the Brooke Road toward Ashland. To all those informants from the north this would point to reinforce the belief we were bound for the Shenandoah Valley and Jackson valiant army.

We made good progress with the road being wide enough for column of 4's but as we got further north it narrowed, leaving no option but to revert to column of 2's. We bypassed Ashland Station and were now close to the South Anna River but before we reached its banks, turned east toward the Richmond, Fredericksburg and Potomac railroad. We had followed 'E' company 4th regiment when they were detached to scout far ahead and some to act as flankers for the main body. Our job was to screen the column but only just far enough away to be in sight of the troopers. We came to the tracks, waited, and listened for several minutes, silent with everyone wrestling with his own personal thoughts. I do not think I was alone in wondering how we would make out. We were now manoeuvring around McClellan's most northerly flank and had travelled twenty miles so far. It was quiet and we waited on the other side of the tracks in a clump of trees for the column to catch up. Stuart urged us on again and this was a definite sign, as we were now travelling in the wrong direction to reinforce Jackson. We pushed on with flankers out and point riders scouting ahead to wait at Winston farm 2 miles east of the tracks. The column caught up and the order was to make bivouac but strictly without campfires or naked lanterns.

Our leader left us then and rode off with Rooney Lee to visit the wounded Wickham on their family estate of

Hickory Hill. He was back before daylight and eager to get staff and regimental officers together. It was now that he enlightened them to their objectives and the mission to penetrate far into the rear of McClellan's army. Just how far and for how long was another matter, and one he would be keeping close to his chest. After a peaceful night we were alerted by the Captain well before first light, he was saying the column would be in the saddle after the second signal rocket but our little troop would be in the saddle and out on the road on the first signal. Company 'E' had sent back a rider with the all clear ahead and information that the bulk of the cavalry patrols and pickets were further south. Our march was relatively safe and the orders were to proceed towards Hanover Court House. Mosby, the Brigadier's pet scout was detailed to accompany a section of 'E' company, reconnoitre the approaches, and gain information on enemy strengths and fortifications. We were tasked with working around to the north of the settlement to prevent escape of enemy personnel and finally to cut back onto the road well to the east and establish a cut-off point.

On Mosby's approach, Federal cavalry observed him as he crossed some open ground; they were alerted and made to join the road leading to the east. However, Stuart on receiving the report from the scouts had despatched Fitz Lee to outflank the position and cut-off any retreat. However tactically this sounded there was no allowances made for the terrain and our regiment with Fitz Lee became bogged down near Mechump Creek. The situation was so serious the bog held up the horsemen for long enough to allow the Yankees to make it onto the road further east. It was their intention to leave a scout party to observe the head of Stuart's column while the others ran back to the east. This country was difficult and did not lend itself easy for flankers and as the road went through thick undergrowth and dense forest it became hard for the 9th cavalry regiment following to reconnoitre. This is where we stepped in as we were already in position in hiding and just waiting for the US troopers. As they came up on our concealment, they were only a few yards from us. We fired a volley into them from our carbines and then rushed them with pistols. We were badly outnumbered but came out of it unscathed accounting for 10 killed and 2 wounded. This was no gentleman fight but short, bloody and brutal and we took several prisoners.

I was impressed with the new Sharps carbine, as it was a well-balanced, efficient breech-loader, being carried easily from the cross belt and the rifle sling attachment that allowed the carbine to hang from the right side within easy reach. This still did not make reloading when mounted, very easy but as we all carried four revolvers the Majority of the enemy were shot using these. I was also impressed with the Remington revolver as this could easily be reloaded with a spare, loaded cylinder while still in the saddle.

The enemy horsemen made off at the gallop following the road down to the east. The Captain questioned some who had surrendered, and it was discovered they were from the same 5th US cavalry we'd previously had the pleasure of dancing with. This was familiar ground to us and we were able to advise the officer in charge of the 9th there was likely to be a cavalry camp close by as the last time we were here our scouts had observed their patrol activities and how they operated. The column formed 4's now and made a faster pace towards Old Church. The 9th regiment was in vanguard leading the pursuit of the Yankees but we were again charged with trying to use cover off the road to prevent any ambush. This became possible only in parts but we were used to doubling back soundlessly as we wore no spurs and our equipment was checked and checked again to ensure we moved without a whisper of noise. We were always far enough ahead but never too far to be able to warn the column of any danger.

We now discovered the enemy was about half troop strength and had seen them detach riders to gallop on further to the east. The Captain had detailed one of the lads to ride back to the 9th and let them know, while we worked our way around further to the east and then waited in cover at the roadside. It was not long before we heard them coming down towards us from the east, Old Church. These had to be reinforcements from the camp but the Captain envisaged we could trap the Yankees between us and the bulk of the pursuing 9th. It went like clockwork just like we were again in training back at Richmond only this time it was kill or be killed. Many lads in other regiments, it seemed were not as savage as us but our training was all based on quick cut and trust manoeuvres, hitting hard and then disappearing to some vantage point where the next move could be worked out. Fight or Flight.

Just after the reinforcements got to us, the 5th US were up close to us. They were about 80 men strong and our detachment numbered around 50 horsemen. We drew pistols again and as they came level, in column of 4's we fired into them. They reeled and taken completely by surprise struggled to return fire, we had separated them and were now joined from the east by the rest of 9th regiment. It was a rout and what was left of the Yankees made off towards the east again.

We took some prisoners and had us a little look around at what the Yankee armaments were like. They carried sabres and had Sharps carbines but with longer barrels than ours. We could not see any point in taking these but helped ourselves to pistols and ammunition. I and three others still carried our Whitworth rifles, as the Captain had been insistent on this and wanted a marksman section for taking out enemy officers and gun crews at long range. To compensate for the extra burden in weight, we had discarded all kit considered unnecessary. Sabres being first to go, left behind, reserved for those reviews so popular with the Brigadier when we would parade by regiments.

Chapter 22

It is now that the memory of the bridge comes back to haunt me for some scouts had come in from 'E' troop and had told us the Yankees had joined with another troop from Old Church. Their best possible means of stopping Stuart would be at the bridge over the Totopotomoy Creek, the very same one where I had waited for them only a few days ago. We informed the column of the threat and I later found out their second in command a Lieutenant E. H Leib, had the best tactical option open to him by placing dismounted cavalry on the ravine sides on the bridge approaches. This threat slowed the column but it was now the turn of the 9th to fight on foot to dislodge the Yankees. We joined with the mounted troopers from the 9th and with their lads pouring fire down on them; we were able to force them out of their positions. We pressed on now with the 9th having sent 2 riders to reconnoitre our front. The main column resumed its march and Stuart himself on seeing the position could not believe there were no Yankees to greet him. I wonder if he noticed any signs from any action, either of the 9[th's] or ours from only a few days ago. The 9th still had a half troop dismounted and these were coming up in the rear with horse holders nearby bringing up the mounts. In addition, were in pursuit of Leib towards Old Church. As we paused to listen it was plain to everyone there was a cavalry troop coming up the road. Equipment probably not secured properly, the slap of sabre, jingling of harness and that distinctive humming made from the passage of a company of horsemen travelling at the gallop, through a canopy of dense forest. We met them on the road and pressed home in column. They were in column of 4's as were we and the clash when we came together in the confines of the trees was like the noise of a 4 gun battery firing at the side of your head. They were surprised and unready, we set about killing them with our revolvers and I quickly emptied one. Reached for another and started all over again. There were horses panicked and rearing up, bolting trying to free themselves from the tight throng of men intent on killing each other, men falling, being stepped on, others screaming out wounded, sabres flashing down cutting the ears of horses and connecting with flesh or other blades.

There was little room to manoeuvre and in sabre attacks, your enemy must be on your right side for the most efficient killing stroke. This is hard when everything is so compressed by trees and the first to break into panic are usually the men with the least training and less of a pain threshold. We were trained better than they obviously had been and our hardiness and drive must have excelled. They broke and some of them simply let loose the horse's reins allowing them to bolt away with their riders holding on for dear life. The 9th lost a few men and their officer Captain Latane was killed, shot by the Yankee officer after he himself had been severely wounded by Latane's sabre. We give chase, as they broke, and then tried to reform in an opening at the roadside, bare of trees but we were too close and did not allow them to organise. Again, because of our training we were able to hit them twice. They were not very good and as the second troop came up to support us; while we were still engaged, it was soon finished.

It was a fierce encounter and afterwards you are often left shaking and feeling empty with little recollection of some of the details. You have been moving and fighting to stay alive, you have checked your body for wounds but it is like your brain is separate from your body and you can see from above, yourself below, going through all the motion of combat but in slowed down time. We pursued the remnants of the Yankee cavalry and they led us through their own campsite from which only minutes ago some had only just rode out to attack us. We had time to relax a little and again we rummaged through everything they had left for us. After taking what we fancied the camp, tents, stores or equipment was put to the torch.

Our Captain was concerned we were in a bad position as the retreating Yankee horsemen would surely raise the alarm, and a force of bluecoats could soon be upon us. Has it happened there was a column of infantry sent out to intercept us but our scouts in the rear had observed them and they were soon outpaced and left behind

Fitz Lee questioned some of the prisoners and of course found they were the 5th US, the same regiment reorganised, as he himself served in before resigning his commission to fight for the South. It struck me, as being strange and I could not understand the polite manner and respect he showed one of the junior officers. In our unit the feeling to a man was that the quicker you killed every Yankee you could see then the sooner you could go back home. I suppose it's gentlemanly conduct, something that reminded me of it all being a big game of toy soldiers to them, where chivalry and fair play ruled the day but without reality or realisation of the dreadful consequences that I was sure, some of them had not grasped. There was nothing chivalrous, gentlemanly or West Point about the way our Captain had trained us to fight as we took advantage of every weakness and ill-advised manoeuvre the enemy presented. We were not so much fighting for the Confederacy but more so, our Family and homes, for our unit, comrades and survival, the trooper riding next to you in line and the one that would be covering your blind side in those bloody savage fights. He had shown us this, as it had happened to him years ago when forced to leave a regiment and men he loved so dearly. He always said your fight was for comrades in arms, not governments or countries. This became even more unreal when we learned that the only Union commander in a position to block us on this ride turned out to be JEB Stuart's father-in-law Brigadier General Phillip St George Cooke.

I can remember I got the chance to speak to the Captain for a moment, and he was still very worried but this didn't seem to bother our leader who seemed even more intent on gaining the rear of McClellan's army. We hadn't gone far when we were all called forward to speak with our commander Stuart; he wished to discuss with his regimental officers and all the scouts just what he intended. I can still see the look on some of their faces, I thought it was amusing but didn't get much of a chance to laugh as one look at the Captain brought me down to earth. JEB wanted us to ride completely around the Yanks. I couldn't believe it and I wasn't alone as the Captain looked like he was now even more concerned.

I often wondered if our great leader had any prior intention of swinging right around the Yanks and not to return the same way or by any other cross country route. We had only just returned from scouting this area and knew how bad this country was for cavalry. The ground was difficult for it consisted of heavy forest with many low lying water logged areas. These meant roads were the easiest method of effective travel. Meaning that an enemy force could easily bottle us up, this meant that we could have easily been surrounded by an enemy force and would have had a hard fight and an even harder escape route as every Yank this side of the James

River would have been on us. It had been a different matter when we had last operated here, as there had only been twenty five troopers. Now we were twelve hundred troopers and the number was growing by the hour being swelled with captured horses and enemy prisoners.

For all we knew old JEB could have been working on this for days but that was how he was, he thought on his feet like that time at Bull Run when he'd put us into them New Yorkers in the funny pants.

Our leader gave us the reasoning behind his thinking and it made sense as the enemy would be alerted now, and to escape further to the North was unpractical because it involved a dangerous river crossing at the Pamunkey. He further explained that we would have to go deeper behind the Union lines to the east before we could hope to turn south again. Before the meeting ended the Brigadier spoke openly with the Captain and asked his opinion on being able to cross the Chickahominy at Forge Mill. I knew what our Captain would say and he wasted no time in relaying the fact that the bridge was down and that the river was in spate, with much deep water flowing at the only ford. This didn't seem to give the Brigadier any concern even though in our report we had given details of this ford belonging to the Christian family. As if by magic an officer emerged to the front beside Stuart. He was introduced as Lieutenant Jones Christian whose family owed the farm near the ford. He was to make sure we could all safely get across but my mind went back to the time when the Captain was nearly washed away downstream on the very same river crossing.

That was the end of the briefing , orders were given for regimental commanders to proceed at once, gathering as much information as we could on troop dispositions, supply lines and to gather up any munitions, horses, prisoners and food supplies we could carry out with us. This is how it was as our position didn't seem to worry him whatsoever. He had already issued his orders so all that remained was for us to turn on our heels and mount -up.

The brigade now moved out at the trot and I remember hoping and thinking to myself if our luck had run out. We made fast progress towards a place called Tunstalls Station. I knew, as the Captain had said that Mosby and some 4th regiment scouts were again in our front. This eased my concerns a little and the Captain seemed to be enjoying himself setting an even faster pace which I had trouble matching, as he would manoeuvre past anything or anyone in his path, often to the shouts and curses of the men and horses he had brushed aside. Our main job was to keep up with our leader and be in a position at his side should he need to dispatch us with any orders for other officers who might be anywhere in the column. This was madness, here we were in considerable numbers, miles behind enemy lines and the General feeling of our officers was one of great joy. They were all in such high spirits it was as though we were on review back in Camp Ashby.

I had had a chance to speak with Mosby before he left and what he said made me realise we were all in the hand of the gods, any one of them that was the best suited to this sort of dancing with death. It turned out that none of his previous scouting missions were this far east. However much information was gathered on our last patrol this was boosted by having guides with the brigade who actually lived in this county. Here again it turned out that one of those gods I had been talking about must have got the message, because at the last minute before Mosby left he was joined by two troopers from the 9th who were actually locals. They had been ordered forward by Stuart to accompany his pet scout, Mosby.

I hope you can begin to see what I have been saying about our leader, the Brigadier, to be a good officer and make it easy for men to believe in you, the officer has to be in possession of certain qualities. Charisma is one, luck is another but the only thing is they both cannot last forever.

We were making for the York River Railroad at a place called Tunstalls Station and I was glad we were not anywhere near the Yankee prisoners or herding the captured horses. Riding with the Captain meant we were always close to the head of the column; it was the best place as the dust kicked up by our passage was not as bad as it would be further back. Officers and scouts had been told at the last meeting with the Brigadier that we were in an area right behind the enemy and astride the supply lines stretching between the Pamunkey River and the US 5th Corp's lines north of Chickahominy River near a place called Mechanicsville.

We were not alone on the road now and wagon traffic belonging to suttler's, seeking to sell their wares to Yankee soldiers was causing some confusion. The contents of these wagons were too much temptation for many of our troopers and they were only too happy to relieve these peddlers of their supplies. A few troopers helping themselves to the delicious cooked hams, bacon, coffee beans and liquor. Stuart was ahead of the game and he sent the Captain and me back down the line to bolster the troop Sergeant's authority and get everybody mounted and back in the column. It was madness, like one of those cartoon sketches.

We had only just got forward again when our leader sent me back again to find the few scouts in reserve, still with the column. I had orders for them to scout forward towards to the river to a place called Piping Tree Ferry as he wished to discover if this was being used by the enemy as a supply depot for hauling food and ammunition. I had asked the Captain if I could go with them but he had refused saying we were to ride with the advance guard to another place further up-stream. This was another location likely to be in use by the Yankee's for unloading supplies. It was unlikely the scouts would find anything at Piping Tree unless things had changed in the last few days.

I was happy to be with my own friends again as here was Joe and some of the others I had trained with. We greeted one another but this was cut abruptly short as the Captain led us out at a breakneck pace.

We cautiously made our approach towards the river and were suddenly aware of a ghostlike figure only just visible in the tree line. This was one of the scouts who had been sent out with Mosby.

His talk with the Captain determined our next course of action, for we were ordered forward to watch for any signs of enemy activity. The area turned out to be a supply depot and there were actually three schooners being unloaded and a waiting long line of wagons ready to receive stores

I was ordered to return to the column and inform our Brigadier. He ordered two squadrons, one from the 1st and another from the 9th to attack the supply depot and landing.

I was to accompany them and I was so excited my mind was racing. When I returned to the Captain, Joe recognised this fever in me and warned me to get control as it could cost me my life. He told me to keep on his left side and not to take my eyes of the Captain. We had flown back down the wagon road and were soon in company with the advance guard again. They confirmed that nothing had changed. The Captain had seemed to sense that something was not as simple as it looked and he detailed one squadron to make their way around to the far side of the depot nearest the river. The other would be further divided into two, one half to remain in cover and mounted while the other advanced on foot to engage the enemy pickets.

I was with Joe and our Captain; we were mounted and waited for what seemed an eternity before the firing started. We moved out of cover with pistols at the ready. Our dismounted troopers had already put to flight the few Yankees in the guard and the rest were either shot down or were quickly taken as prisoners. Suddenly other shots rang out from the direction of the river and wharfs where our other mounted troop had gone. We rounded the corner of a store house and saw they were being engaged by a squadron of Yankee cavalry. 'Follow me,' the Captain shouted and I remembered what Joe had said to me. I manoeuvred the horse with pressure on his flanks from my legs and this seemed to be working as he was jumping and swerving his way into a line that would take us up alongside Joe, just behind the Captain. I had just enough time to look up and see this Union cavalryman swing across to my right side in a classic manoeuvre to put me within the arc of his sabre.

The blade was arching backwards ready to be slashed at my head.

It's difficult to explain exactly what happened next but I felt the Remington revolver buck in my hand and I saw through the smoke from the barrel the Yankee was swaying in the saddle. He passed by us between Joe and myself and the sword had dropped from his grip but was still held to him by the sword knot chord.

Almost immediately there was another enemy rider, His horse was rearing up on its hind legs and it appeared as if he was just waiting for us to level with him. This was happening at breakneck speed, but for me it was as though it had been slowed down, my senses so tuned I was anticipating every danger. We flew up to this rider; he was again in the air with his horse up on its rear legs. Joe was being forced to take a different line by another Union soldier's horse shoulder charging his mount and forcing it to side step to the left. This was putting him instead of me in the exact position to receive the enemies sabre slash. This time I could remember my mind being really clear as I cocked the action on the revolver, levelled it at the horseman's chest and pulled the trigger. I then had to try and stop the horse for we had come close to the edge of the wharf. The enemy cavalry had broken and were in full flight as our lads on foot were discharging some carbine rounds to help them on their way.

There was the Captain, he was shouting something but I couldn't hear what he was saying but as I looked around there were some soldiers on the wharf and they had cut adrift one of the schooners and it had already moved out into the current and was being borne away on the tide. Some of us shot down these men but it was too late and the Captain was shouting for us to Cease Fire.

Chapter 23

We had captured around seventy five wagons, two schooners, more horses and some prisoners. This was annoying me as I looked on it as foolish because it took a good man's attention to look after and guard an enemy prisoner. I was praying that I wouldn't be given the task of playing guard to these.

The Captain was pleased with us although that was hard to know as his next order was to burn everything, wagons, schooners and all the buildings. The smoke was soon spiralling thirty feet into the air and it must have given the rest of the Brigade the good news. Stuart had taken the column onto Tunstalls Station and by the time we had joined him again things were under control and nearly finished. At the offset Mosby and the advance guard of the 4th regiment were put under pressure for some time but they had been able to dismount and fight off a company of cavalry and some infantry. However when the 9th got to them they showed their heels and turned away. The remaining troops surrendered to Stuart's staff while the fun of pillaging the vast amount of stores and equipment was left to us troopers. The Captain ordered the telegraph wires to be cut and I was detailed for the job. I thought it would be easier than it was. I got my legs around the pole and was able to take my weight as I pulled up my body weight with my arms. I became a little more efficient at it as I got higher but when I got to the wires I had to let go and use the bowie knife to cut the copper wire down. I almost fell to the ground and Joe and a few of my company were splitting their sides laughing at my predicament. After some effort I managed to cut all of them, just in time, for the Captain to come riding past. He looked up at me and just yelled 'What the Hell are you doing? 'Get down before you break something'. We were allowed a little rest here and there was much high spirited behaviour. The wagons and buildings were searched thoroughly and anything worth eating, the clothing, ammunition, equipment or in fact anything that could be carried was brought away. There were some bad incidents when champagne was discovered and it wasn't long before some troopers were out of control and one blind drunk. Discipline was soon resumed and the drunk was left in a heap where he had dropped. The perimeter guard had come in to report to the Captain that there was a Yankee locomotive coming in. He ordered some troopers into a detail to man a makeshift barricade while he organised others to try and dismantle some rail track. There wasn't enough time but they still managed to pry loose two rails. However not having the necessary tools the efforts were futile. I thought it would have been good had we had some explosive with us but apparently the Captain had indicated that Stuart wouldn't hear of any suggestions along these lines of extra stores or equipment and most of the staff became reluctant to voice their true opinions. I knew in my own mind that if our officer had been given his own way we would have been blowing things to pieces.

The train was in sight now and some officers were in a mind to attempt to stop the locomotive by flagging it down. This seemed to be working at first as it slowed. This however was short-lived as the engineer seemed to sense something was not right and accelerated. We were then ordered to open fire on the train and the box cars and flat wagons were riddled with bullets. Several soldiers were seen to fall; others jumped and tried to get away. These were either shot or surrendered to our jubilant troopers. The locomotive was approached by an officer armed with a big shotgun and he fired into the cab. This killed the engineer but didn't stop the train as it merely rumbled away towards the east. Our celebrations were soon brought to an end as the Brigadier was ordering his regimental officers to ready the men and get the column going again towards Talleysville. We had now captured two hundred and sixty horses and mules and had pressed into service some wagons to transport all the captured supplies. In addition we were encumbered with one hundred and sixty five prisoners. I was concerned at the start of this patrol about our actual size and this being too, large but now we were even larger and it was harder to go anywhere without being observed but so far we'd been lucky

The Captain was up alongside me and he was showing some concern. This was not so obvious and for any other person who didn't know him it would have been impossible to observe. I on the other hand new his moods and how he behaved differently under pressure and concern. He mentioned the ford again at Sycamore Springs and I had to admit that the same concern was foremost in my mind too. He was quiet for a while and then whispered about the bridge pilings at Forge Bridge, ''That's it,'' he said ''we can build it again and get everyone across.''

Riding towards Talleysville during the night it was obvious the Captain was worried; this was being transmitted down the chain of command. The regiments had become really separated and this was not good as if we were to remain an effective fighting force we would need all the sabres together to stop the enemy being able to annihilate us section by section. We also had the wagons and horses which did not make for easy control.

Our Brigadier ordered a halt as we pulled into Talleysville around midnight so as to wait for all the trailing elements to be able to catch up. We all must have realised that the Yankee's were close now, especially as we'd left a drunk of a straggler behind and there were plenty of people who saw which way we were heading. It's one of them things you just put out of your mind if you're going to be able to carry on

I was further surprised, as when the rest of the column showed up we were given time to enjoy what we'd taken from the suttler and the supply depot's. I grabbed a few minutes sleep with the horse reins tied around my leg. We were soon on the move again and on our way in the darkness toward Forge Mill. I told you before about the bridge and the ford across the Chickahominy River and if you remember I said they were both going to be unpassable in their present state. The river was in full spate and very dangerous, there would be no possibility of getting any part of our columns across the ford at Sycamore Springs. However the Brigadier had listened to us when we mentioned about it but this is the first time I have to admit, when he looked really concerned. If we were even delayed for an hour it would give the Yankee's more of a chance to close with us. The Lieutenant whose family owned the farm that used the ford regularly was living in hope. We had seen the river only days before and it was high then, since it had rained again so there was a good chance the level would be higher still, not lower.

This was proved but not before our Colonel had attempted to swim his horse across. He soon gave it up and this allowed our Captain again, to come forward with his plan. The Brigadier was really in a state as only we knew that his jovial exterior was a front to inspire confidence in his command. He sent a galloper off to Richmond to explain the situation to Lee and possibly arrange for a diversion to be put into action. The Captain asked permission to speak and explained about the bridge downstream at Forge Bridge, still having pilings intact. On arrival we were ordered to start ripping down a plank warehouse nearby and some of us were to organise a gang of prisoners to help lay the dismantled timbers across the bridge spans. After probably three hours we could start to move wagons across. Once these were on the other side the horses and mules were moved; the whole command apart from the guns were across by midday and these were manhandled and pulled through the water using ropes, to the south bank by 1:00 pm. The rear-guard then set fire to it all and spurred after us as Yankee cavalry appeared on the far bank and started shooting at them. We were again required to ride within site of the Yankee gunboats on the James River but we were in high spirits and their shelling caused us to break out laughing. We pulled into Charles City Courthouse at the Buckland Plantation and here the Brigadier ordered a couple of hours rest. All of us had been in the saddle for over thirty six hours and we rested until sundown. Our officers were rousing us then and our Brigadier was issuing his next commands.

He left Fitz Lee in command and explained to our Captain that he wanted him to accompany him and Captain Frayser, who was a native to this country, to ride to Richmond. They left us and rode out at breakneck speed for Lee's headquarters at Dabb's Farm. We continued our march through the night and arrived back in our own lines on the 16th June.

Our Brigadier, in the company of Captain Frayser and our Captain Robinson spurred through the picket lines before sunset on the 15th June, having galloped twenty eight miles with only one stop for a cup of coffee. Lee was so happy to see him and talk to him of his very anxious moments the day before. He was that concerned he congratulated both Captains, sending one to Governor Letcher with the news of Stuart's successful mission, and our Captain was instructed to relay the good news to Mrs Flora Stuart of her husband's safe return.

The General was so impressed with the action that these two officers were being presented with new sabres, the very best the armoury could provide.

He came to us again the night of our arrival and thanked me for taking care of the boy Jacob. I felt bad about it as I had forgotten about him completely and I had not even given his safety one minute of my time. He looked at me then, and I started to colour-up. He started to laugh and said "I know you didn't even think, did you?" "Good job he can look after himself with Silas's help eh!"

It was this night after we had been left alone he started to tell me about his regiment in the British Army. He said they had gone to Russia to the Crimea to fight these people. He then went on slowly about a charge when they were put against a line of enemy gun positions and infantry lines. He seemed to be looking through me and away into the distance and his voice was strangely quiet. His account of the action was shocking as the odds they had encountered that day seemed unbelievable, but I did not doubt his word. He told me of his men not giving up even after many of them were wounded, some more than once and getting through the shell and grape fire, they were attacked on the way back, repeatedly by lancers, dragoons and those Cossacks he was always on about. His attention came back to me slowly with his eyes seeming to focus again, but then continuing, speaking through his hands pressed over his face saying that most had been killed or wounded and that out of six hundred men, only just over two hundred got back to the British lines.

He must have felt like talking that night as he went on to say about how he'd been forced to leave the regiment, not as was customary, being allowed to sell his commission. Almost penniless he drifted around in England for a while but couldn't earn a living. His wife had left him as her family could not stand the shame, and he was heartbroken but very angry about how they had been treated by higher-ranking officers in the cavalry.

On their arrival in Russia, he and his wife had been accommodated in tents sometimes on the cavalry lines or sometimes in only just liveable squalor, housed in a small village close to where he called Balaclava. Not everything was perfect but his wife did the best she could to make their rough quarters always comfortable. Things were manageable and she was liked among the other officer's wives and was well respected by the soldier's wives who she helped all she could, providing little comforts, food and help when they fell sick. They were both friends with another officer's wife who was married to a Captain in another hussar regiment. This lady enjoyed much freedom owing to her very forward personality and her popularity with all the officers. She would be allowed to accompany staff officers to vantage points overlooking the battlefields, one in particular Lord Raglan the Commander in Chief of the Cavalry Division was content to allow her free passage anywhere she wished to travel. This situation helped his wife also as our Captains wife spent much of her time in the company of this most popular lady. They were both happy until the night of a regimental accompanied mess dinner night where all the regiment officers and others from the whole brigade would be present as guests of the Commander Lord Cardigan.

The next statement surprised me and for the third time that night, I was amazed at what he told me.

He had been ordered away from the dinner table to attend to some trivial matter. This gave the Commander, Cardigan the opportunity to direct his attentions upon an unfortunate junior officer. The commander was a renowned bully and womaniser, although he was never associated with any public scandal involving other officer's wives from the brigade, it was public knowledge there had been an affair with a married woman only a few years previous.

He went on saying that this poor officer was the centre of an abusive attack, completely unwarranted and out of place in the Officer's Mess. However not being able to stand this verbal attack on her friends, our Captain's wife spoke out in defence, answering back across the table.

Things must have happened that he did not tell me of but it transpired the Captain had returned to the Officer's Mess to a growing argument and an irate Cardigan who was then blustering orders for the two wives and the junior officer to be removed. This proved too much for the Captain, all he needed to retaliate to defend his wife. The commander ordered for his arrest and disciplinary hearing for ungentlemanly conduct. He was put under house arrest but allowed to ride with his men on any engagements. If he survived then he would afterwards be court martialled for his conduct. They were both sent back to England after he had recovered from his wounds enough to be able to travel. They embarked for England before the remainder of the cavalry to face further indignation and unfair treatment. This was to result in their marriage break-up and the Captain seeking out another countries army where he could hopefully make something of a military career.

So that was his story and with this told, he got up, wished me good night and walked away. I was left staring at his back with those words still ringing in my ears.

Chapter 24

Throughout the month I don't remember a single day when our cavalry was not in contact with the enemy. Constantly day and night, we watched his troop concentrations and reported his every move.

The Captain seemed to be at General Lee's headquarters at Dab Farm a lot, as he was on JEB's staff now and would have to sit in on meetings. These were often over breakfast or supper and he never forgot us, as he'd always get Jacob to bring over tasty bits of food he'd brought away for us. Our horses were in good condition as we were still managing to feed them by still being able to find good fodder within the city. This was fortunate because the surrounding countryside was being sucked dry from the thousands of them Blue bellies being sat around so very close to our lines.

I had been elected to be a Corporal now and remember I had mixed feelings at the time on whether I was capable to do the job. However the boys in the company seemed to accept me and I was always given the respect due to my new position. The Captain would explain certain things to Joe and me about how we were in a dangerous position and the fact if the enemy had any other commander, other than this McClellan we would have even more to worry us.

The situation was, we were surrounded by two main armies, but foolishly they were separated by the Chickahominy River. He would tell us of the folly in dividing before a determined enemy and the ease with which one army could be annihilated before the other could be brought up to reinforce it. What truth this held, as we were going to experience this more than once before our fighting days were over.

On the 23rd June, Lee and all his Divisional Generals had finished their planning. Orders were issued the next day and our lads started to deploy. Jackson was to be secretly brought down from the Valley and to close with the enemy's right wing. The intelligence we brought back from our ride with JEB going a long way in providing vital intelligence for this manoeuvre. Next, our forces around the city would be redeployed so as to weaken our right in front of McClellan and reinforce our left to support Jackson. This would mean the Confederate strength would be 55,000 men against the enemies 25,000 in that section. The Yankee General Porter wouldn't know what hit him and Jackson's men with a bit of luck could press on down the Peninsular on the north bank of the Chickahominy and sever all the supply lines of McClellan's army leaving him surrounded this time.

Like in all laid plans, there are always weaknesses; this whole operation had to be carried out by precise, coordinated movements requiring good communication between every element engaged. We didn't even have good maps in those days and the weather was so hot and humid it drained your energy. This affected everyone but especially Jackson's men as they suffered terribly from heat exhaustion, the distances and time they were to be completed by. Yes it was true these were the 'foot cavalry' of the Confederate army but this fame was won in the clearer air to the north west. I don't know if any of you have experienced this kind of mind numbing lethargy which is very likely to affect any person struggling with such physical burden, in this country at this time of year? Well take it from me it was a daunting challenge, to ask them to cover distances of over 60 miles in those conditions. Perhaps it was asking too much even from these soldiers because their efforts caused them to suffer, what can only be called an illness which not only brought down the foot soldier but all the commanding Generals as well.

We were roused early by 'Boots and Saddles' the morning of 25th June, being required to throw a screen across the centre and flank of the Jacksons Valley army. There didn't seem to be any urgency and the Captain was not present then. We were ordered to draw sixty rounds of carbine ammunition but we had learned to hoard revolver ammunition and opportunities were never wasted that could result in us finding extra supplies. Bodies were always checked relieving them of any primers, ball and cartridges. Only three days provisions of corn poke and some coffee were drawn but I knew Jacob would have secured some bacon for us. We reached the bridge over the Chickahominy by the Fredericksburg Railroad and rode through one of our infantry brigades, AP Hill's. They were waiting for something to happen and must have been bored, as when we rode through em they took it out on us. "Make sure' yar look after 'thar nag as it's got heaps more brains than 'yer under 'tha cap." We reached Ashland station before dark and this had been a struggle with all the roads being blocked and congested with troops and pickets causing many hold-ups. We could now see the dust cloud that was being thrown up as Jackson's men came from the Valley. He was behind schedule by best part of a day and should have been leaving Ashland that morning but here we all were with his men who were preparing to bivouac. We skirted around behind his supply wagons and escorted them into Ashland.

Our orders were to screen his flanks and that is what we did moving out towards the railroad and Hanover.

The Captain left us that night, and we enjoyed the bacon Jacob had stolen for us while our leader accompanied the Brigadier to a meeting with a very weary General Jackson.

The next day 26th June we were roused early, well before dawn and in the saddle moving down the Hanover Road around Wickham's Mill before it was light. Jackson's columns crossed the Railroad seven hours behind schedule but they had made their way from out of the valley and late or not they could be relied on to give a good account of themselves.

We were in good company having with us again the 1st, 4th and 9th Virginia and riding with us rode men of the Cobb, Jeff Davis and Hampton Legions. Our brigade was completed by the Stuart Horse Artillery commanded by Captain Pelham. It was a lot of men, probably around two thousand, but didn't we make a grand sight trotting north on that Brook turnpike.

We were up ahead of the infantry having been in the saddle since before dawn. We were in the vanguard with the Captain and had stopped in a little patch of woods to gobble down some coffee beans and drink some water. This gave you a bit of a lift, and as the crushed beans entered your empty stomach we heard the sound of the Yankee bugles sounding reveille.

Those bastards would be scoffing bacon and biscuits no doubt. We pressed on and came down the Ashcake road to Merry Oak Church. The infantry should have been with us but as was often the case, we were alone.

We were just west of the rail lines and well in the operating vicinity of Yankee patrols. There were two or three roads, the main Ashcake road having some further branches which all had to be scouted to gain any information that would assist Jackson's line of advance. This was our kind of work for we had practiced this so often. Our little Georgia patrol was divided and I ended up with Silas. This put me at ease because I knew I could rely on him and his experience to get us out of any kind of hurt the Yankees could throw at us. Good cavalry are experts at placing point troopers well in advance of the vanguard. In conjunction to this there will be flankers in twos or threes well spread out down the length of the route being reconnoitred, exploring any branch roads that might lead off. This network of alert troopers will be connected by other gallopers who move between the units providing a constant communication all the way back to command in the rear. Here you would find a large enough cavalry force to be able to look after itself capable of handling enemy resistance or holding a position until reinforcements arrived. This way we were well prepared for any surprises the enemy was preparing. However, we had learned not to take things at face value and never to rush into situations that would be impossible to get away from. Our leader had often explained that the trooper who allows him to be drawn into a trap has probably cost the lives of many of his fellow troopers. It goes a lot deeper than that, even for one moment of carelessness and a single second of lost concentration could alter the outcome of a whole battle. We found ourselves again with Fitz Lee and also in the company of our friend Mosby. The 9th with Rooney Lee, alongside the 4th with Captain Chamberlayne formed the main squadrons being followed by the rear-guard consisting of the Jeff Davis, Hamptons and Cobb Legions. The guns under Pelham were in the rear. It was a good formation as reconnaissance information was passed between gallopers all the way to Stuart who was never far from the forward units. We reach the railway at sun-up and send a galloper back to inform Stuart we have bumped some cavalry pickets. They circle us firing a few shots but do not close with us. We ride after them but they have no spirit for a fight. There is now a force of cavalry at Tallieferro's Mill. Our galloper came in and said they were on foot and in defensive positions. I couldn't wait till Fitz Lee got there and as they pulled up we joined them in dislodging them. We lost a few lads as we charged them but we flanked 'em and caused them to remount and pull-out, they were good and the Captain who had ridden to the sound of the rifle fire said they had to be regulars. It was a running fight but we pushed them back three or four miles. Stuart joins us now and we clear all the roads around Shelton's corner.

The rifle fire is brisk all morning and then around noon our scouts come in with the news a mixed force of cavalry and infantry that are drawn up at the bridge spanning the Totopotomoy. They are in firing lines and have deployed so as to be able to cover their engineers, busy setting fire to the bridge timbers. Stuart is told of the Yankees attempt and it is obvious that this is vital, the bridge must be secured to aid Jacksons advance. We now form on our officers and are again under the Captain's command. Dismounted we join the regiment and using cover, make our way toward the Yankee line. We come into position around 500yards from their lines. They are steady and well-disciplined so we select targets and from cover start putting down accurate fire, concentrating on officers and non-commissioned section leaders.

There is nothing more demoralising for a soldier than to see his comrades go down right alongside him. The Captain was moving carefully amongst us calmly giving us our individual targets, fire orders. Many of the regiment's individual units had now trained sharpshooters among the ranks, since the availability of more British Enfield rifles. This meant we could lay down fire accurately without wasting ammunition. He told me to take down officers first and then change to the section leaders. He came back along the line and then ordered me to start aiming to wound. I looked at him questioningly but angrily he told me that to wound individuals in close ranks had a bad effect on morale. It was human nature that soldiers would want to help wounded friends and would eventually stop shooting. If you shoot enough of them they will not be able to stand and will break as their nerve collapses.

This is what we did and I still can see the line of men wavering as their volley fire was disrupted. We didn't have long to wait as Stuart sent the 9th Virginia with Rooney Lee upstream to find a ford. One squadron dismounted and joined us while the rest raced around and crossed over to the other bank. These were now in a position to force their flank, but the bridge is now burning. Gallopers have been sent back to summon Pelham and his battery, and he is soon swinging around to unlimber and come into battery. This is a most wonderful sight to watch, guns deploying at the gallop and coming into action. From the time they arrive to the time of the first shot is not very long. They were pouring canister and shells onto the riflemen. They were already leaving the scene and while the rear-guard tried to cover them they broke into panic. The blue bellies cavalry mounted and rode away. Oh! How I would have liked to have chased them. The fire on the bridge is extinguished. An engineer detail is set to fell trees and repair it while we ride across with the guns and start to winkle out any lurking Yankee's.

Jackson's infantry are now up and the advance elements consisted of Hood's Texans followed closely by Ewell's division.

We have to open out now to cover a probe by Stoneman eastwards. The main objectives were to be able to cover Jacksons advance southwards towards Mechanicsville. We had better move on now as it was hard to keep abreast of all the infantry movements that day. The Yankee's under Porter were unmovable. The military chair-bound expert will for ever more cast doubt on Jackson's apparent lack of judgement. He did go into bivouac two mile from Porters line. Ambrose Hill had dashed his brigades against those unmovable Yankees and they performed with unbelievable bravery. Charging up to the Beaver Dam but the fire was so intense they melted before it.

The Yankee positions were well prepared and for these southern boys it was their first taste of action, and they were sacrificed, being smashed to pieces like waves driven onto rocks. The Yankee engineers had constructed obstacles and cut lines of timber down to create wide rides between the trees. These lines would draw the attacking southern boys onto their guns; it was a carefully planned 'killing ground.' Longstreet became involved and brought up his guns to try and take the pressure off Hill. When the sun set it also set on the hundreds of our dead and wounded, Hill's attack was finished. However it was known to the Yanks that their flank was turned and under the cover of darkness they started to withdraw to a second line of prepared defences at Gaines' Mill.

The day before was one of the most frustrating days I had spent since I joined the cavalry., Jackson had ordered us to screen his left flank while he stopped and

206

bivouacked between Hundley's Corner's and Bethesda. True we were in the rear and flanked the Yankee position and had the separate divisions acted as Lee had planned, Porters right would have been engaged as well as his centre. Our Captain had told us how it had affected the Brigadier. He was withdrawn and unapproachable. He paced up and down and constantly scratched at his beard till the skin broke adding blood to the natural red colour of his beard. Jackson himself was strangely withdrawn and not wanting to speculate, even now, I will not pass judgement on this officer as I am not fit or qualified to give an opinion.

Chapter 25

Our Captain's orders were for us to keep in contact with the enemy and to do this we had to creep across the killing ground, like wraiths. It was like we were inhuman. There were many dead left on the field as we later found out there had been well over a thousand casualties. The wounded cried out as we tried to avoid them and sometimes you would stumble over a bloody bundle that had once been a human being. The injuries caused by canister shot were horrible beyond belief, sometimes causing you to look down at them simply because they were just so unrecognisable. I shuddered with the cool of the damp night and the creeping mist which added to the eerie atmosphere. If there was ever a reasonable set of circumstances offered why a person would believe in the supernatural it would have been strong on this night. We moved silently into the trees, the Yanks had set-up traps to entangle skirmishers and many were still there. Some had bodies twisted in the branches as they had been shot struggling to get themselves free. The Yankee rear-guard never heard us and we came up on them as they strained to see into that blackness. You have to wait a long time for your eyesight to be able to function in that kind of pure black. It is like someone has put a blanket over your head and then asked you to start walking.

I had become used to moving in this pure, velvety cloak, so thick you felt as though you could reach out and touch it. There were muffled, anxious voices now, close and you could almost sense their fear, smell it. I was with Silas and we had been ordered to leave the horses and make our way towards the enemy positions find their strength and how far their line extended.

Silas was gripping me with his fingers tightening around my wrist. So tight I thought he would stop my blood flow. I put my face close to his and he motioned with his eyebrows toward where previously I had heard fragments of sound. He was drawing the flat bow from around his shoulder and as I stared at him through the gloom I knew he was notching an arrow.

A number of our little troop had practised shooting these weapons with the guidance of Silas and Joe but I had never been required to make a shot count. Silas was sniffing at the air and I instinctively did the same. There it was, Tobacco and even as it registered in my brain Silas was drawing back the bowstring. I had taken mine from around my shoulders and had attached a shaft to the string. These were beautifully made arrows, handmade to such detail they were works of art in their own right. He nodded in the direction and as I followed where I thought he was meaning for me to look I saw a little glow of red. It was a pipe, I knew instantly but even then the arrow had left the bow with that individual sound that only comes from the release of a bow string. I waited but there was no sound after the 'thud' of the shaft entering something soft. I had drawn the bow back to its full extent and the turkey fletching was touching my cheek just under my eye. I was straining to see through that darkness but it was like a blackboard when teacher has just asked you to wipe it for her. Suddenly there was the sound of a branch snapping just to the left of the direction where Silas had released his shaft. It was caused by a human and he made the mistake of cocking his rifle. The sound was like a pistol shot in the dark and it gave me the direction in which to fire. It's like something has disturbed the surface of a pool like a fly landing and causing a ripple, this is the best way I can describe it and I released the shaft. My heart was pounding and I had to struggle to control my breathing. There was only silence and again that smothering cover of near total blackness.

We inched forward using the Indian techniques shown to me by our Captain, in those days that now seemed so long ago before the war. These worked and having taken probably thirty minutes to travel ten or twelve yards we came up on the first body. On hands and knees we had groped along feeling for anything in your path and working around any obstacles until you were able to move easily, forward again. It was agonising but exciting and for those of you who won't be able to understand it's as though you have just discovered a part of your inner self that would have otherwise lain undisturbed in your brain for all the rest of your life. It made you feel so alive and able to see and feel forces all around you those untrained, inexperienced humans would never be able to know.

The first Yankee was laid on his back between two felled trees. His pipe was still burning but had dropped onto his chest. Silas picked it up and dug the hot embers from the bowl with the blade point of his small knife before stuffing it into his buckskin pouch; I felt around his face and recoiled in horror as my fingers touched the shaft that was sticking out of the open mouth. The arrow had entered through his lips, smashing his teeth and continued through his mouth to exit through the back of his neck, severing the spine. Silas wanted to make sure of the other one and I followed him around the felled trees to where we thought the picket had been standing. It took us another thirty minutes to find the body I put my hand into a pool of blood and was moving to extend it when I touched his arm. The arrow was again in the upper part of the body, this time however it had penetrated into his throat just to the side of the Adams apple and again exited out of the back of the neck. It had severed arteries and feeling the amount of blood close by, he had probably bled to death. Silas removed both shafts, wiped them on the soldier's uniform and then slipped them back into his arrow pouch. In groping around in the blackness we had also gained information on the extent of the picket lines. The rear-guard were still in position just as dawn was breaking but we heard our boys coming and had to alert them to our own presence; as these were what was left of the Texans that had suffered so badly the previous day and were definitely out for revenge. We joined them and put down some accurate volley fire. The Yanks must not have had their coffee yet as they were rudely awakened. They started to pull out and our boys started to hunt for any weapons or good bits of kit they had left for us.

The Yanks were again in good positions on a plateau behind Boatswain's Creek. This is where the Gaines Mill is that I told you about, and all around is that hells hole of swamp land somebody called Powhite.

The infantry were engaged all morning but they again were blown to pieces. Divisions of both Longstreet and Hill were dashed upon those guns. Jackson's men were in a position where they could be used as an anvil if Porters forces could have been dislodged and driven toward his position; but this didn't happen and Jackson waited. However they attacked in the late afternoon but it was already too late for the thousands of Confederates who had fought their last battle. We were pushed out again and rode over a wide front, sometimes as far up as Old Church. This was not new territory as we'd been there only a few days ago. We were close to the guns at one particular time. I loved being with them they were so spectacular. At the gallop, horse's manes stretched out with the speed of their passage, the gun swerving and coming back into line while the limber and caissons plunged up and down throwing huge clods of earth and grass skyward.

They were in action as we closed with them, acting as a screen. Captain Pelham was good at his trade and knew his business. The enemy were coming up from Grapevine Bridge and the Captain had seen them. He wheeled around at a speed you'd have thought would have resulted in all the wheels being torn from the carriages, but there they were with our lads hurriedly unlimbering them and coming up with ammunition from the caissons further away. After what must have been only seconds the guns crashed out. One was a captured Yankee Blakely and the other a 12 pounder Napoleon, both guns, only recently having changed owners. They had only fired one round each when several enemy batteries returned fire. These were good gunners so must have been regulars as their incoming rounds were playing havoc. A limber was smashed and a shell fell in-between several of the battery horses killing one. The tricks of the trade with gunnery is to fire and then manoeuvre to another position and repeat the operation; this way the enemy is unable to get the range in time and so it allows you to knock them out before they do it to you. Pelham had to repeat this fire and manoeuvre three times before they had had enough. However this position was the scene of a bigger fight as more guns were sent up and this hot and bloody duel lasted all afternoon. We pulled out and were grateful to get away, being sent to Jackson to help him come up into position, hopefully to be able to take the pressure off Hills and Longstreet's shattered divisions. We watched as Jacksons skirmishers broke out and felt for the enemy. You could just hear it as it started, still very low on the wind but it steadily grew in sound till it was making the hair on the back of your neck stand on end and sending little shivers down your spine. The lines of screaming men came running on the extreme shattered left of what was left of our brave lads. But they came on again, what was left of them and further away we saw that Lee's divisions were advancing.

We had been tasked to find a point where there could be a passage forced between the stinking Powhite and the Boatswain's creek. I was again with Silas and we had two other good lads with us. We were close to their lines and could sense there was a definite weariness about them. Previously our presence would have attracted much attention in the form of musketry if not a report from a gun, but now there was this lack of interest. It was just possible that there was a strip of slightly higher ground in front of their lines. I studied it through the glasses which the Captain had found on the body of a dead Yankee and had passed gratefully to me. It was possible, and I sent the two gallopers back to inform Hood we would wait and show them the gap.

The Yankees suddenly woke up and fired several times at our gallopers but they were good at this and were soon out of their line of fire. Hood came with the Texan's and Georgians. He was on foot at their head and we dismounted and showed them the way. They rushed out like ants on the move turning right and left, enveloping the enemies plateau position with the battle flags waving through the gun smoke. The enemy was broken but not beat and they still had a number of guns in battery position, these must have been running short of ammunition as cavalry could be seen deploying to ride through them to allow for them to withdraw.

It just so happened that this cavalry were our old dancing partners from when Latane was killed. Here they came down the slope at the gallop probably about three squadrons. They looked real pretty but I couldn't help thinking they had not learned very much. The Texans must have still have had good disciplined firing lines as they poured controlled volleys into them. The centre of their line was shot to pieces killing and wounding all the officers. They had had enough and regulars or not they turned and galloped back through the gun batteries. Shame really as they panicked all the horses that ran off leaving the gunners to their fate.

Porters Yankee's were battered but still fighting and we were ordered to maintain contact as he filtered his division into the heavily forested area around the Chickahominy. The Yanks had been sent some reinforcements but it was too late and nearly dark. However the fresh troops acted as his rear-guard allowing him to cross the river By Grapevine Bridge. We watched his progress in the dark and sent gallopers back.

The army was drunk with victory and weary from the efforts to dislodge this worthy opponent Porter. He had left most of his wounded and his dead. We later found out that we had been awarded twenty-two guns, thousands of good rifled muskets, and other small arms and some nice horses. Talking with the Captain later that night he warned us of how close a thing it had been. Lee had been unable to throw in his divisions until it was nearly too late and had that idiot McClellan seen fit to send reinforcements to Porter earlier the outcome of the battle would have been different. McClellan had his army all together on the south side of the Chickahominy with Magruder's army between him and Richmond.

You didn't have to be a military genius to realise our armies were exhausted. McClellan had a clear line of retreat to his bases on York and James rivers and the York River line was easily supported by naval craft. However McClellan being true to form had been greatly affected by Magruder's professionalism over the last week and as the Captain said our little ride behind his lines will have worried him and made him so nervous it must have influenced his decision.

We were allowed some respite and given a few hours rest. On the night of the 27th we were again pushing out troopers in two's and three's right up to his forward positions. There was something not quite right and Joe, Silas and I were with the Captain on patrol very close to their picket lines. We could see where there had been much overcrowding and that many men had been confined in that evil mosquito ridden, bad land. It must have been another reason he did what he did. The Captain was sure we should take a captive and persuade him to tell us what he knew. Silas and I were now accomplished veterans of the covert operation and so he ordered us to infiltrate between their pickets and wait for the opportunity to snatch an officer and bring him back with us.

It was a dark night and again similar to all the others we had patrolled on in these Bad Lands. Silas and I again felt our way through the inky blackness; slowly moving by allowing your weight to be suspended on one foot while you carefully lifted the other high placing it down a tiny bit at a time and then rolling the foot so as if there were any twigs or branches underneath, your weight would not break them sounding like a cannon shot in the blackness. It took hours to be able to cover only a few yards and this was agony but preferable to being discovered and jeopardising the whole mission. You could hear them as we got close and Silas wanted to shoot them with our bows. This time however there was no tell-tale glow of burning tobacco. I forced my decision to leave them alone as it looked to me there would be an officer making his rounds before long.

We waited in the darkness and I knew Silas was handling his Bowie knife, fondling it in the dark as though it was a sweethearts hand on a dance night. Suddenly there was a challenge shouted out from one of the pickets and an officer appeared out of the gloom with a shielded lantern. They approached him and he was telling them that they were to wait one hour and then make their way through the line to a muster point for their regiment. I was now in two minds of what to do. To snatch the officer, take him back, or turn tail immediately and go back to the rendezvous with the information. I decided and Silas was already readying his bow and fixing an arrow. I had to go along with this now as I couldn't really afford to have an argument in which to get a point over. They were still in a group when we shot the men down assisted by the small light coming from the lantern. The officer was startled as his men went down in front of him with arrows sticking out of their bodies. We had aimed at their chests as this area offered the largest target. Silas was leaping over the low bushes even before I realised he had moved. I saw the officer's mouth open to shout but it was too late for him as Silas had already swung the tomahawk and it was coming down, flat bladed onto the Yankee's head. He collapsed into Silas arms and as I got to them he was ordering me to bind his arms and legs while he fashioned a neckerchief to gag his mouth. We carried him between us until he regained consciousness. Silas put the bowie knife into his throat drawing blood and I simply explained he would lose the whole of his Yankee head if he didn't walk with us as he was now a prisoner of war. We reached our horse holder trooper and quickly mounted urging the Yankee to do likewise, but securing his feet and hands to the saddle. A lead rope was passed to one of us, to be able to prevent his escape.

We got back to the Captain and he questioned the officer. When he came up to us his face was not pleasant. We will ride for Lee's headquarters immediately as there is no time to lose.

Chapter 26

On the 30th there was another dance at Fraysers Farm on the Charles City crossroads. This was a day of savage fighting again where Hills and Longstreet's lads were in the thick of it. Magruder didn't have much effect on the outcome but there is some doubt whether Jackson's boys could have given them a hiding had they crossed White Oak swamp in time and come in on the Yankee north flank. We got to know from some of Imboden's cavalry boys that they had found a good crossing point in the swamp that was not even guarded. Hampton's scouts were active on the same mission and they too found another good place, he could have used. The outcome was the Yanks were allowed to get further south where they took up good positions on Malvern Hill and were able to cover the retreat of their wagons. On the 1st July they were safe south of this position and the Yankees gave us another very bloody nose.

We were busy and from the 26th June were almost continually in the saddle. We chased down towards Despatch Station road on the 27th looking for a supposedly retreating Yankee army, there were many enemy stragglers and our orders were to round these up and escort them back to our lines. The roads had to be picketed and we left patrols along the White House and River roads. Our Brigadier returned with the other regiments and received further orders at New Cold Harbour. He had to send us some more boys as we couldn't cope with the amount of Prisoners of war. We now got orders to cut the York River railroad. The 9th Virginia was with Ewell's Division marching to the railway while we were with the Brigadier towards Despatch Station about seven miles north. We had some good fun and picked up some good looking rifled guns that the Blue coats had left for us. There were always enemy stragglers and these were troublesome because you had to escort them back to our lines. With these being so fluid it was often a while before you could get back to the troop. Luckily I was seldom tasked with the job. We arrived about noon and were greeted by a cavalry squadron dismounted and drawn up in firing lines. Our Georgia cousin's boys from the Cobb Legion. We laughed as they expertly manoeuvred onto their flank and forced them to wheel smartly away before they were flanked. The noise from there whooping attack was probably heard in Richmond. There were plenty of new carbines left for them and I couldn't believe how they had thrown these away, some complete with carbine slings.

I was with the Captain, Joe and Silas and we were occupied tearing up the rails and climbing up the poles to cut the telegraph wires. Our Captain couldn't believe how easy it had been and kept saying it didn't make any sense as this was one of his supply lines.

We were to find out from prisoners that there were cavalry and infantry ahead on the White House road. It was thought Stoneman and Emory were there and as we had been engaged with them over the past two days our Brigadier decided it was within his orders to pursue them. So we were now off again this time bound for White House landing, the only place we didn't get to when we had come through behind their lines weeks ago.

This was good fun and I loved the way we would overrun the marching infantry and the lumbering wagons. A section would overtake them well on the flank and circle around to block their path. Then we would ride into them scattering them but they would be stopped by the blocking troop, being either shot or throwing down their weapons. The wagons were a nice treat, like Christmas. There were also Suttler's wagons and we helped ourselves to their goods. We pressed on leaving the wagons to be turned and escorted back to our lines; we had so many I wondered how long it would be before we started to fire them. Our Captain was in a fine mood and we raced through Tunstalls Station where we had entertained the Yankee's only two weeks before. They had constructed earthworks and rifle pits so we must have impressed them on our last visit. We raced out the other side and as we approached the Pamunkey River the sky above the whole valley was full of smoke from the fires of burning stores on the landings.

There was a need to patrol around and close with the landing and as we came up on a deep stream bank, where the road crossed a bridge we saw it had been destroyed. It was covered by an elevated position on some small hills and I noticed there were cavalry deploying around a battery of guns. I galloped back towards the Captain who was busy restoring some swift justice and regaining discipline over some misguided troopers who thought they could sample the drink in a suttler's store. He rounded on them punching and kicking them into the saddle where he slapped at the horses rumps with the flat of his sabre. He chased them all the way back to the bridge. I was ordered to ride for Pelham's guns as the regiment dismounted and Rooney Lee prepared to fight on foot.

I loved to ride with the guns, and as we came up on the hill overlooking the bridge Pelham swung them into position, unlimbered and came into battery. Within sixty seconds a salvo of shell and canister was being flung over their gun position. The Bluecoats cavalry had no stomach for it and they dispersed out of range. Canister falling in the underbrush on the forward slopes also upset another troop of dismounted men and they followed their comrades. We were sent downstream and found a crossing point where our Captain led us around and into the attack. We dismounted and again did what we did very well and sent some long range accurate rifle and carbine rounds down amongst them killing the officers and gun layers. They soon got the message and brought the guns off and retired after their cavalry. We were stuck now as we couldn't get the guns across and everyone was exhausted. We needed to rest and feed the horses so the Brigadier allowed us to camp at the bridge and relax for the night. Everyone had taken what they needed and more from the Yankee stores en route and we had bothered to bring up a wagon with horse feed. We sent out pickets to all compass points to watch our position but every one of us was amazed by the fires and explosions from burning ammunition which kept us without sleep most of the night. However as we had been continually in the saddle for three days, sleep did finally come.

There was more fun the following day as the engineers got the bridge ready for the guns to cross we had already rode toward the open plain where the Yanks had built their supply bases. For two miles all you could see were burning heaps of Federal army stores. Riding through the smouldering heaps we must have been noticed by a gunboat on the river. They started to throw big shells at us and we danced about laughing at the force of the explosions. Our Captain comes up now with a full troop of the regiment. He shouts to Joe to fall in, column of fours and follow him. He led us to a position that had a slight rise to it above the river and we form a skirmish line on foot with horse holders for every five horses. We are in our element and our little sharpshooter section along with the rest of our troop puts down accurate fire on the sides of the gunboats deck and cabins. On board are the last troops to have been embarked and I was hoping these would be a New York regiment. We could see our fire was taking a toll on the men crowded on the gunboats decks and some could be seen falling overboard and huge surges of humanity being swayed one way then another as panic did its work for us.

Pelham's guns now wheeled into battery in the cover of the nearby woods and started to fling shells over the gunboats decks, these were adding to the panic which we had already started. The Yanks were in no shape to stop us from out there on the water and as we took aimed shots we saw them launch three boats and start sweeping towards the shore. They were loaded to the gunwales with men but Pelham shortened his elevation and started to drop shells right over them. It was a beautiful piece of gunnery but they were not in agreement as they quickly pulled back to the sides of the ship where in their panic one boat was capsized before it was loaded. It didn't end there as Pelham raced after them. They had weighed anchor and were beating out into the current but we hadn't finished either. The Captain was directing fire orders and required aimed volleys to be directed at the ships wheelhouse. I know for a fact some of my rounds entered that space but I was not rewarded with any evidence for a confirmed kill. The guns were now delivering shell after shell to air burst over the decks, but as the range increased and the bend in the river hid the target Pelham ceased fire and pulled out of battery to trot away back to the treeline. We trot back to the landing and dismount organising horse lines and posting sentries. The Captain sent out cavalry pickets to watch our position and act as security.

We roamed around the wrecked wagons and smouldering piles of equipment. There were abundant undamaged stocks of food and we gorged ourselves on tinned delicacies of every description. There was even ice and ice making devices it was unbelievable. Our horses were well catered for with plenty of long forage and oats, they had been in such a haste they had left us horses also. These were good looking animals and a big improvement on the ones they were riding at Bull Run. There are also thousands of rifled muskets of good quality, almost new and some British Enfield rifles. Our rest was soon disturbed as we were required to mount-up and ride with the 1st regiment and Rooney Lee. We had been ordered south again to find the enemy. Our destination the bridges and fords on the lower Chickahominy that we knew so well between Bottom Bridge and Forge bridge, the latter where we had had so much fun that night with the Brigadier. White House is still a prize and so our Brigadier remained there all that day 29th June.

Orders will have been issued as JEB is in the saddle to ride towards where we are keeping watch along the river between the crossing points. Pelham is much engaged and I seek permission to scout for him with Silas. There are exchanges of gunfire with the enemy on the south bank and a gun carriage is wrecked but we have still two light howitzers. Around 3:30 we hear sounds of a large engagement towards Charles City crossroads, and we get the order to cross the Chickahominy to screen the army as it moves towards the James River. The roads in this part of the county are switchback and difficult to navigate as you are never sure of the way they will lead you but we had some good troopers with us who knew the country and led us out to where we would be the most useful. We had been joined with Munford's command and that of Jackson's division cavalry. We were required to cross at Forge Bridge and make our way towards the river, but as the roads were of no use we detoured to the east and came up on the Malvern Hill action. This as I told you died out before nightfall but there was no rest for us as we pressed on toward Haxall's landing right on the James. We pulled up in the dark and observed the fires of what could only be Federal troops.

We were exhausted, having covered over forty miles since boots and saddles. We bivouacked in a corn field and put the horses out to graze, we were just east of Turkey Creek and had not bumped any enemy but we were not in contact with any of our forces either and not even sure where they were.

Staff officers were sent to find Jackson while we made the most of a well-earned rest.

Chapter 27

The entire time I have been telling you this story my old friend from my cavalry days, Joe, has been fighting his own personal battle with an all-consuming illness that has steadily robbed him of most of the body weight from his entire frame. Over the last two months I have seen him change from the man he was before to shrink into a shell that can be described in no other way but that resembling a living skeleton. I talk to him every day and we discuss what he would like me to do and if he wants me to end his misery by shooting him in the head. I think this time is very near and I have to search the inner depths of my thoughts to ask myself if I will have the courage to do this.

I have contacted our Captain and informed him of the ill health of our old army comrade. He now lives in Virginia and has done well for himself as he manages a large tobacco farm in the Valley. After we returned from our quest to find my lost family we drifted apart and I perhaps would hear from him possibly once a year. We have perhaps seen each other only a few times in the past ten years but he would always want me to come up and visit and I would never take him up on the invitation. It struck me strange that this man who had always had his differences with the upper classes from society had married into a rich Virginian family who through the whole length of the war and the struggle for survival afterward had managed to hold onto their position and fortune.

I knew him well and understood how he felt and how his mind worked on nearly every subject for you don't go through five years of war with a man and not get to know exactly what makes him tick. All those nights together by the campfire told the story of who he was and exactly what his morals and ethics were.

He was going to be here with Beth and me soon as he was travelling down by train and he would be coming to stay for as long as we both needed him. I married my sister's friend Beth as you will probably have gathered and this was about the same time as the Captain went north. He was there at our wedding and I was proud to have him there. Just as proud as I was to walk down the aisle with Beth for she was so beautiful and still is for that matter. We never were blessed with any children as my state of mind was, for so many years severely damaged. Beth had nursed me many times and she knew every part of me, including the insides of my head and every scar, as she had tended my wounds just as professionally as any doctor.

The Captain had married soon after we had found my family and when he had returned to Virginia. This made me think of how he had found the time to find such a high society lady. Then it came to me and I remember thinking of all those times when I'd be on courier duty and had been required to deliver messages to JEB Stuarts Headquarters.

If you can remember there was always a party atmosphere around his quarters and there was music and entertaining and candle-lit suppers where ladies were often invited. It all made sense now and this high class lady of our Captain's was probably the frequent dinner guest at fine houses in Richmond where our officers were often the guests of honour. I wish him well as he is my friend and can only hope this relationship will in every way replace the one that was taken away from him by another aristocratic system belonging to people who believed they were born to rule others and it was their God given right to carry it out regardless of any right or wrong. The war had changed many people's opinions but it was greed and power that caused those less fortunate to suffer and after the war the Southern peoples suffering was a prime example of this wrong which one human being is capable of forcing upon another, less fortunate.

I do not think he will have changed, and if I know him that lady wife of his will share his opinions on fair play, equality and sense of justice, the same justice we both fought for all those years. He will know what to do and will be able to support Beth and me through a funeral. I am going to visit Joe today and Silas will be with us as he came yesterday. He never came back with us from West Virginia but left Mosby's regiment to join a Cherokee unit that required some military leadership and the last time I heard from him he had married a Native American.

I rode over to Joe's little cabin that afternoon and was shown to his bedside by a Negro lady who had been his companion since the end of the war. I never knew exactly what the relationship between them was and simply didn't want to. They were both happy and that was all it was about. There was a smell of death in the room and Joe's skin colour was a pale yellow. He looked ghastly. Silas was sitting at his side and they had just finished laughing together about something which had caused Joe to struggle for breath. Silas had taken him by the shoulders and eased him forward into a sitting position. This had cleared his airway and he lowered him carefully back, so his head was again on the pillow. I was uncomfortable and he could sense it because he motioned me to sit on the other side of the bed. "Don't worry I'll not be long now," he said, "Just waiting for the Captain."

He knew I was talking to a journalist telling our wartime stories, and he seemed to be in approval but when I mentioned Seven Pines he didn't agree with me especially when I started to say that nobody knew why Jackson hadn't come in earlier at Malvern Hill. He argued and his voice took on a more authoritive tone and seemed to get stronger, more so than it had ever sounded in a month. "We gave them something to think about though, remember when we had all got dressed in Yankee greatcoats over our shirts and those boys off that monitor lying at Haxall's landing didn't suspect anything was wrong till we took em all prisoners?" He was in his element now and we spent an hour talking about how we had come across their cavalry again south of Malvern Hill and bumped them, riding into them from ambush and using our revolvers. "That rain was heavy and it made observation really difficult through the woods but by nightfall we were scouting between the landing and Charles City." I said, but Joe added, "Yes, but our boys had to go over to keep Stoneman's cavalry from getting the drop on us." Joe added. "You lot had all the fun as the Brigadier wanted to get Pelham's only gun onto them heights at Evelington." Silas now laughed and slapped his thigh. "Just imagine what those gunners could have done with even a four gun battery." It was nice to see Joe come out of himself but he soon became tired, and his nurse came into the room and briskly ushered us out. He was asleep before we had reached the porch.

The next day we visited again and took up the story of how we had dismounted and held the heights while Pelham lobbed shells into their camp. Joe was loving every minute and spoke out. "Pity that McClellan wasn't in his tent as one of those twelve pounder shells burst right above."

The truth of it was we had to stand in the rain and shoot those Yankees as they came up. It took us from nine in the morning till two in the afternoon to change their minds. We were low on ammunition and the gun crew had fired everything they had.

The day dragged slowly and we tried to get Joe to drink and take a little soup. He became agitated and even though he was so weak, the force with which he made it known, he simply wanted to be left alone was surprising. Silas and I talked outside and we were both in agreement he was getting worse as his breathing was such an effort now but he would fight through these attacks. The effort was taking its toll and that afternoon he suffered a particularly severe one that we all thought would take him. However it was while we were all outside on the little cabins porch that the buggy trotted up the road and stopped inside the yard.

I was expecting the doctor as he'd been sent for an hour since but this was another figure stepping down and walking swiftly around to the other side of the carriage to hand-down a lady and set her feet firmly on the ground. I looked in amazement as they both walked up to the porch steps. He had aged but the years had been kind to him for he was not bent over or favouring one limb more than another as Silas and I were. His back was straight and he still carried himself with that manner of someone who had spent all his younger life in the military.

He ran up the steps and threw his arms around me squeezing me till I thought my chest would cave-in. My mind was a million years away, and for a split second we were asking my mother for permission to travel north to join the army. "Well lad what have you done with the Sergeant." But he had brushed us aside and disappeared into the cabin. Even the Negro lady, who previously had protected her man with the valour of a female mountain lion with cubs, was taken aback and so subdued by his authority she curtsied as he called out. "Where is he?" There was little need for explanations and the next thing we heard was Joe's voice, strong again and so full of his old self. Silas had left me on the porch looking into that beautiful face and trying to break my obvious stare. She must have known how much I had been shocked by her looks, for women who resemble goddesses as she certainly did, must be so accustomed to this kind of reaction from members of the opposite sex.

She gave me her gloved hand and automatically I was leading her up the steps onto the porch as though I had been accustomed to doing it all my life. It was easy to be a gentleman in her company, as her subtle, natural actions gave out signals that informed you exactly what she expected. Just like being on parade when you would get an order in advance, 'company will move to the right in fours,' preparing you for the next command, 'right turn.' I was completely captivated by her.

I hardly had time to gather my senses, as she was in a hurry now to get inside and find her husband. She swept into the room and everyone's attention was immediately drawn to her like a magnet being dropped in a nail barrel. The Captain broke the spell. "Gentlemen allow me to introduce my wife Isabella." "My dear, these are my comrades."

She immediately took over and gave orders as easily as any Commanding General; sending Silas to meet the doctor who apparently they had requested the previous day by telegraph to his offices in Atlanta. Her next task was to organise his bed and clothing ordering the Negro woman to find fresh linen and a new nightshirt. Not that he needed these as she was so particular about his appearance but she was just as influenced by this lady as we all were, and merely went along humbly with her every request. The doctor arrived in a great haste and we all assumed Silas had been responsible for this as he hovered in the background with a wide grin across his face. Our presence was short in the room as Isabella emptied it as though a shell had exploded.

The doctors report was shocking and he told us he had probably only got a couple of days left for this world. He left us with some opium mixture and told the Captain's lady how it should be administered. We talked things over around his bedside and Silas knew exactly what was going to happen. "I am happy to do as they want." He said and then continued with. "I was only hanging around for our Captain and now he's here my fight is nearly over."

The conversation followed on how best we could grant Silas his last wishes. The Captain was intrigued about how I was talking to a journalist from the Atlanta newspaper, which was featuring weekly articles on the war time experiences of our little Georgia Sharpshooter's. He agreed with Joe that it would be too much to fully go into detail on every action but we would be better to describe the most exciting, dashing and daring exploits we lived through with our heroes JEB Stuart and Mosby. In any case, as Joe put it, he didn't have the time or energy to relive it all and his own personal 'Boots and Saddles' would be calling him any day now. The following day we invited the journalist to

Joe's bedside and he was honoured to be able to record what was to be a collection of memories from a group of veterans of the war. Throughout the following day and well into the night we talked of how the war had gone for us following these two men and it is now that I will let you read something that will be very close to the articles published in the Atlanta Journal.

"Why not start with Pope's coat." The Captain said and this started us all laughing. A bottle of fine sipping whisky appeared and Isabella handed us all a glass and then wheeled round pouring a full measure into each. We agreed that each one of us would tell a story, starting with Joe, he would tell us about the ride where JEB lost his hat but gained a coat. I would do Second Bull Run, followed by Silas who would tackle Brandy Station leaving the Captain to handle Gettysburg and then Yellow Tavern and the death of our leader. With this Joe started to explain about how some of McClellan's army had been withdrawn by naval craft and we were mainly engaged with watching the James River and the nearby roads.

He still had men around Westover but if you've ever been there you'll be able to recall what a hell-hole that place is, the mosquitoes and the hot weather would soon account for more casualties than we ever did. Failing that the typhoid and malaria would take over where the other left off. Most of us were withdrawn back to the camps at Richmond because Lee considered McClellan was done fighting. Richmond had an air of joy and laughter about it. Our officers were invited to all the parties in the houses of the important people while we swaggered around in our ragged Confederate grey with the Yankee's equipment and side arms. Parades were the order of the day and our Brigadier had us riding through Richmond to the pleasure of the whole city, we felt like, and were treated as heroes.

We welcomed the rest and chance to catch up with the mail. Our horses were looked after and we had them to the farriers and horse doctors. Mine was a little thin, like most of the others but were still all very fit as we had been able to feed them well from the Bluecoats. There seemed to be something in the air, and the Captain had hinted as much saying there was probably going to be a new offensive in the west and this General Pope was taking liberties with the civilian population. Land owners and farmers were being ravaged by a new army that was provisioning itself almost entirely from the land. It was rumoured people had been threatened, attacked and even imprisoned. While this probably boosted the number of new recruits from Virginia it still needed to be put right.

The railroad was our main supply route, and Pope's new army were manoeuvring to cut this artery which we so depended upon. We now were back with Fitz Lee and at the end of July our boys were dancing with the enemy cavalry from our bases around Hanover Courthouse. Our orders soon came and in August we were riding toward Fredericksburg. Remember that day we were all together doing what we do best and had been fortunate to gather information about enemy cavalry at Beaver Dam Station. A large patrol had ridden into the Station and captured one of our men. It was poor old Mosby who had been waiting for a train. This was a bad raid as houses were destroyed, crops taken or burned and livestock stolen or killed. It was the new style of warfare the Yanks were using. JEB was with us then and we had gained further intelligence of Yankee's around Port Royal. We rode that day and surprised him taking it easy in the town. It was a laugh making most of them prisoner and again questioning them for information. We learned from them there was a large wagon train en route toward the railroad again by the Telegraph Road. The lad and I were in the vanguard when we came up with them around noon. It was unbelievable they had no point or flanker troopers out, and we easily came into an attacking position filtering through the woods on either side of the road. Fitz Lee gave his orders and our Captain shouted for us to form line. It was like a storm of locusts as our leading squadron hit them before they realised what day it was. The Bluecoat infantry are probably still running. There was further intelligence gained from the prisoners and we learned there was another supply train travelling south with a main force of infantry so we were ordered after them with a battery of guns.

It didn't take us long to catch up with them but it looked like they were going to put up a fight as the rear-guard stayed put. The Yanks sent some reinforcements back and we were engaged, but were told to withdraw steadily drawing the enemy with us. It was beautiful as they took the bait and our guns were able to fire and manoeuvre using every bit of high ground. Those boys knew their jobs and the Yanks suffered badly till we got back to where we'd flounced the first wagon train. The enemy had had enough and we got away with around 20 wagons and a few nice horses. Pushing about eighty prisoners we moved steadily back to bivouac at Bowling Green and spent a good night's rest there.

Chapter 28

This had been enough and we would have to wait now till the following day for Joe to finish his story. He was tired and the nurse gave him his medicine making him comfortable for the start of her night shift. The Captain and his lady had stayed in a hotel in Roswell the first night but I had persuaded them to stay with Beth and I, and we left for our farm after Joe had been settled for the night. Beth was pleased to meet the Captain again and the two women just seemed to like each other from the very first minutes. I couldn't help noticing Beth had dressed for dinner and she was wearing a gown that I had not seen before. Or maybe I had, but thinking the better part of valour would be to say as little as possible, while still complementing her on how lovely she looked. The Captain's lady wanted to refresh and change before dinner and I was really pleased I had built on another bedroom, when we extended the farmhouse a couple of years ago. This addition was now where they both could be together in relative comfort with us, their old friends.

Beth had come from a family who had enjoyed something of a comfortable life style before the war and since, right through the troubled war years they had still managed to make a reasonable living from their estate. When the Captain and I came home to Georgia we were carrying a lot of money in US dollars, this was courtesy of the Army paymaster and I will tell you about that a little later. The money was used to finance our trip north to find my mother and sisters but I gave a large amount to Beth's father to help him with the business and to pay off the land agents. The arrangement of repayment had enabled Beth and me to start over again and make a go of the farm.

The dinner table was one of elegant proportions and the linen and tableware were items I had not seen before. I dare not ask too many questions as she had done a fine job and put on such a wonderful dinner it was unbelievable. The Captain's wife came from the bedroom in a beautiful evening gown and it crossed my mind this was going to be the latest Richmond fashion and probably imported from a Paris fashion house. She wanted to help Beth and refused to allow her to wait on the table on her own. So the two of them served their men and I became increasingly uncomfortable. Our Captain and his lady were used to having servants and a chef to prepare their meals, but I had little need for concern as this did not spoil the evening. We enjoyed each other's company so much it was one of the most pleasant evenings of entertainment, Beth and I had ever experienced.

We returned in the morning and were greeted by Joe's Negro nurse. She was pleased to say that the patient had spent a comfortable night and that he had already been given his daily medication.

We entered the room and Joe's face lit up. "I have been thinking," he said, "we were with Fitz Lee, when JEB had gone off on his ride."

Joe was talking about how we had been allowed a little time to re-group after the action along the Massaponax and Po River. Popes army seemed content to concentrate along the Rappahannock and Rapidan but we later found out that he had been ordered to react more aggressively to cover McClellan's withdrawal. In fact the two armies were about to combine.

Stonewall was engaged in some manoeuvring that would put him in contact with a some of Popes divisions around Culpepper, but things did not go well; probably owing to the uneasy relationship between him and AP Hill. The weather was another factor as it was unbelievably hot and humid. This, and the fact there was ample quantities of strong applejack available all along the route of the march, strongly contributed and hampered the Confederate advance. Hill was put under arrest, Robertson's cavalry were engaged and there was a savage action fought at a place called Slaughter Mountain when our lads under Winder collided with the Yankees under Banks. It was a hot engagement and went hard against our boys, and as far as I can remember was one of the very rare occasions where Jackson himself had to rally his own men personally. Banks was finally worn down and was forced to retire as reinforcements bolstered our firing lines. The Yankee withdrawal was covered bravely by a brave cavalry action. The 1st Pennsylvania suffered heavily in this, losing seven out of every ten troopers that were engaged.

I'll leave it up to Joe now as we were ordered up to do what we do best. "We were with our beloved leader again and it put everyone in high spirits." Joe started. He went on to talk about how our little troop was again in action.

We rode like the wind towards where our boys had been held up the night before. We were with some of Robertson's regiment and they were good lads. Coming up we were able to see enemy pickets. "Can you remember lad, how we rode them down?" "Swinging around in a wide circle until we were on top of his outposts." It was exciting and I don't think any of us worried about not coming out on the other side. We shot them down if they looked like they were going to fight. Those that didn't either ran away or threw down their weapons.

Another action followed at Cedar Mountain and this time Jackson was obliged to withdraw having come up against superior forces. We screened them back towards Gordonsville but Jackson had pressed on and we were engaged with their cavalry again. These seemed different somehow. They had better horses, and the men were not as easily turned like the majority we had fought in past battles. Jackson was hoping Pope would follow him as this was one of his favourite tricks, but Pope was now waiting till McClellan's army was up with him providing an advantage in numbers. This put him on the north bank of the Rapidan. Our Captain broke in at this point saying. "We had probably got more men at this stage than the Yankee's." "Because we were reinforced from Richmond by Longstreet's command."

Joe continued explaining the idea was to turn on Pope quickly and destroy him before McClellan's army came up in force. We were supposed to be deployed to the front of Longstreet's divisions but our baggage train had been directed away from our new operational area, and worse than that we had not eaten properly in days. Orders were received but whether Fitz misunderstood we'll never know, for the result was, we were allowed to ride towards our wagons to re-provision.

Well, Old JEB had intended to rendezvous with us at a position he thought we'd be in on the 17th. I believe the order was misinterpreted, but regardless, there was no chance we could have been there to meet him, as to go towards the supply train and then return in time would be doubtful. As it was JEB and a hat full of staff officers were unfortunately put in a position of grave danger. They were riding east on the plank road towards Racoon

Ford where he thought we would be. Popes army was over to the west and so he didn't consider them to be a big threat. However he was concerned because it was now nearly dark and they should have fallen in with his regiment before now. Just before dark they rode into the little village of Verdiersville, perched alongside the road and about ten miles from the ford on our Fitz's line of route. He stops for the night and seeks intelligence from some local villagers. They have nothing good to tell him as no Confederate cavalry have come this way. I and our Corporal, the lad here had been detailed to scout far in advance of the column and as it happened we had seen enemy cavalry patrols all along the route, but heading away from our regiment's line of march. The lad had decided we would reconnoitre the village in case there were enemy patrols or a squadron outpost there.

Meanwhile JEB and the officers were making themselves comfortable in a house just back from the road. Our friend Mosby had been a prisoner, but he had managed to get himself free in an exchange of prisoners, and when he reported back to JEB he was promoted to Captain and ordered onto the staff. I don't think he liked this and especially when he was made adjutant a little while afterwards, but there's another story.

"You know about JEB just being sent a new hat from his wife?" Well this night he'd decided to sleep wrapped in his cloak and without his favourite new hat. This he had placed carefully to one side where it would be less likely to be trodden upon. It was not a cold night and some of the officers had foolishly unbuckled their pistol belts in order they could rest more easily. Luckily the horses were not unsaddled but had been secured in the little yard at the back of the house. Around midnight we heard pistol shots not very far to our front. We had ridden into the cover of some trees and were sat quietly listening for anything which would signal danger. Suddenly there on the road to our front we see enemy cavalry with a Confederate officer in tow. The lad recognises him to be a Major on JEB's staff and we immediately get the wind-up. We found out later these Yankees belonged to a squadron under a Colonel Broadhead and who had been on a reconnaissance of the area for several days. They must have felt real proud of themselves with the Major in the bag. We were just outside the village now and shadowing the Yankees when something just not right attracts my attention. I had seen him before and knew who he was as soon as he came out of the treeline. It was Mosby. He quickly ordered us to ride back and get reinforcements while he alerted our beloved Stuart and the rest of the staff. The Corporal persuaded him that there may be a need of another set of pistols and he agreed that only one of us was to ride for help. I was with the two officers now and we were flying along towards the house in the village. Pistol shots now and the sound of bullets flying past. We round into the street where we are met by the Big German officer on his huge black stallion. We are in danger of being cut off and JEB and the remaining officers are now with us. I lead them down a small track which opens out into a fenced yard. We put the horses at the fence and all of us gallop away across another field which is also surrounded by a big fence. I put the mare at it even though I knew how tired she was. All I could do was simply empty my mind. I knew and trusted her and had little doubt she would get me away.

We had lost them, but JEB wanted to look down on the scene which was now lit-up with lanterns held by running soldiers and cavalry. He was very angry as he drew our attention to the porch where only a few minutes ago they had been all resting. A Yankee trooper was whooping for joy and trying JEB's hat on, pulling it down hard to alter the shape to his own head.

He looked over at me and nodded. I slipped the Enfield rifle from its slip. The range was long, over six hundred yards but I thought the shot was still possible. We had practiced many times at these ranges so I was reasonably confident. I placed the rifle stock on a little stub of a broken branch just at my height, being still seated in the saddle. The sights were set at seven hundred yards and I waited till the Yank was stood still trying to see his own reflection in the window looking out onto the porch. I held my breath and controlled my movements, then when I had exhaled every bit of air from my lungs I took in a small amount of air. Just for that split second everything was perfect and aligned; I squeezed the trigger. The new owner was still admiring his new cavalier, broad brimmed hat as the bullet entered and exited his body. I had aimed for his high chest area level with the shoulder blades. The bullet had dropped slightly and had probably taken out his heart and part of his lung followed by a huge spurt of blood that now ran down the shattered window pane. JEB looked over to me and laughed, but at the same time turning his horse and spurring away with such speed we were hard pressed to catch him. My horse was not fresh like theirs, and they soon left me behind, but Mosby came and stayed with me all the way back to where we finally came up with the regiment and Fitz Lee. JEB was annoyed with him and the exchange of words was like cannon fire between them, even over a distance you'd normally consider to be out of earshot, the conservation could still heard by most of the command. We left Joe to rest now after deciding the next part of the story would include Pope's best uniform coat. The

Captain and his lady came to our farmhouse again that evening and we enjoyed another wonderful meal together. The ladies acting as perfect hosts serving us as we sat at the table talking and laughing, helped by another fine bottle of expensive sipping whiskey. I couldn't help thinking I would have to pay for this laziness after everything had returned to some normality but there would be a funeral to attend very soon. The morning was on us before we were ready that day and we both were subjected to a sharp tongue lashing from these two ladies. Beth was smiling as Isabella rounded on the Captain like a battery of Pelham's guns. I hoped she was not too annoyed as the silent treatment she normally doled out as punishment for this bad behaviour was more than I could stand these days. We were again welcomed into Joe's bedroom and given the news of the nights nursing. He was still managing to sit up unaided and was eager to finish his part of the arrangement. The journalist was there already and he was keen to hear about the General's coat.

Chapter 29

Joe began by explaining that Pope's army was reliant on rail supply from Alexandria. His left flank was vulnerable and we had been in contact with the blue cavalry all that week. It would have been around mid-August when Baynard had crossed over Hazel Run. The Yankees had the better of us in numbers but we had engaged their five regiments with our four. They were not used to the way we fought and were reluctant to stand for us even when dismounted and were in firing lines they did not stand for long. We just had a real time as we forced their pickets and outposts taking prisoners and whatever else they left for us. I had been with the Corporal for a day and we had moved like spirits through the countryside avoiding all contact with their pickets and patrols. We learned that Pope's main army had now crossed at Kelly's Ford and Rappahannock Station and there was a good chance he had pushed his supply trains well ahead. Our beloved leader had sensed the opportunity may be there for the taking, for if we could flank him and get into his wagons and supply depots we could play the merry devil. Orders came after we had had a wonderful rest day when again some mail had reached us and we re-supplied from our wagons with ammunition and rations. We were to ride in brigade strength with Beverly Robertson's. The 7th and 3rd regiments had been left with the army. We were joined by Pelham's two gun battery. We crossed at Waterloo Bridge and with us in point and flankers out the column rode another twelve miles before dark to the little town of Warrenton. Here we were received very well. The ladies were very attentive and the officers were engaged in much flirtatious conversation. However we hadn't time to dilly dally and were occupied gaining as much intelligence as possible from the locals, concerning enemy troop movements.

We were with the Captain now and our little troop was together again. Our objective was out towards Catlett's Station and because we were well behind Pope's army there was much need for stealth and reconnaissance. It was a dark night with some heavy rain and this helped to keep us concealed. At Catlett's Station we stopped and watched. When Fitz Lee came up he ordered our Captain to take a troop around the opposite side to act as a cut-off section, to stop Yankees escaping and fetching reinforcements down on us. The regiment charged into the Station and the Yankees were taken completely by surprise. We were waiting in concealment as the majority of them came racing out from between the buildings. The Captain ordered us out in a fan like formation and we shot those of them that looked as though they were going to be trouble and took the others prisoner. There wasn't much time to spend here as JEB had now come up and he wanted to know if there had been any intelligence collected from locals or prisoners. Well there had been and it was good information from a reliable source.

It was unreal, but Pope had located his headquarters only a short distance from where we were. He had tents for his staff there and a wagon park containing a large number of vehicles, mules and horses. In fact the informant believed the General's own personal re-mounts were there also.

This was too much for JEB and we were soon in the saddle again.

Rooney Lee's regiment 9th Virginia was to attack the camp while our troop with the 1st and 5th Virginia was to ride with our Captain to another camp located not far from the wagon park. Wickham's 4th Virginia was to ride toward the railroad bridge spanning Cedar Run.

We raced into the tented camp from one side while the Major led his own attack from the opposite end. The Yankees didn't stand a chance and we collapsed the tents by cutting the guy ropes. One of the best uses for these sabre blades, but as we didn't have much time a lot of stores and equipment were put to the torch. Everything was so wet it didn't burn that well and fortunately we got another short opportunity to collect valuable stores, small arms and ammunition. Wagons were collected and teams harnessed. Heavy horses were rounded-up and we took everything that we could remove easily, the rest we burned.

Rooney Lee had a great success as his cavalry rooted through all the Yankee officers' baggage and loaded many trunks and crates onto some wagons. Among the prisoners was most of Pope's staff including his Quartermaster. Personal letters, files and books were also taken and all loaded for shipping back to Warrenton. There was only enough time to cut the telegraph wires after the wasted attempt to destroy the railroad trestle. If only we had explosives.

Our scouts in the rear had reported all crossing points on the river were in danger of flooding making it a dangerous situation, for if we were caught on the wrong side of the water with the Yankees on our back we may not have been able to fight our way out. With this in mind our officers organised us into column and with flankers and point troopers out we turned around and headed back to Warrenton. We reached the town just after sun-up and were received warmly by the local inhabitants. The wagons were unloaded and all the booty was inventoried. Our beloved JEB was beside himself with joy when we found an officers frock coat amongst some personal belongings. This was fresh from a Washington tailor and of the finest quality. This fine looking coat was a Major-General and could only have belonged to one person, it was Pope's.

The journalist was enjoying Joe's story and showed a demanding fascination by anything concerning our leader JEB Stuart. With this in mind I decided to step in and tell the tale that not many people had heard. Even to this day no accounts have been published that disclose details of this part of JEB's Chambersburg Raid.

The Captain had been allowed to keep us together and we were in the company of some good boys from the 10th Virginia. These were expert scouts, probably just as good as we were. We made up a company of twenty five hard men who had been in the saddle since the day before. It was now just before dawn on that October morning and we were in concealment overlooking a large force of Bluecoat cavalry on the opposite bank of the river. The place was McCoy's Ford on the mouth of Black Creek on the Potomac and around twelve miles from the Pennsylvania State Line. There was a chill in the air and a mist was rising all around us from the river which was a blessing for it was shielding us from the enemy pickets. The Captain had explained we were to cross dismounted in a small party led by Lieutenant Philips. This lad was good at his job and had gained the respect of us all. The mist seemed to cling to you as we waded slowly across the stream. "I was with you Joe, and off course Silas here."

If you have ever tried to walk through freezing, running water reaching up to your hips without making a sound then you will know how hard it is. I reached the far bank and sinking into some bushes tried to get some feeling back into my numbed leg muscles. The enemy were close, and I waited hoping that the rest of the lads would not be discovered as they came up behind me. We gathered around, some of us still in the water under the stream bank. The Lieutenant urged us forward and we knew what was expected. Silas was ordered to shoot the farthest pickets taking them out with his flat bow. Joe and I were to take care of the nearest ones without making a sound. I selected the tomahawk that Silas had now given me; in fact both Joe and I favoured this weapon over any other for this kind of action. I crept forward using my hands to clear a path moving any obstruction that would make a noise if my weight was put on it. My target was only three feet in front of me now and was placing his carbine against a tree. I realized what he was about to do and I had a funny pang of guilt that I was about to kill a man who was just about to urinate. This seemed to propel me forward and I swung the blade of the weapon into his neck. He died instantly and I was pleased he would have felt no pain.

Joe had accounted for the other Yankee and I knew the other pickets would be dead as we both had heard Silas's arrows as they left the bow string. We signalled the Lieutenant and the rest of the boys forward. He ordered us to fan out and move through the trees. I had just come around the trunk of a small tree when I came face to face with a Yankee soldier. He had his carbine at the ready but it was not pointing in the same direction to where he was looking. He learned too late from his mistake but the sound of my revolver was a shock even for me. Pistol shots rang out now all around and I strained to see if there were any more enemy soldiers within range, Just then I heard the regiment splashing through the water and the voices of the boys of the 2nd Carolina under Colonel Butler, yelling as they crashed up the bank and fanned out through the trees striking down those bluecoats. The column crashes through behind them and we sit astride our horses watching a two gun horse battery followed closely by Rooney Lee's and Grumble Jones's men with Pelham's guns in the rear, followed with a small rear-guard. We join the rear-guard and are soon found by the Captain, who orders us to move far out on the right flank.

It's getting light now and we press on toward Hagerstown Pike. Shortly we observe a signal station perched on a hill top near a place the Captain said was Clear Spring. Here we come into contact with Hamptons men and he orders our Captain to ride around the far side of the hill to act as a blocking force while he rushes the station through the ever present mist. We take the signalmen and their officers as they rush down the slope away from Hamptons charge but fall right into our loving arms. There are some good horses here as they are the strong mounts used by the enemy couriers, and we take them along with us. We are now approaching the Pennsylvania State Line and not far away from Mercersburg. We soon cross the line and after another fast gallop enter the town around noon. This is where Hamptons boys re-supplied themselves on the towns shops and trades people but we had been warned there was not to be any foul play and Confederate dollars were given in exchange for all supplies.

JEB now called a regimental staff meeting and our Captain was considered important enough to sit in. He soon approached us and gathered our troop of scouts together. We were still in the company of the Lieutenant and his boys from the 10th regiment. "The situation is not good," he said and continued with, "we are probably going to be surrounded very soon and need a distraction to attract the Yankees attention." "You remember Stanley," I said excitedly, "we could all see what was coming next." You then asked for volunteers to ride towards the depots and camps in the Hagerstown area. The mission was almost one of suicide as the whole place was crawling with Yankee cavalry and infantry. We had found some explosives and we were going to be with an engineering Captain who knew how to place them. Our mission was to make as much noise and cause as much disruption and chaos as we could. It was to be a carefully coordinated operation involving Hampton's regiment as he was to come to our assistance and with the luck of the gods on our side we would be granted our survival. That night under the cover of darkness we rode out.

Our travel arrangements were the same. Flankers, point and rear-guard troopers were always deployed. We travelled as fast as was possible by night and then before dawn, laid-up to wait for the rest of the troop to catch up and the day to come. We would then make sure where we were and bring in all the scouts and guards replacing them with fresh people. This would lead us into another 'briefing' session where the Captain would let us know what he wanted, but still he would ask for suggestions from the men. It was to be a dangerous mission as the depots were on the railroad and would include quartermasters, cavalry, infantry and artillery supplies and troop reinforcements. We watched the town and the enemy tented camps all that day and witnessed much activity and troops being loaded onto railway cars that trundled north towards where JEB and the rest of the command would be.

That night we got into position and from cover and concealment we watched the scene below and took-in every piece of information we considered would be of interest to the Captain. All night we remained hidden and my excitement was high as I thought about what we were to be involved with in the days to come. Never considering we would be caught. If anything my greatest worry was being shot but not killed outright as I often woke covered in sweat and shouting aloud from dreams of being under the surgeon's knife.

We would give our reports to the Captain as normal and information was thrashed out at the next briefing with our Captain sorting through all the relevant points, obviously disregarding the stuff about the latrines but pressing the information out of us about guard's posts, picket positions, mobile patrols and outposts. We would then learn in detail what was wanted and from this intelligence a layout of the depot was produced drawn out in the soil. For us to get the most accurate knowledge, it was important observation was continued through the day and the information these lads supplied was vital.

These were experts at concealment and here again, the Captain had honed in on those individuals who were most suited to this work. Many of them being only just one-step away from the law back home but now were, like most of us dedicated to the cause of ridding our homelands of this epidemic of Yankees and if we needed to kill as many of them as we could in order to make this possible then this was the order of the day. We who were considered expert shooters would take out the guards and any officers who presented themselves but shooting all at the same time this being at the time of an explosion caused by a planted charge in one of the storehouse buildings. This would hopefully bring in the mounted pickets and the other guards.

It was beginning to take shape as the Captain sorted the order of things in his planning. We were part of a coordinated diversion but at the moment we were alone with hundreds of Yankees. The target consisted of railway depot, wagon parks, supply houses and a tented camp area. We were to set a trap for the cavalry pickets by attacking them as they were relieved by the new detail coming from the depot, and would ambush these on the road, then securing the whole perimeter sealing the exits also, tighter than a drum.

The explosives were to be placed by the engineering officer and two lads who knew their stuff as all were tradesmen in the use of these devices. Two others who were also masters of their particular trade would escort them through the guards and any off duty personnel. These lads were experts as we knew from serving with them over the last few weeks. Knife throwing was never my best skill and if I had a choice then it would be the tomahawk. I had witnessed these two at practice with their knives and they had perfected skills with those weapons that had to be admired. Therefore, they would take out any unfortunates, which were in the wrong place at that particular time.

Therefore, the reader can be easily reminded of the individual qualities of the men in our little command and see what exactly made our little company different. Each trooper was a specialist in their own right. The men were allocated to positions and individual tasks, some of the most important of the group would be the horse holders, whose job it would be to ensure the others had a horse on which to ride out of danger. Another detachment would cut-off any enemy from reinforcing the area, protect us and help our lads get any plunder, captives, horses or guns away before the enemy could retake them. I was a little doubtful we would be bringing much out with us for if we came out of it safely mounted on our horses it would be a miracle.

Chapter 30

Dawn the next day was set for the attack; I was to take out sentries, officers or any other valued targets. As usual, Joe and I had the section of expert shooters and we were ready to make good, every shot from our Whitworth and Enfield rifled muskets. We numbered six men counting Jacob and two others from the Lieutenant's troop who were also renowned shots. There were other sharpshooter sections covering all the cardinal points on the depots perimeter. We had eaten before dawn, cold rations of jerky washed down with water, now we were as ready as ever we could be and had checked our weapons and quadrants of overlapping fire. There was what we knew to be a guardhouse and officers' quarters around 300 yards from my position. The rest of my little section had weapons at the ready and brought them to bear on the enemy individuals that were in plain sight. We were waiting for the explosion that would demolish the large storehouse and would signal our sniping to start. Suddenly there was the most ear splitting noise and our attention was shortly distracted towards large, rising fireball and flying debris which was sailing up in the air to over 100 feet. This was our signal to open fire and I had not to move the fore sight on the rifle barrel very much to line the rear leaf with it and an officer's body, who had just come into view. I squeezed the trigger, a primer cap cracked and then the noise and muzzle flash of ours and the other marksmen muskets together. Men were falling, some were wounded but many more were down and very still.

There was much confusion in the depot now but we had not time to enjoy the scene, as it was rapid fire drill now. We were ready again and the firing was now individual in sections as each leader gave the order to his own men. Our own troopers were amongst them now and I could make out the effect the lads with the knives were having on the panicked Yankees. It felt like we had been firing for a long time but I knew we had shot-off, four controlled and aimed volleys. We had succeeded in breaking up any attempt to rally a defence and blue-coated soldiers were already panicking. We had seen the blue cavalry pickets set off to relieve their comrades from duty but I do not think they ever reached them, as there were now loose horses running around. Our riders had come in now and were assisting the lads as we fired, moved and reloaded as fast as we could. The Captain was directing fire orders and we shot at every Yankee that presented a threat. Many were confused and wanted in their panic to surrender, but we could not risk having to take prisoners, and these joined their comrades who had put up a fight but had been shot down. We were getting ready now to move forward so our Whitworth's were slung on their straps around our shoulders and we were moving out with our beloved LeMatt's and other revolvers taking a heavy toll on the enemy. We were in a bad position and the Captain was shouting for us to get to the horse holders who were on foot firing into some cavalry who had been alerted from nearby and were now threatening to cut us off completely. There would be no chance of any Yankee equipment being brought away as we would be lucky to get out with our lives.

A Yankee seemed to rise out of the ground in front of me but I had the revolver on him and fired instinctively. He staggered back with the charge of buckshot ripping into his chest. Others were trying to run through us as they were coming away from the clearing action of our lads down in the depot, but we were there to stop them and many fell to the fire from our revolvers. I only had one LeMatt with me and it was now empty but I had decided to try out the Colt .44. I was now leaping from cover to cover in order to get into the main depot compound. The Captain appeared from nowhere and was shouting at me to form on him as some of the Yankees had regrouped and were now organising a small firing line. We raced around their flank and the Captain led us down their length firing as we went and accounting for a great number of their company. I was impressed for the new Colt seemed to be accurate at longer ranges than the LeMatt. Everywhere I looked there seemed to be enemy soldiers running around in panic, many of which had not had chance to get dressed and were still in undergarments. This was of great amusement to our lads and they were laughing and shouting, "If they liked our Captains bed-time story?"

We now threw ourselves onto the backs of loose horses to herd together as many others as we could and drive them in a stampede towards the railway depot. The confusion gave us some protection and most of our troop got out without a scratch. These were some fine looking animals and would serve us admirably for re-mounts if we ever got out of this mess. Our own mounts had been left with the horse holders and these boys were now joining us in galloping away, being followed hotly by some more concentrated fire. The Yankees had started to wake up. Through the dark acrid smoke and the press of horses and running men we crashed out into the railroad depot yard. I was so relieved by what was in front of me I shouted with joy. Our flanking screen of cavalry from Hamptons regiment had taken care of everything. They had not only destroyed by fire, all the buildings and rolling stock in the yards but had set fire to all the cord wood intended to fuel the huge locomotives. These they had only enough time to shoot holes into the water tenders tanks or gash them open with the engineers axes. As we passed many tenders were empting streams of water down onto the ground.

Everyone was in high spirits but there was much firing on our flank and again the Captain was ordering me to gather my men into a troop and join him.

We quickly forgot all that had just happened as we were flying after our leader as he took us into action again with the blue coats. They were out for revenge and we drove into them with a sickening clash. I groped for the pistol bucket expecting to come out with a LeMatt but instead it was my Colt. Not having had time to realise what was where, I just had a fleeting glimpse of a Yankee seemingly determined to severe my head from my shoulders. The .44 surprised me as I had fired, its action was different and lighter and I was happy to see the attacker had been stopped with a wound in his chest. On now at break neck speed, dodging sabre swings and bumping from enemy horses that nearly un-saddled you but I could make out the Captain with sabre and pistol fighting with three Blue troopers. I put the spurs in and Clem's horse leaped me to within firing range of them. I levelled the Colt and fired. It was good at its job and I again fired taking out both of these troopers. The Captain had succeeded in manoeuvring his attacker onto his sword, right swing side and I saw his sabre flash and then it was cleaving through cap, hair and scull to finish it. We were outnumbered but had ridden right through them. The Captain was shouting for the recall, our bugler succeeded in rallying us again, and we turned back into them with the charge sounding, in arrowhead formation. There was no time to think and everything was instinctive. I fired the Colt and it was soon empty, but I had had time to return it to its bucket and grab a loaded LeMatt. I was now up with the Captain and he looked magnificent, the classical example of a cavalryman, with just sabre in hand he was cutting a swathe through those Blue uniforms. His experience was so obvious you could see his practiced manoeuvres defeat his attackers every time and I was there to shoot at any of them that came up on his blind side.

We were again through them and they had broken leaving us stunned and exhausted from the action. I was happy to see that my old friend, Clem's horse was unhurt and that I still with my own section of lads. We had not come out of it unscathed as there were many loose horses a lot of which were ours.

We raced after the column and came up on them as they were herding some captured enemy horses. Everybody was in good spirits and among our lads there was much laughing and carrying on. Joe and I let them be as they had all done well and deserved to let off a bit of steam as we had pulled off a suicide raid into enemy territory and given him a bloody nose bleed.

We were still not out of trouble as the Yankee's would be trying to estimate our intended line of march and would be deploying cavalry to cut off both our party and JEB's from escape.

The Captain and the other officers were worried but Hampton just laughed, shouting a question to them asking if they wanted to live forever? "We have to rendezvous with the Brigade and we'll do that by doing exactly what the Yanks least expect." He ordered our line of march to be north east to cut the Hagerstown Gettysburg pike due east of South Mountain.

We pressed on away from the burning town and depot as it was essential we put some distance between ourselves and those angry Bluecoats. We formed column of fours and sped out on a bearing of roughly north east across an empty landscape. It would not be that way for long and I wondered if our luck would hold long enough to make good our escape. Joe and I were again detailed to organise flankers and point riders while the Captain and the Lieutenant waited for us to disappear into the night before he rode back with the rear-guard along the way we had just come. The column rode all night but we sent a rider to find our Captains rear-guard and gather intelligence on what the Yanks were up to.

Just before dawn we knew what they were doing and our scouts had seen they had sent a large force of troopers after us, but they were travelling more due east towards Mechanicsville. The route they would take would be through two separate gaps in the South and Catoctin mountains. We came in to join with the command just after dawn. The Captain made his report and we made sure Jacob was allowed to select one of the captured enemy horses for his re-mount. We also changed horses and were ready again as soon as we'd transferred saddles, weapons and equipment. Hampton had interpreted our information and thankfully he relieved us, to fall-in with the vanguard while fresh troopers took over. Our Captain was with us and he explained we would drive on eastward until we reached the South Mountain. This would put us further north than the pursuing Yankees but well in front giving us enough time, to both send riders to contact Jeb's column and also to turn south and ride to intercept the Yankees who would by then, be coming through the gap in the Catoctin Mountain just west of Mechanicsville.

If we could hold them long enough with a rear-guard action there in the gap, it would allow the rest of the regiment to rendezvous with JEB's force on the pike below Gettysburg.

We reached the gap in the mountain and were astride the road well before noon the following day. Our Leader despatched an eight man patrol to catch up with the brigade and then ordered our Captain and the entire Lieutenants troop from the 10th regiment, to draw extra water and ammunition and any hard rations that may have been available. We were to ride south with a number of horse holder troopers and spare re-mount horses to the gap in the Catoctin Mountain where the Yankee column would be approaching. It was only about eight miles and we reached the gap within the hour.

The Captain gave his orders and Joe and I helped to position the boys into good firing positions with overlapping arcs of fire. He also detailed another section to go into positions at the far end of the gap so as to bottle-up the first riders in the Yankee column and destroy them completely before their fellow troopers could reinforce them.

We didn't have long to wait, as presently we heard the sound of horses coming at a steady trot along the muddied road.   This was the point troop advancing towards us and we would allow these to enter the gap and ride through it towards where the road once again spilled out into the open countryside. There was a big space between these point troops and the main column following. They were in ranks of fours with flank guards out, but we could see these were a good distance away from the main troops. I was with Joe and Silas and we had been ordered to stay with Jacob and make sure he got out of trouble when the firing started. Half of us would fire into the gap while the others kept up steady volleys onto the oncoming troopers. As normal the orders were to put down officers and non-commissioned section leaders first. Next would be to shoot to wound, and make sure enough troopers were on the ground but not killed outright, merely wounded. This, he would say always unnerves soldiers for a while, to see their comrades go down under the horses legs screaming in pain. Our Commander Hampton had made sure we were all armed with either Enfield or Whitworth rifled muskets and were all confident we could keep the enemy away from five hundred yards and cause heavy casualties.

Our chance came suddenly with the sound of musketry from the other end of the gap. It sounded strange and echoed around but this was our signal to open fire and while some watched the road into the gap the rest of us opened on the Yankee column. The range was around 600 yards but these bullets at that range are still flying at a pretty flat trajectory which means that you cannot fail to hit soldiers who are in ordered ranks. The routine for this action is for everyone to fire at one time and then to revert to independent fire where each sharpshooter selects a particular target of his own choice. We had fired two volleys into them and then the boys behind us opened fire as well, shooting the remainder of the advance force down as they attempted to get back to their comrades. Fire and load as quick as you can was what we normally did but horsemen were now galloping up to our firing positions in ones and two's. Small groups were forming and charging down to fire at us from their horses. The Captain ordered that only every other man in the position was to fire at these people, which meant that there would always be some of our company with loaded rifles. This drill meant there would never be a time when our fire stopped altogether because as one trooper fired his next in line would be waiting for another target to present itself. He called this a 'rolling volley' and we had not done this work in earnest before but it was proving to be effective as the dead and wounded bodies of our enemy were piling up in front of the firing positions. "We'll expect to receive skirmishers now lads." The Captain shouted, and sure enough they came running from cover to cover to get close enough so as their carbines would be effective. We watched and waited and took them down as they exposed themselves, never wasting ammunition but simply concentrating on those that presented the best targets. The majority were pinned down now in every piece of available cover in our front. We were reinforced now with the lads from the other end of the gap and they took up positions alongside us giving us a chance to gulp some water down and take stock of how much ammunition was remaining. We had plenty of carbines and ammunition as we had taken this from the dead Yankee troopers, but one by one our sharpshooter section ran out of ammunition.

The Captain was now up with us and he didn't have to explain how dangerous the situation was. Yankee cavalry were bound to be around and the force we had just beaten would probably be joined shortly as a troop had ridden away down the road in the direction they had come from. It was time to withdraw down the gap and we disappeared in ones and twos while the other lads kept the Yankees busy. Every one of us assembled around our two officers. "We will stay here until nightfall and then mount-up and head for the rendezvous."

We exchanged fire with them all that afternoon and into the evening. They were pretty good and I must admit they died bravely even though we were occasionally shooting to wound. Their morale did eventually breakdown and many of their troopers were shot in the back whilst running away. This was unreal because of the fact they died from their own regiments arms and ammunition. As it got dark we stopped firing and allowed those left alive to surrender to look after their wounded. It was a ghastly business and I admit I had some conscious pangs of guilt, but they were only very short-lived.

Chapter 31

Under the cover of darkness we mounted on our freshly watered and rested mounts and with the Lieutenant leading we pulled out and set a bearing on a distant star, somewhere over the road we would meet with JEB. We reached the road ahead of the brigade and the Captain started to worry in case we had missed the column. We scouted up and down the road but could not find any evidence of a large cavalry force having passed that way. Only there was concern enough as we came across sign of around well over a hundred cavalry having passed within the hour, heading north. Our column would have been coming from the direction of Cashtown which was also to the north and we could not help thinking if these had been Yankees then there was a good chance we had been discovered.

Having rested at Chambersburg the night before JEB would have turned south to cut the Hagerstown Gettysburg pike and then coming back down the road south westerly to rendezvous with us at the junction where the pike joins the Emmittsburg road. Our concerns were soon over as in the deadly hush of the night we heard the sound of galloping horses. It was the vanguard of the Brigade and we made it very clear to them, we were Confederate cavalry. Our leader Hampton was up with them, and I could hear him laughing with the Captain as they greeted each other under that clear night sky. The night was so full of twinkling stars it looked gigantic, so vast it made you feel very small and insignificant and I couldn't help wondering if there was something or someone looking out for us up there.

We were allowed to rest for a short while that night and the Captain asked permission for us to light small fires for coffee brewing. These were allowed on the understanding that if they smoked or were too bright they gave off any reflections, the whole troop and its officers would be put under arrest.

Our Captain made sure we lit the 'snake hole' fires we had shown the other troopers and the same fire he had shown to me back in those mountains. A time now that seemed a hundred years ago.

So on reflection I can safely say our training as a unit with this officer was one of the main reasons I was still alive, together with some of our original section. The Captain shared our captured Yankee rations with us that night, sitting around our 'snake hole' fire. He was in a good mood and spoke to us congratulating every one, and then asking what we thought of the action and if there were any suggestions on how things could have been done better. To a man, the Lieutenant's troopers told him they were grateful to him alone for having got them through the last action and very proud to serve with him.

We had lost some good lads, some of them had died later of their wounds but we had brought them off the field when we withdrew. At least this allowed them to die with friends around them and be all buried together, but many others were left for the Yankees to take care of.

Well before dawn the following morning we were roused early by our officers. The Lieutenant had become so popular with the troop and his men real good lads, fitting-in with us really well. The Captain told us he required intelligence again and we were in the saddle, off doing what we do best. The situation was still very serious as the Yankees would have deployed cavalry and infantry to cover as many escape points as they could think of that were likely be on our line of march. We would soon be crossing back into Maryland. The dangerous threat would be from the west as forces would now be pushing towards Mechanicstown which was only four miles away. Our Captain had also stated there would be a strong likelihood troops would have been put onto rail cars at the Baltimore & Ohio railroad, these troops being ideally positioned to cover the crossing over the Monocacy river from Frederick. It was with a very deep concern our officers turned the column, as this threat was merely five miles from where we would most likely attempt the river crossing. We were eight miles east off Frederick when we turned towards Rocky Ridge to the east. Our troop was in the vanguard with the Captain in command. He wanted to push on towards the river crossing and then if this was clear send another detail with fresh horses further to the Frederic road, north west of Liberty.

Joe and I with two more good lads on fresh mounts cleared the river and raced for the road junction. Here again we came across signs there had been cavalry using the road and not too long ago.

We scouted along the route, north east and south west but there were no contacts. Satisfied Joe and I watched as the column came up with us. We joined the road and followed it south west but after five miles turned south east towards Liberty. Luckily we had a string of useful enemy horses being herded along with us and these were able to provide remounts as our boy's horses became blown. The battery horses were also changed as we had taken many good draught animals along the way and these were fine strong animals which ensured the horse artillery could always be with the column and ready for action. We were now tasked with scouting the railroad south of New Market which we had skirted around. There were no signs of enemy troops either in the town or along the railroad tracks. Joe sent back a galloper and it wasn't too long before the command with Stuart at the head came to meet us. There were no further stops and everyone apart from point and flankers had been called in. Stuart had come well over thirty miles since leaving Emmittsburg and the command was now continually in column of fours.

By now the reader must have gathered our officers were not of the usual type and I'll expand on another episode where this fact will be reinforced. JEB, even though we were under pressure from enemy forces from all compass points, wished to swing towards New Market. The Captain and our little troop were detailed to make sure everything was as it should be. Our leader instructed me to scout forward and locate the house of a Mr Cockey. I was given the description and told to wait for our General, under cover until he got there. When he came alone I was really concerned as it wouldn't have taken much for an enemy trooper to have shot him down. I watched amazed as he shouted up at the upstairs windows. After a few seconds a gentleman stuck his head out and peered into the gloom below. On this our beloved leader started to recite some piece of poetry and on hearing this, the gentleman interrupted and joined in reciting the verses. Two women were now alongside the gentlemen at the window and JEB was warmly giving them his greetings in his usual gracious manner. This was unreal, we were probably being chased by thousands of enemy soldiers and here I sat on my horse watching my General exchanging pleasantries with the members of this household. I respectfully urged the General to end this meeting and for us to return to the column. "You worry too much sharpshooter, isn't this a wonderful night to die." He laughed and turned his horse's head and cantered off into the night. I was relieved as we joined with the column again and when the Captain asked if everything had gone well. I could only shake my head and reply; I had just been to a performance of a theatre play by someone called Shakespeare.

At daybreak the next morning we were scouting Hyattstown and we ran into some enemy pickets. We had been instructed to take prisoners and this was achieved without much of a fight although Silas had been forced to kill one of them as he attempted to fire his carbine, even though we had asked them to surrender. The rest however didn't mind talking and they were full of our praises at what we had achieved but told us confidently we would all be either dead or captured before nightfall. Our officers were able to learn there were cavalry at Poolesville to our south and would be blocking our escape to the river in that direction. We were now ordered out again on remounts this time to the southwest. The mission was to gain intelligence of any threatening forces around or on the approach to White's Ferry on the Potomac. We rode into a forward patrol of cavalry just as we were swinging wide to the northwest and close to the Little Monocacy River. We didn't alert them but merely observed them from cover. They were in bad shape and it would have been easy for us to have killed many of them and scattered the rest as their horses were badly blown. However the Captain ordered us to shadow them. They were making for the ferry and flanking the Potomac on its southerly route.

To our surprise we observe another force of cavalry beyond their vanguard. These are wearing pale blue. The

Captain handed me the glasses and I strain through the morning cool, sharp air to try and identify them. The stillness of that cool morning is shattered by the sound of pistol shots being followed by that eerie sound which even now makes the hair on my neck stand up. The rebel yell! And here they came crashing through the trees and throwing these Yankees into a blind panic. Men are falling now and the grey troopers are accounting for an enemy trooper nearly every time they fire. The Captain orders us forward and we crash into the rear of their command as they sit as though asleep in the saddle. It doesn't take long before what was left of them to turn and run, but they are in no fit state to get away and we allow them to surrender. The staff officers of the column now come up with Stuart in the lead. We are despatched with Rooney Lee towards the Potomac while our General offers to hold off the rest of the Yankees, the main command of the cavalry unit we had just fought. These were under Pleasanton who had pursued us all the way from where we ambushed him in the gap. The Boys are whooping around now as they form up on the road their blue coats explaining the confusion and how the Yankees were caught napping.

We race south for the Potomac and the fords hearing the regular volley fire coming from the rear-guard under Butler. A battery is now in action and this must be Harts gunners as they pour shell and canister down on them stopping us from being caught this side of the river. As we get closer to the river there are infantry drawn up right across our escape route. Rooney Lee orders us into battle line and we deploy. My mind is racing at the thought of another cavalry charge and I check the loads of my four revolvers two on my belt and another pair on the saddle front in new fashioned holsters modified from those normally worn around your waist. Rooney

Lee had sent a galloper to inform Stuart but his reply was that, 'he was to conduct himself as he thought fitting.' We were already now and the longer you have to wait before action the worst it becomes for your brain starts to work on your stomach and all the little butterflies start hatching out and fly up into your throat. These were no strangers to me and I became unsettled, but thanks to Joe and Silas I got my concentration back. The next thing we knew was there was a lone officer sent with his sabre drawn but flying a white handkerchief from it. He went straight up to the front of their firing line and called on the officer in charge to consider his position and save the lives of the men in his command. Pelham by this time is drawn up in battery and ready to fire. Our messenger returns and Lee orders the battery to open fire. The enemy is deployed on a ridge with a commanding field of fire and would be able to murder us as we attempted to make for the crossing. There is the sound of a Yankee drum beating out a rhythm, but it's not for advance. They start to disappear from the ridge leaving us looking on in amazement.

We rush for the river and deploy to all round defence while the rest of the command comes across. Prisoners, captured horses, our own blown horses and the captured wagons trundle through the water. Pelham is now deployed into battery from a little hill and is now shelling the Yankees as they rush toward the ford. There is not much of a threat as the enemy is demoralised and in no physical condition to offer any offensive. The rear-guard and the rest of the guns trot casually across and we give them a cheer as they ride through our skirmishing line.

We were Home again.

Joe was alert, sat-up and in fine fettle, he had enjoyed the story and was overcome with the comradeship that filled the whole room. All of us were affected and very emotional and I was only too pleased that Beth had chosen to stay away. She had agreed to accompany us the next day but was worrying about having to leave all the preparations for dinner to our Negro housekeeper. The Captain had eased her mind a little as he volunteered Jacob to assist. He was not perturbed in the least and I got the impression he was proud to be with us and wanted to be a part of what this would soon become, a final farewell to our Sergeant.

The journalist was so excited about have an inclusive story that had never been released to the public even after all these years. The silence may have repercussions and our Captain warned him to hold the story until after the day when we were to lay our comrade to rest.

Chapter 32

The next day it was the Captain's turn and he was going to tell the story of how we fought at Brandy Station June 30th 1863.

Isabella and Beth were with us today and I felt really pleased she was willing to share with us the last few hours we had left in the company of our dying comrade. I had spoken to him the previous night and he had given me the assurance he would be on parade and ready to ride as soon as the story was finished which covered the death of our leader JEB Stuart. His eyes clouded over and as I looked at him there were tears falling down his cheeks and covering his lips. "I have only one regret and I know you have tried, but isn't it a great pity Mosby wasn't able to come down for my celebration?" My tears came easily now and I couldn't face leaving him until he had fallen gently asleep. The Negro woman came into the room and I helped her to lay him back so as his head was comfortable on the pillow and as I glanced around she had his old Confederate Kepi in her hand and she lovingly placed this so that the peak was between his relaxed fingers. "He sleeps every night with that thing in his hand." She went on mumbling about how it stunk and how he wouldn't allow her to wash it.

It was late spring as we were allowed leave to march away from Lee's army and move to Culpepper County. Two days ride to the east the old man's army was spread out around Fredericksburg but we were jubilant and so proud there was nothing in the world could have worried us, least of all the Yankee cavalryman. It was a time of elaborately staged reviews and our leader JEB was in his element as he would invite all the local civilian population along to share in the grandeur.

We were an army of many thousand cavalrymen who had never before been so prepared and resolute in the belief we were unstoppable, and that our enemy could not withstand our professionalism and courage. I can remember a review on the 5th June when the General had nine thousand sabres on parade and you must all be able to recall what a fantastic day that was. We had all been present on the two previous ones but this was the most memorable I'm sure you'll agree.

Even though the surrounding countryside had been ravaged cruelly by the Yankees the civilians that turned out for us that day were all dressed in their finery. The ladies so excited by the parading ranks of grey cavalrymen they cheered and jumped for joy as they paraded by them in regimental order. Jacob was kept busy cleaning my best parade uniform and I never rested until I had attempted to get new uniform issued to my troop. We were able to acquire a lot of equipment from Uncle Sam but uniform was always a problem. Roswell grey was much sought after and I could only find bits and pieces to issue to my boys. However we did manage to find some cavalry trousers that were light blue and these were good quality, double seat and reinforced seams. They were courtesy of the American army but did complement our grey shell jackets. These were all altered and fitted really well and all had yellow facings on sleeves, collars and across the chest. Rifle slings were all given to us by the Bluecoat cavalry and most of us had carbines also from good northern factories. My lads of course carried rifled muskets on slings over their shoulders. The disadvantage, you'll not argue, being we were required to carry different types and calibre ammunition. This made it necessary to have another cartridge pouch or haversack. The boots were also all from The Yankee cavalry and we were so pleased they could afford to supply not only their own army but ours also.

The morning of the big parade we were ordered to form column of fours and regiment by regiment we made our way to the parade grounds. The crowds were overjoyed and we give them our best. Standards fluttered above the individual regiments and the flashing, polished sabre blades reflected the sun like hundreds of pinpricks of light from scattered diamonds. The horses were beautiful, their bodies shining from healthy condition and hours of grooming.

"I must remind you though gentlemen that we were forgetting too easily a lesson that should have been heeded in March, for if you recall on the 17th we had a visit from Averell with a few thousand Bluecoats." We were camped at Court House that day and when news came in from Kelly's Ford we were under attack we were nearly caught napping.

I just managed to get us away in advance of the brigade and we raced down to the river. It was no exaggeration our forces were outnumbered but before we could act strategically Fitz Lee had come up and ordered us to attack. It was usual for us to form line by regiments and attack by squadrons. This was adhered to with one exception the formation would keep in line until the last moments and just before the horses were at full tilt we would alter the formation by allowing those regiments on the flanks to drop back and the advance regiments would form the point, so as the formation would resemble an arrowhead. The advance troopers would smash into the enemy and open a gap where the following troopers would then open it further and punch through like a wedge until we were into their the rear. The enemy would be restricted to manoeuvre as we would be in close order and their sabres would be unable to engage in independent action which is what usually happens in a mounted battle. We were experts at firing into them as they came to bear and this would have the effect of unnerving them. This action proved different as they seemed to open before us and didn't engage but rallied around and came at our rear, we had to punch through and turn and then the style of fight had returned to independent action. We were lucky as we had trained to fight supporting each other, those choosing to fight with sabre being protected by a wingman armed with a revolver. "You remember lad how we had accounted for them in many engagements?"

That day something seemed different as they didn't break and were better mounted and more determined to fight and not to simply turn and run. It was a hard day and I can remember it took us almost six hours before they showed us their backs. We were outnumbered and had fought for our lives but these Yankees had been recalled by their Commander Averell. If this had not taken place we would have been swept away.

However Pleasonton took command of the Union cavalry after the large scale cavalry raid led by Stoneman failed to achieve anything of advantage for the Yankees. Perhaps here was another lesson that we should have learned from but as it happened it did strengthen some officer's belief that the Yankee cavalry had finally learned from all the direct, hard teaching we had provided for him.

In June the die was set as Pleasonton prepared to cross the Rappahannock with his whole cavalry Corps. It was early morning of the 9th June when the table would be turned against us once again but this time it would be the biggest struggle of the war involving the cavalry.

Beverly Ford was where they came across the river led by Colonel Davis. The crossing was being watched by some lads of Grumble Jones 6th Virginia. It was misty and the visibility was short but our two lads on duty heard them coming across. In the night around 30 infantry had come as quietly as they could through the ford. I had been sent to bring a communication to the officer Captain B Gibson. The picket had come to report the Yankees were crossing but they had not interfered with them. I suggested we rouse the men to horse while we both took a look at the infantry.

They came out of the water and we watched them scout up the bank and creep quietly down the road for 25 yards. I touched his sleeve and squeezed his arm. When he looked over at me startled I slowly shook my head. The Yankees slowly retreated back across the river and we let them go. As dawn broke we were drawn up in attacking line at the edge of the tree line where they would be forced to come into the open ground. A galloper had already been sent to warn Stuart camped along the Beverly Ford road, and Gibson's regiment around two miles away; we felt sure help would be there soon with the whole brigade.

It wasn't long after first light that we saw them nervously manoeuvring amongst the trees, and our point rider had come in from the ford to say they were crossing slowly in force with a gun battery. As they formed into column and just before the order to march was given we hit them. Our horses were committed and they hadn't even seen us.

I had suggested to Captain Gibson that the men with carbines should fire these first. We were coming up at an angle towards where they were deploying but out on their left flank. The mist was still thick and swirling low over the ground making visibility difficult. Either they must not have seen us or had mistakenly taken us for their own skirmishers, but from 50 yards we give them a volley. I had explained that we would not make close contact but by riding parallel to them each trooper would simply have to point and shoot to achieve a hit. Men were falling from their horses but we picked our line and I drew my first pistol. We turned away from them and circled around to gain enough space to enable us to come back at them at the gallop. Hitting them just as they were trying to recover, we added to the confusion by firing the revolver into them as we collided. If you remember I always wanted you to fire when they were close and keep the barrel pointed at their stomachs. If you pulled the trigger on the high point of the horses rise, the bullet would hit your target high in the chest or even better in the neck or head. With six shots I saw five of their cavalry go down. The other lads were having results and we were holding them together with our cool discipline. There wasn't much time as the Yankees were soon recovering and there was a steady stream of horsemen coming up from the ford. We disengaged losing two horses and three men. One of the unfortunate lads managed to swing his leg clear of the stirrup as is horse went down and his messmate circled and came up to him whereupon he leaped expertly up behind the mounted man and they both bore away followed by some wild shots from the Bluecoats. Two regiments of Yankees in column of fours were racing after us. They were hemmed in between a stream and the woods close to the edge of the road.

We saw ahead of us the artillery camp of Stuarts horse artillery commanded by Beckham. I raced in between the guns and where a confused officer was running around rousing his gunners. "Get a gun into action and cover your withdrawal as your about to be overrun." I shouted and wheeled around to see where the Yankees were. They had stopped for some reason and were shooting into the tree line from horseback. These gunners were good at their work and it didn't take long before a Blakely 12 pounder was calmly lobbing canister into the two Yankee columns.

It was poetry to watch and another gun was brought to bear on the enemy and it too started to drop canister and shells onto the Bluecoats forcing them to deploy quickly into line before they were torn to pieces. "The column of fours was a bigger target and by deploying into line a force of cavalrymen would not only be ready in attack formation but it meant enemy fire would be less effective." I explained for the journalists benefit. "There would be fewer casualties in this formation as the regiment would be spaced out in line as opposed to being held tightly together in sets of four men in a tight column." The problem was the ground didn't actually lend itself for this formation and their line was very disjointed. The gunners had managed to limber-up the battery horses, hitch up the wagons and gather most of their mounts, Beckham wheeled them out of the trees and they raced away up the road. I stood by and waited for the two rear-guard guns to disengage but the Bluecoats were amongst them slashing at the gunners as they dodged sabres by diving under the cannon barrels and defended themselves with pistols or fighting them with sponges, rammer staffs. I had reloaded the Remington as I had acquired two spare cylinders and promptly set to work helping our gunners. A fiery

Bluecoat Sergeant had just cut down one of Harts gunners' right in front of me. I thought this was a little too much and rode up behind him. He turned around still laughing at what he had done to the boy gunner, but it was his last laugh as I put a shot into his head right between the eyes.

They were forced to leave some of the horses and a wagon but managed to pull the two guns away in such good style and skill it was unforgettable. A classic example of fire and manoeuvre, what we used to call 'pepper potting' where one gun covered the others withdrawal and then they changed over as the first gun engaged raced past the first one away providing alternate, accurate shelling. It was a wonderful sight and I respected Captain Hart's skill as I cantered up behind them well out of the line of fire.

I was greeted by the main body, Captains Gibson's regiment. There were probably about two troops and I smiled at their turn-out as most of them were in various states of undress, without boots, jackets, hats or sabres but every man able to shoot either a revolver or a carbine.

This, I explained again for the journalist, was not good as to go into a cavalry engagement with only one pistol meant that when your weapon was emptied of bullets the rider was rendered ineffective and would result in him having to withdraw, but if armed with a sabre the rider could always continue to fight. I had fought for months to be able to get regimental officers to realise that danger was always uppermost in the early hours of the morning before daybreak and that troops were so vulnerable. The British exercised a policy of calling sections to arms before dawn, calling it a 'Stand To' and in some regiments it was practiced regularly on campaign and would be called a 'Crash Stand To' when officers and non-commissioned leaders would rouse the men routinely every morning. 'Crash', denoting urgency. JEB did listen to me and I was glad it had become standard procedure since January, that one regiment in every division would leave horses saddled overnight with their riders sleeping near to them having secured the reins or a halter around their arm or leg.

This practice was to save us that day, as this regiment also in Jones brigade the 7th Virginia was able to quickly form battle line and support the 6th regiment. I was engaged now with the boys and we were flying into a large Yankee formation, the 8th New York belonging to Buford's wing.

The discipline was fantastic and we rammed into them, broke up and fought pretty much in small isolated pockets. This was where I longed for you lads as we were so accustomed to operating as a unit we were able to look after each other. The fighting was vicious and as I said before they were not breaking as easily as they had done so many times in the past. I shot them with my Colt revolver making every bullet count and then took up my other one which was the Remington. I emptied this very quickly and had to disengage to draw my sabre. This is, as you know, when you are most vulnerable but I managed, and was lucky again as most of my assailants were not as experienced, making it possible for me to come out on top every time. Suddenly there was a change in the enemy's behaviour and they started to disengage and make a turn back down towards the river. Their officers were attempting to rally them as it was not pure panic as yet and I witnessed a high ranking officer being engaged by a Lieutenant from the 6th Virginia. I later found out the Yankee was no other than Colonel

Davis and our boy was Lieutenant Allen. It was another classic example of revolver over sabre. The Yankee swung at the Lieutenant's head but he ducked down expertly under his horse's neck, like a Cheyenne 'dog soldier' and shot his enemy in the head. We were being steadily outflanked and there was danger we would be drawn after the retreating New Yorkers. 'Old Grumble' made it plain we were to disengage and regroup.

Meanwhile Beckham had deployed his batteries on a long ridge, about three quarters of a mile back, and the sixteen guns were throwing shell, canister and ball into the Yankees who were forming up all around and lurking menacingly in the woods. He told me afterwards they had been fortunate in being issued with Yankee ammunition and in particular some shells. These were equipped with better timing fuses which were more reliable than ours making it so easy to drop explosive projectiles accurately to explode in the air above the Bluecoats.

We learned later that the death of the Yankee Colonel had worked in our favour as it put them in a bit of a state of disorder. They had pulled back and were waiting on the reserve brigade led by Whiting. Their 1st brigade was shattered and demoralised and even though we were dropping back it wouldn't be them that could follow us as they were incapable.

Chapter 33

It wasn't long however before they got infantry and guns across. "Oh how grand it would have been had we been able to deploy Beckhams batteries within a thousand yards of the ford as they would have been funnelled down into a near perfect 'killing ground' and would have been cut to pieces. Things were warming up now as Bufford sent a regiment of cavalry and two guns to cut west and deploy on a hill covering the advance.

We were now being engaged by around two thousand bluecoats. Regiments were forced to provide dismounted skirmish lines and I wished again for our little sharpshooter troop. Our position was like an open triangle with Jones boys on the right facing north while Rooney Lee's lads faced east, having been reinforced with a regiment of Fitz Lee's but well over, close to Hazel River south west of Wellford's Ford and covering the road to Farley and the approaches to Brandy Station from the north. Hampton's regiments would come from the south and deploy to Jones left when he heard the sound of the guns.

We were now counter attacked directly by a Yankee regiment and Jones ordered our skirmishers out, but I was unlucky here as he also spotted me and sent me with them. I made plain my objection but he wanted me to call down fire orders on the most worthy of targets. It became another shooting gallery. We raced from cover to cover using all the natural features that presented themselves ditches, fences, folds in the ground and the woodland edges. I gathered a good section of lads under a Lieutenant and we advanced stealthily to contact. Suddenly we came up out of a slight fold in the ground and there in our front charging in column of squadrons were the Bluecoats. Our fire was directed in enfilade and concentrated on the flank, their ranks two deep. These as you know gentlemen can be devastating and unnerving for soldiers as their attention is concentrated to the front. The trick is too fire in a rolling volley every other man firing then alternating as the carbines were reloaded. The range was around five hundred yards and their weapons were accurate. A new issue of ammunition had seen every man was using high quality silk wrapped cartridges for the Sharps breech loaders, many of which were 1859 models and in first class order this improved accuracy enabled targets on horseback at this range were achievable by every trooper. Some of us including me were in possession of the Enfield rifled musket and I directed these lads to target officers further out in the line. You had to time it right as if you were taking a toll on them they would soon realize and try and outflank and then ride you down. Fire and manoeuvre was called for and four controlled volleys and then running was how we did it.

We watched as Beckhams guns began to slow them down and when suddenly they stopped firing we knew the reason why as the 12th Virginia hit them right on the treeline. It didn't last longer than a few minutes and the Yankees drove our boys off making them suffer by the look of the number of loose horses riding with them as they withdrew.

Jones still had two more regiments and he now threw in the 35th and the 11[th]Virginia but the Yanks had reinforcements and the whole treeline on the edge of the plateau was filled with the sound of fighting cavalry, the white tell-tale puffs of smoke from small arms and the sunlight reflecting of hundreds of flashing sabres were made even more noticeable against the backdrop of green from the wooded slopes. Luckily for us he couldn't deploy his guns and the first time he did they were sent packing with a few salvoes from our massed batteries.

It was still only around 7am and a small Yankee cavalry regiment had been deployed into the trees to try and get us out. I had the lads all prepared but we were running low on ammunition and could only give them two or three good volleys. I ordered them to fire in the rolling volley, this way we would still have men with loaded muskets when they were on top of us and at a time we would all be frantically trying to reload. They never caught on and as half of us fired they rallied and came at us again thinking we were finished. They got a shock, and by this time the other half of our line had reloaded and were able to cover us as we ran through the trees performing the classic 'pepper potting' I told you about before. I have seen it so many times and have experienced the overpowering force that can take over in your brain to drive both the horse and you to chase after a retreating enemy. The only difference today was that we were not in panic and couldn't believe it as they came thundering through the trees intent on splitting our skulls but not looking where we were leading them.

As we filtered out of the treeline they thundered out trying to cut us off but this put them in direct line of fire of Beckhams batteries and he wasted no time to open fire. Our lads of the 35th, 12th and 11th Virginia had stayed in contact but they now realised the Yankees big mistake and joined in leading them onto the guns. This was an old trick of Stonewall Jackson's, and these Bluecoats never seemed to learn even though they were getting braver they can't have been around the day when the quartermaster had issued brains.

Jones and Hampton's brigades were now deployed in battle formation and the Yankees were charging bravely but with great stupidity into the jaws of death. The Virginia regiments were too close, so this is probably why the yanks were not all cut down in a few minutes, but Hart was able to open the elevation and drop shells and canister safely over their heads so as not to hurt our boys. They reeled too late as our three Virginia regiments rounded on them. The 35th taking them from the front while the 11th and 12th hit them on the right flank.

I had to find my horse now, and I had no idea where the horse holder troopers could be after we had been in action for over an hour. The obvious solution would be to get onto the plateau and on to Fleetwood House and try and find Stuarts Head Quarters. I knew you lads had been attached to one of Hampton's regiments and I had left Jacob with the horse holders before the skirmishing action. There was definitely a lot of activity across the Fleetwood Hill and I had not gone far when I saw Jacob leading two horses. He tells me excitedly that Stuart has been asking for me and I have been requested to report directly to him. He is still down at St James Church and we spur away down the slope. He rushes out and greets me with, "I believe we are turned Stanley," "ride for Hampton and stop that blasted English, Soldier of Fortune.

He was referring to Wyndham who you will recall I had the dishonour of playing the fool with in the Crimean. The 12th Virginia rides up onto the ridge and Stuart and I follow them at the gallop. I rode toward Hamptons formations and as Buford had been persuaded to go back this left the Brigadier pining for action. I met him and we quickly exchanged greetings. "Was that you down there with the rolling volley?" He roared. We'll have to go bear hunting soon Stanley, you'll love it." I told him nothing he didn't already know and it was Gregg we needed to stop now with Kilpatrick and Wyndham. "Let's away then and upset them."

Colonel Harmon had been badly mauled by the Bluecoats and the Yankees were already astride the ridge. Martin had his three gun Yankee battery in action and they were playing havoc with our boys. Harmon had cobbled together two squadrons and they rode into them again suffering some heavy losses, but not before they had shot most of them, leaving only very few to run away. Shame as their cavalry came to them but it was too late for the gunners.

We flew onto the ridge now in column of squadrons and I went to him for orders. He was angry now and shouted for me to hit Gregg's flank. The troopers of Hamptons from Carolina and Mississippi drove all before them off the ridge and flew at Gregg's unprotected flank. I was with the Brigadier, he was laughing and completely out of his head as we swept them aside and smashed into a gun battery that was in Gregg's reserve. They opened fire and we open ranks and swallowed them up. Their horses were taken and most of his gunners were cut down. Hampton's men would only use the sabre and we engaged their right wing and centre and the fight lasted it seemed a very long time. I had fired two of my pistols by this time and felt that I should fight in accordance with his standing orders and deploy the sabre. The smoke was so thick and swirled around above our heads. It was a question of who would break first and I was unsure how it would all end. Suddenly in front of me I saw Joe, he was firing into a Yankee and then in a tight little unit there you were, all together. I was amazed and overjoyed you had been successful in collecting Jacob who I had not had time to think about. We converged on each other and fought our way through to some open ground. "You remember it was hot and the smoke so thick it chocked and stung the eyes till you couldn't see."

At last there was a flow away to the east and there was an easing in the fighting. They were pulling back. Hampton broke away and galloped for the ridge, we had no choice but to act as escorts and all of us followed at that same breakneck pace. He wanted to see where that Soldier of Fortune was and although we were too late as our right echelon had dealt with him sending what was left of his men onto Barbour's Hill. Harts battery, my favourite gunner came charging onto the crest followed closely by McGregor and Chew's guns. That Englishmen's bluecoats saw the opportunity and attacked the unsupported gunners of Harts battery and flew back down the slope to join Gregg. They now engaged them in unison and poured shell and canister down on them wishing them farewell.

Poor Old Grumble and Rooney had been kept amused as they had been engaged in a rear guard action with Buford's divisions. Rooney Lee was wounded badly in the thigh as he was leading a counter attack to clear the Yankees from the northern end of Fleetwood Hill. The Yankees were forced after some bitter cavalry fighting to give ground. Pleasanton pulled them all back across the river but It was not without cost, as throughout the whole day there were losses in officers which would be irreplaceable, Farley, Butler and Frank Hampton, not to mention over five hundred men.

 This tale left us all exhausted, as for us it was easy to imagine you were back there on that ground. The ladies fussed around and we were treated to several bottles of our Captain's good whiskey. I helped the Negro's to settle Joe for the night and we talked briefly. He was very weak as the Captain's story had left him very breathless but he admitted the story of the death of JEB would be his bugle call to ride out of this world. I didn't know what to say to him and was so happy when he fell asleep.

Chapter 34

We had talked together that evening as the sun went down and the whiskey was shared around. The ladies had allowed us to enjoy each other's company with more than one bottle; because there was a strong feeling we would not be seeing Joe around for very much longer. The doctor confirmed this; saying in his opinion the man was near to death and would most likely leave us sometime the following afternoon. It was with this in mind that we all agreed Silas was to talk to us all on the death of our beloved General JEB Stuart the very next morning.

This as you can remember was at Yellow Tavern only a few miles from the Capitals defence lines and in those dark days when our spirit was slowly being washed away by one endless disaster after another.

I had intended this information for the journalists benefit but it resulted in creating a melancholy atmosphere that seemed to eat away at you leaving us all very depressed and withdrawn.

Silas had prepared for his story and was ready that morning as we drove up to Joe's cabin. The Negro nurse was in a state of concern as her patient had spent a very uncomfortable night and she had thought on more than one occasion that Joe would not be able to fight any longer. However when we arrived he was a lot stronger and was eager for us to start.

Silas began with some derogatory comments regarding one of our old sparring partners Kilpatrick. "Hell, even his most seasoned troopers called him Killcavalry." Was Joe's justification, but he went on about Custer and fringed on some of our next exploits that were beside the point and belonging to another time. I tried to move him away from these but he came back at me arguing the journalist must be made to appreciate how things started.

We were with JEB in the Wilderness and had fought Sheridan's Bluecoats dismounted in the woods. They were firing Spencer repeaters, breach loading carbines and the rate of fire was something to behold. The thing with repeaters is that the soldier can easily get carried away and burn-up much ammunition to no effect. We had been trained to draw his fire while at the same time make our shots count. The ground over which we were fighting was heavily covered with thick brush and low trees with little open ground. This meant there was not great opportunity offered for the guns to be deployed. Our marksmanship excelled here and our Captain kept the section together with his coolness directing our fire and moving troopers around to where they could inflict the most damage to the Yankees.

The next day we were in the saddle and with Fitz Lee's Division having been ordered to cover the army's right flank. Grant was trying to outmanoeuvre Lee. We had ridden at the gallop closed-up in column of fours along narrow forest roads. Our little Georgia troop on point, watching for the Bluecoats who would soon be coming towards us by the Brock Road. We clash heavily with Tolbert's men on the 8th May around   Spottsylvania Court House. We have to hold them and manage to survive till Longstreet's, Anderson's infantry come up. Now Torbert is reinforced with Warrens command but we are in a good position on the right of Andersons men and again dismounted we take on the Bluecoats. Our gun batteries at last find some good ground and we at last can start to reverse the odds a little as repeating rifles are no match for canister and shell fire.

This position was not as bad as the one we fought over in the Wilderness but it still was unsuitable for cavalry action. Our little troop again was called upon to bolster the firing lines and with the Captain's directions we were able to bring down very controlled and accurate fire onto the enemy. Our leader seemed distracted and one day he was mounted on his horse for at least four hours just behind our firing lines. He was in the company of his aide Major McClellan who we supported on Fleetwood Hill at Brandy Station. The Major would be despatched on courier duty for most of the time and would return to his side on an ever tiring horse. The bullets were snapping pine branches and bringing a constant shower of pine needled onto both these officers but it didn't seem to concern our General as he would be seen to smile and then again send off his Staff Major with yet another message.

We were again pulled out of the line and required to scout far to the right of the army. We are close to Telegraph Road and hear through the trees below us the sound of cavalry moving at a steady pace and unhurried. Our observation is masked here by the forest and we have to move silently through the green curtain to gain a better viewpoint. Suddenly as we come out into a clearing which commands an uncluttered line of sight along the road we see them for the first time. There are hundreds, no thousands of them. In column of three divisions, steadily advancing towards Massaponax Church.

The Captain knows there may be a vedette here and I send one of the new troopers, only a lad of fourteen, off to warn them and order those to send word back to Stuart. In the meantime we shadow the Yankee column.

I am ordered to make contact with Wickham's brigade as a messenger comes in from Stuart. Our leader has drawn in all available cavalry now, Fitz Lee's and Hamptons Divisions and together these may number between four and five thousand troopers. Wickham instructs me to take them around to the rear of the enemy column which is around thirteen miles long. We soon reach a position and form into squadron line around one thousand men trotting forward towards the enemy. He hasn't seen us yet but some rear-guard trooper's find us drawn up in battle line and shoot at us, riding away to warn their regiment. We were riding at the canter now and the officer shouts for the regiment to gallop. The charge sounds on the bugle and we are committed, the horses at full tilt and I am picking out a Yankee trooper about one hundred and fifty yards to my front. The LeMatt revolver is in my hand and I have cocked the shot gun hammer ready to fire. Their line is formed now and I flinch for a split second in anticipation of the collision. Some of them are firing their repeaters at us but we are in amongst them. I had already realised we were badly outnumbered but it was too late to worry about it now. Right in front of me there is the Bluecoat who I had marked and as we came into position. He was coming at me now with the sabre at the point, blade outstretched over his horses head and pointed straight at my throat. I ducked down along the horse's neck on the Yankees blind side and watched the look of surprise come across his face. As the horses clashed together violently my brave gelding swung his head into the other rider's horse and bit it on side of its head. The startled beast swerved to its left to avoid those snapping nashers and this caused its rider to be off balance just at the wrong time.

It was easy to line him up and I pulled the trigger. He never knew anything about it as his face disintegrated in a spray of blood, bone and pieces of his brain.

I had to regain my wits very quickly as we were being pressured and had to fall back to regroup. The cost was far too much and one we could not sustain. We formed again and gave them a volley from our carbines before screaming into them again. This made it worse for us as they were able to use their repeaters and took a terrible toll on our company. Horses without riders were milling around us and I noticed a lot of them were theirs. We got in amongst them again and most of us were now using the revolver. Every time I pulled the trigger a Bluecoat left his horse and a lot of them became cut-off and threw down their sabres, holding up their hands in surrender.

The main body were unstoppable and as the rear-guard was reinforced they simply trotted away up the road. They turned due south at Chilesburg toward the Virginia Central railroad at Beaver Dam station. They decided on some favourable defensive ground near to Mitchel's Shop and take up good positions. We throw ourselves onto them but are thrown back by their rate of fire and the easily defendable position they have chosen.

Our General himself joins with us and overlooks the situation, with him he brings Fitz Lees, Gordon's and Lomax's brigades, probably between four and five thousand troopers.

He quickly describes that he wants Fitz Lee with two Brigades to follow the bluecoats and orders Gordon's men to follow him toward Davenports Bridge on the North Anna River. From here he will come up with the outnumbered Fitz Lee and my good self.

Sheridan had pressed on though, and was now marching south towards Negro Foot and probably Old Mountain Road. This was all familiar territory to us and our leader had second guessed the enemy intentions to the letter. Our leader Fitz Lee was summoned and he disengaged some of us. I shared my breakfast that morning with what was left of our rations, some bacon fat and the last flour and water biscuits, frying them as I washed down some good quality coffee which I had taken from a dead Bluecoats haversack. I knew our leader was away as my Captain had found me during the night and told me we would be together in the morning to escort JEB back to the Division. He was visiting his wife who had only given birth to their daughter around the end of the year. She was only four or five months old and he had named her Virginia Pelham Stuart and a pet name of Jemmie. This was obviously in honour of his brilliant artillery officer who had been killed before Brandy Station. I rode out with him before first light and we rendezvoused with Major McClellan near the house where they had all spent the night. They consulted the rolled up maps and between them they came to the conclusion Sheridan was heading for Richmond. As we rode together on that morning I couldn't help notice there was a definite change in his demeanour as he was so reminiscent, talking of places we had all served and the wonderful joyful times in winter camp when he would often entertain us with singing and the banjo music of his own minstrel. Fitz Lee even had his own personal Negro minstrel troupe who would travel between the campfires and entertain us. He would round on us listening out for good baritones or sopranos for his headquarters choir. Poor old Sweeny had died of pneumonia in the winter and it was sad not to be able to hear his music on the occasions you had been detailed to report to the Generals quarters.

You must agree though lads that there had been a drastic change, not only the fact, that it was now the Yankees who were doing all the raiding but the realisation we couldn't kill enough of them to make any difference. This column was so long, it took hours to pass any given point. The other big problem was the horses; we could not rely on remounts coming from Texas or anywhere else now as all roads were blocked to the south. We were blockaded from the sea and there was little hope of any help from the west. We were on our own now as even though we had killed so many, it appeared there was no shortage of others to replace them. We as an army were being steadily worn down.

I rode a little way behind them but our old Commander appeared deeply concerned. Our Captain told me we would be joining our troop soon as we would be riding with the regiment at last. The General leaves Gordon to follow the tail of the Yankee column while we are welcomed back by you. Our brigades head for Hanover and we reach it on the morning of the 11th. We are actually ahead of Sheridan. We are ordered to march with Lomax and form on the left side resting along the Telegraph Road. Wickham was on the right with his position extending along the high ground facing northwest and southwest. We could muster about three thousand cavalry and a battery of guns. Such a small force with which to try and hold the Bluecoat hordes. The place was called Yellow Tavern and I want you to make sure you get that right Mr. Journalist. It was called that because years ago it was a hostelry painted that colour, but this day it stood alone, run down, desolate and just a ruin.

They came in mid-morning and we were engaged after 10:00 am. We were dismounted along the road and fought the force of Sheridan's troopers as they tried to weaken us with their skirmishers but we waited till they had emptied their carbines and then looked up and took them down. They came at us mounted but we stood our ground shooting them down as fast as we could reload our breech loaders. Our Captain ran up and down the line and we were all so proud to be with him that day as every other one. He would select targets and give us fire orders and you could see the effect our controlled volleys were having on their people. He would use all he knew, some we knew but for the other men this was all new. He would order every other man to fire, the others to wait for the Yankees to pop up out of cover. They always presented us with good targets as they would think they were safe because we would be busy reloading. Then he would order officers to be targeted with our rifled muskets and with these, Bluecoats five hundred yards back were hit. Sheridan's mounted troops rode around our flanks trying to turn us but the guns spoke to them and they soon changed their minds. They broke in but were taken. I killed three men with the tomahawk who thought they knew better than us.

By mid-afternoon reinforcements were coming up to Sheridan. He had obviously studied the ground and thought his best option would be to attack on our left, right where we were. It must have been around three in the afternoon when we were allowed a little rest as the Yanks had pulled back a little and resorted to firing at us from three hundred yards, just about effective with the Sharps but a bit less efficient for their repeaters. The Captain had seen what was about to happen as he had allowed me and our troop to circle around well out on the flanks and try and get some intelligence. We saw the new cavalry were Michigan men belonging to Custer and we watched until we were satisfied of his intentions and then rode back to the division.

Suddenly they broke out of the tree cover and swarmed down towards us. We took cover again and picked them off but the pressure was too great this time as their skirmishers were coming, and in large numbers.

Lomax ordered we give some ground and we covered each other as we 'pepper potted', each regiment covering the other in turn, so as accurate fire was always put down on the enemy attackers while one section ran for cover. These would then wait for the others to come through their lines and protected them from being cut down from behind. We were left with another small company and were in serious danger of being overrun, but our Captain held us together and under his expert guidance we were able to withdraw in good order. The enemy troopers had overrun the gun battery on the road and we watched helplessly as they cut them down with the sabre. Our leader had asked for permission to mount and try and save any of the lads that were left alive among the guns. He came around now with another troop, they were with Captain Dorsey but just to their right there sat tall in the saddle our beloved General. He was shouting encouragement to us and we mounted up behind him and spurred out to follow him and the troop into the 'killing ground' we raced up onto their flank and they hadn't realised the danger. As they thundered past us we were able to fire into them enfilading along their line. They were joined by another one of Custer's regiments and we gave them the same treatment at less than 100 yards. There is a big dust cloud and probably that's why we were able to fire into both regiments as they flashed past. Suddenly there is a commotion and a distinctive sound of our boys venting all their anger by giving them the 'Rebel Yell' we look toward the Captain and he leads us to join the regiment.

I let my horse settle into line as we crash through the grass and small trees. We are around 200 yards from them now and they have manoeuvred into line to accept our attack. You don't have much choice when the horses are committed, but if you can pick a horseman in their line on which to aim for it keeps the regiments line straight. We hit with a sickening crash and I am immediately engaged with two Yankees. My revolver accounts for both these men and I am propelled deeper into them. We are in a little tight group and each man is taking down these Yankees. That is how we were trained by our Captain here, and it was this training that saved us.

The regiment fought these Blue coats till we could gain the advantage and they faltered. They started to disengage and streamed away back the way they had come. Old JEB was shouting encouragement as we turned on them and chased them. There were many Yankees running back through our lines without their horses and I was just about to call out a warning when this Sergeant stops, ten yards from the General and levels his pistol at him. I tried to get there in time but the shot had hit him in the belly. He was still mounted when we got to him and Captain Dorsey takes hold of the mare's bit. She is skittish and is uncontrollable. We lower him out of the saddle and get him onto a steadier mount but he is unable to support himself and we lower him to the ground. An ambulance is brought up and we get him onto it. We escort the ambulance through the position avoiding any enemy concentrations. The Yankees are coming on again and we are ordered back into the line but Dorsey stays with him and greets Fitz Lee as he comes up on a lathered horse.

We learn he has the strength to raise himself to rally some men who look like they are going to break. He shouts at them 'that it is better to die than be whipped' they are hard pressed to get him away from the Yankees but they succeed in reaching Richmond. The doctor can do little for him as he is shot through the liver and the following afternoon he is near death. His wife Flora had been attempting to make her way from Beaver Dam Station over twenty five miles away across the countryside that would have been alive with Yankee pickets. Having been forced to take a very circuitous route she was unable to get to his bedside in time. The poor woman never got to say goodbye to her beloved.

We were all consumed with sadness and the grief even after all these years was still as deep. Even the journalist was infected and the ladies had long since rushed out of the room holding handkerchiefs to their tears to stop them cascading down their cheeks.

They came back into the room and this probably distracted us from Joe's bedside. The Negro nurse suddenly gave out the most piercing scream and we jumped around to look in her direction. She was stooped over Joe and was kissing his forehead, the sobs of her sorrow making her ample frame shudder. I stared at our old comrade and saw nothing but peace, all the lines on his face from constant suffering had disappeared and he looked almost young again.

He must have died the moment Silas had ended his account of the battle and how our beloved leader had passed from this world without having had the chance to hold the hand of his dear wife.

We were stunned and still in shock but the Captain took over ably assisted by Isabella and my Beth. The whiskey bottle came out again and while Beth handed the glasses out our Captain poured a measure into each one. We all took a glass and waited for him to set the empty bottle down. "Georgia Company," we stiffened to this old familiar command, and he continued "Georgia Company, attention." We were all conscious of our officer's right boot striking the floor making the decanter and water glass on Joe's bedside table crash to the floor. His expression never changed as he called out, "I give you Sergeant Joe of the 1st Virginia cavalry, who like us all present here, never surrendered."

We contacted the undertakers and Joe was laid out in his own bed and washed by the Negro woman. They were to come by on request the next day and all of us sat drinking most of the night in his company.

It was his request that he was to be buried in the Confederate cemetery in Marietta and that is where we took him. There was a small private service in the chapel and we were again reminded of how much we had all loved him. The journey to the grave side was the worst part as Jacob and I; Silas and the Captain shouldered the casket and marched slowly along the path to the burial plot. Here we laid him to rest alongside his fellow soldiers but before we lowered him on the ropes to the final rest, the Negro lady placed his old confederate Army kepi on the coffin lid and we couldn't help staring at it until the ropes went slack and he had been finally been mustered out.

Chapter 35

It took us a long time to return to normal but sadly we went through all Joe's belongings and gave them to the Negro woman. She had loved him and looked after him all these years from the end of the war to when he finally left us. The cabin was given to her and I had made her accept that I would help her with money and food and that she would be allowed to live out her life there at the cabin, in comfort. This we all felt was what Joe would have wanted, but she insisted that I give her employment either in Beth's household or in some capacity on the farm. To this I agreed, and she was so grateful she had been given an opportunity to feel she was not taking advantage of her dead partner's friends.

The only thing left to talk about before the Captain and his lady returned to Virginia was to finish our stories for the exclusive newspaper article. I took it on myself to finish the war stories by narrating the few last months of our war. We as the small special unit under the command of our Captain had been granted leave of absence to join another regiment. The 35th Battalion Virginia cavalry, commanded by our old friend Mosby. He needed experienced troopers to train and bolster his unit and we had been granted, under a Senate approval and in accordance with the Partisan Ranger Act of 1862, permission to leave our parent regiment, the 1st Virginia and join Mosby's men. Silas was to leave us, as he had also obtained permission to join as an officer in a Cherokee regiment and this would be the only time we would see him until now, at Joe's last farewell parade.

Mosby was in daily in contact with the Yankees and very often fighting the men of Custer's regiments. We journeyed west to rendezvous with him in June 1864.

Mosby had formed the battalion in June 1863 and since had conducted some brilliant cavalry actions against the Bluecoats. These were even praised by our General probably as they resembled, on a smaller scale some of our famous rides. This is not surprising either as Mosby rode with us from the very beginning and even when he had been taken prisoner he didn't stop gathering intelligence wherever he could. When he was freed in an exchange of prisoners some weeks later, he brought the information with him written in a report which he gave to General Lee.

These actions and his ability to remain undetected while deep in enemy country was to gain him much favour with both Lee and Stuart, and it was definitely their blessings that enabled our little company to transfer out of our regiment. This procedure was far from normal and unheard of as once mustered onto a particular regiment's muster roll it was seldom acceptable to transfer permanently.

Our new area of operations was Northern Virginia, actually around Washington. His men were all resident in the counties where we operated. This made it difficult for us as we were strangers and had to rely on friends and comrades taking us into their own homes and giving us food and shelter. Yankee cavalry constantly operated everywhere and would make a habit of harassing farmsteads and homes not only to rob the owners of anything they fancied or considered useful; but to arrest the occupants if suspected there had been any involvement in guerrilla activity. This not only put pressure on our comrades but would involve their families also. We hated this and in the end, especially after a large scale operation we would simply live in the woods so as to spare any reprisals being carried out on innocent farmers. The procedure before an operation would be to arrange for couriers to deliver messages to all the company troopers' homes, or there would be a prearranged meeting place. This was very strange for us and we would volunteer to ride with the men detailed as couriers just to gain some experience of the lay-out of the land and the whereabouts of settlements and homesteads.

At first it was very difficult as we were mistrusted by most of our fellow troopers. The Captain decided he had to try and alter a situation that was not getting any better and was having an effect on our morale. Fights would develop out of the smallest of arguments, and there were some serious incidents. Knife fighting was our speciality as we had trained together in this art. Joe was in one such fight some weeks after our arrival and his opponent was badly injured with deep slash cuts on arms and across his chest, If Joe had been serious then this trooper would have been dead within a minute but hopefully a lesson would be learned in the weeks it took for the muscles in his arms to heal and he was again able to control his horse. The four of us talked together the day after, and we reached the conclusion if we were to continue serving in this unit it would act in our favour if we could prove our worth in battle and let them see we were all on the same side.

We did not have long to wait before an opportunity presented itself. On 2nd July we were summoned to a secret meeting with Mosby. He told us of the proposed invasion into Maryland by Old Jubal, Lt. General Jubal A. Early. "I intend to assist this action by hampering the Yankees lines of supply and communication." He said solemnly.

We were detailed to ride with the couriers to help warn everyone there was to be a rendezvous at Rectortown early on the next day. I was impressed by the numbers of men that responded as there must have been well over two hundred troopers at the rendezvous; Jacob was with us and had made sure his Captain's horse was well and healthy. He was a good lad and he had always been in our mess except when the Captain had been lucky enough to have been allocated his own tent or quarters. He had fought with us since first Bull Run and we had come to trust him knowing he would do the right thing when in a tight situation.

The command rode out just as light was breaking and as usual we were able to demonstrate our skills in scouting ahead or skirting wide out along the route, in order to be able to see the enemy before they discovered us. We rode all day and managed to reach Purcellville before nightfall. We camped for the night having put out a good screen in all-round defence about our position. These lads were relieved after four hours and we took over from some of them at one thirty in the morning. The atmosphere between us and Mosby's men had become a little easier since the fight but some of the younger ones were really hostile. This command in General was manned by youngsters and there were not many troopers who had served in regular army units. We spent an anxious night till dawn and then waited to be relieved, to go off duty. Our Captain turned up instead and told us we were to ride out immediately for the Potomac River close to the settlement of Berlin.

This was achieved without incident and Mosby deployed fresh pickets and scouts to patrol the river in both directions while we rested in good cover with pickets deployed. When they returned with the news there was a Union force at Point of Rocks to the east he ordered us to move out and make haste towards the area. The Yankees had some infantry, probably around two companies with another two companies of cavalry. In all possibly total strength, not more than three hundred and fifty men. We had done this so many times before and our Captain's caution was taken notice of. We watched from cover while the main body of the command hid themselves in amongst some trees fifty yards from the road.

There was an island in the middle of the river which had been occupied with around one squadron of their infantry. They had prepared rifle pits and some log defences. The other squadron had occupied the small earth fort which overlooked the canal on the far side of the river. The cavalry however didn't look as though they were too serious and had made a camp around the village and could be seen lounging about and taking things easy cooking food and brewing coffee.

Joe said they would soon be sorry as the Captain would make them pay for their lack of attention.

We returned with our report for Mosby and he ordered the attack to begin. We had a little six pounder deployed on a bluff commanding a good view of the fortifications. It started to drop shells into the camp and causing some real confusion. The Yankees were running about all over the place trying to remember where they had left their rifles. The Captain led us out into the shallow water of river, formed up into a skirmisher line but keeping good spacing between the men. The light gun was working wonders and with the accurate volley fire we were giving them they started to think about running. Suddenly they were bolting for the small bridge that spanned the canal parallel to the river on the Maryland shore. As they ran across this, some of them started to rip the boards up to deprive us of its use. Mosby was having none of this and another line of rangers jumped into the water and made a dash for the opposite bank.

We joined the vanguard as our horse holders had splashed across holding the mounts. We swung up into the saddle and followed the officers across the bridge which was being repaired by some of Mosby's men. The Captain's mount had taken off and I watched one young lad as he was knocked aside and his fellow trooper jumped into the water to escape having his head knocked off. I laughed at them as I raced after the Captain and thought this was highly unlikely to repair any breaches in our relationship with these men. There was around ten of us including the officers and we collected ourselves before the village. One of Mosby's troopers put rowel to horse and catapulted towards the cavalry horse lines. We were coming under fire now as the enemy started to defend themselves but this was too high and you could hear it flying past, above head height. We leapt away chasing him, I was laughing my head off and for anyone that doesn't know, and it would appear I was a lunatic. Mosby's young trooper was up to the flag, flying from a pole close to their horse lines. He set about hauling it down and bundling it into his haversack while we were joined by some more of the rangers and charged into the mounted Yankees. They were no match for us and had no spirit for a fight. We raced around to cut them off but a few got away, but not that many. The rewards were good as there were loaded canal boats and bulging store houses along the waterway. This was a wealthy place and the home of some prominent Unionists. We joined the rangers in looting everything we could carry away, but Mosby allowed us to load it all into three wagons for shipping back to Fauquier County. This booty would be sold and the proceeds shared among all the lads who took part. The warehouses held a variety of supplies for the Yankee army and in the Unionist's homes many fine articles of calico cloth, and this stuck through the years as it is still now called 'The Calico Raid.' What was left we set fire to. As we pulled away, huge columns of smoke were spiralling sky wards being chased by the hungry flames. We crossed back into Virginia and camped for the night near Leesburg.

The following morning the Captain ordered us into the saddle and told us we were heading for the Potomac, to cross at Point of Rocks once again and then continue raiding deeper into Maryland. Mosby had sent a signal to Old Jube to assure him the rangers would act independently but in support of his manoeuvres. The loaded wagons were already on their way back home escorted by one hundred rangers of the command.

By mid-morning we had arrived and carefully sought some vantage point to enable us to reconnoitre the objective. The smoke was still thick and was curling up from the twisted and blackened remains of the warehouses and barges on the canal side. This wasn't our concern however and as I studied the position, silently mounted at the Captain side, I could easily make out they had been up to something in the night. There below us was a cavalry regiment and by the look of them they meant business

Mosby and the command were told by a galloper we sent back, but the young lads in his battalion just wanted to attack no matter what. I recognised there was a little insubordination brewing and had no doubts how our Captain would have handled the situation. Mosby merely organised them into a formation and we charged down towards the river bank. Here we dismounted and with the horses under cover we prepared to send them some Minnie balls. They were using the repeater breech loaders while most of us were still armed with the Sharps carbine. Here again unseasoned troops will always rapidly use up ammunition if not properly under command of good experienced officers and NCO's. These Yankees performed exactly like the many others I had fought against that had been issued with repeaters. Their rate of fire was very quick but we were in good cover and could afford to take our time. The Captain had ordered a troop to protect our flanks and they were to stay mounted within a short distance so as to be able to warn us if we were in danger of being turned.

This was what we did well and our rifled muskets were brought into action. Counting the Captain we had five of these weapons and he had already started to give his fire orders, picking out experienced NCO's and senior officers.

The range was a comfortable three hundred yards and no challenge for our weapons. For the Yankees this may be a little different as their weapons were a little less accurate at distances like these. I lined up on a Yankee Captain and set the sights for 300 yards. I was already loaded with a percussion cap on the nipple. I cocked the action and waited for the order. Our leader had assumed command and he was being taken notice of now even by the most troublesome of the young rangers. He moved down the line instructing each of our boys and then returned and lay down next to me and levelled his weapon. Suddenly his command rang out like a howitzer. Over one hundred carbines and our rifled muskets crashed out a volley together, in perfect harmony. As the smoke cleared he was shouting to reload. This time when he instructed specific targets it was not to shoot to kill. He wanted some wounded on the ground and screaming in pain. We fired again and each volley was aimed and controlled, shooting at selected targets. The smoke was thick now but we were allowed to fire independently towards the end, but only when our cartridge boxes held no more than twenty shots. The action had lasted for one and a half hours and as the ammunition started to run low our Captain pulled us out. Not altogether, but section by section, so as there would always be men shooting from our position right up till we were all mounted and ready to withdraw.

Mosby was full of praises and our little demonstration had gained us the respect of the entire command. He told us he wanted to head for Catoctin Mountain to the west of Leesburg. We'll spend the night and arrange for ammunition to be brought up. We had received reports from scouts that in Leesburg there was a Yankee cavalry force.

Mosby wanted intelligence so we were deployed to watch their movements. They moved out early next morning and we shadowed them leaving one trooper to give our report to Mosby. The Yankees were heading for Aldie. Mosby ordered the command to ride to intercept them. Instead of acting on intelligence he presumed they would be returning the same way as they came in. However he was informed by some local residents that the Yankees hadn't come this way and so it became necessary for him to send a galloper to find us. We were shadowing the Yankees and watching them from good cover as they rested on a small ridge, half a mile south east of Gum Springs.

He found us without alerting the Yankee skirmishers and we gave him a rested horse so he could return to Mosby's command. He soon rode up accompanied by the Colonel who quickly made his plan. "We'll deploy the howitzer on that other ridge over there and then we'll charge 'em." We formed column of fours and with flankers out charged down towards them. Our flankers rode into their pickets and there were some pistol shots, but we had caught 'em as they were just preparing to pull out. In the confusion we unsettled them a bit but they formed up in attack formation line abreast, two men deep. The gun now had a good target and started to drop shells on 'em. This did the trick as it upset them even more, and they changed formation again so as to be able to defend themselves. The Captain was shouting for the fence to our front to be dismantled and in the end we jumped down and started tearing the rails apart. Other troopers got the message and joined with us. Minutes later we formed the famous phalanx and slammed into them. We rode into them as they were dismounted and shot them down where they stood. I emptied both the LeMatt and one of the Remington's and was just reaching for the Colt when they broke swinging up into the saddles as the horse holders came up. We chased 'em southwest and they ran into cover in the woods just southwest of the pike. We drove through the trees into a clearing and there they were, mounted this time to meet us. They had all drawn their sabres and came at us, as though they meant it. I had two loaded revolvers and prayed to the Gods these would be enough.

I was taken on by two Yankees, they were manoeuvring me onto the sabre of the Bluecoat on my right, and I realised that if I didn't counter this I would be cut down; as if I concentrated on my attacker on my right the

309

trooper on my left would swoop in and take me on my left side. Something told me to shoot the trooper on my left first and then lift the revolver up and away from my horses head and shoot the other just as we were passing. This was a risky movement and one we avoided by fighting in pairs. I had merely seconds to live and without thinking anymore I fired at the left hand trooper. The shot took him in the chest but there was no time to watch as the other troopers horses head was level with mine. I remember just pulling the trigger relying on my training which assured me the revolver was automatically lined up and on target with this enemy directly in my line of sight.

The horses slammed into each other and they shoulder charged each other as they crossed. My horse was the most aggressive and she lashed out with her head and I saw briefly a spurt of blood come from the other horse's neck.

We seemed to have an easier time of it after the Point of Rocks action and we were boarded on a homestead in Loudoun County near Rectorsville. For the most part the men were beginning to trust us and accept the Captain as an experienced officer. Mosby had done everything he could, and now, as he said, it was up to us to try and persuade them to accept us.

There was much activity now as the supply of food and forage for Sheridan's cavalry was drying up. The whole countryside of Loudoun and Fauquier Counties had been ravaged by the foraging parties of the Yankee Army. Homesteads and farms were targeted and livestock and crops were either destroyed or carried away. This obviously made it extremely difficult for us but the people were with us and they started to hide supplies of food for us and we would have caches of supplies distributed throughout the region in secret locations.

Chapter 36

Towards the beginning of August it became seriously obvious to the Yankees that they were going to be required to provision their army by deploying wagon trains despatched from supply depots in Washington to Harpers Ferry. From here these would head for Winchester where the supplies would be further distributed to the individual units in the field. We had been watching these operations for weeks and on many occasions had been working in the company of one of Mosby's scouts, Russell. On this particular day we were together again and had the good fortune of coming across a particularly large train travelling towards Winchester in the vicinity of Berryville. We left it alone and made our report to our Captain who then informed Mosby of the enemy's activity. "It's a large train." Joe said, and I added. "Probably five hundred wagons." We sent out couriers as was normal, and that night we set off to intercept the wagons, riding west into the Shenandoah. From a well concealed vantage point we watched them throughout the following day, the 12th August. Their progress was slow as they were herding cattle with them and also some re-mounts. We made a quick count of their strength and estimated this to be in the region of over two thousand men. Mosby had deployed three howitzer light guns but somehow there were some problems with the carriages and they were only able to get one of them into position on a bluff overlooking Bush Marsh Creek. Through the night we watched their camp fires and in the early hours of the morning around 01:00, they started to move around. The smell of brewing coffee and bacon frying reached our noses and I had to tighten my belt to stop my stomach from making noises.

Mosby organised the attack and detailed 'Dolly' Richards to lead his men in from the front while we joined with William Chapman and attacked the rear. The signal to go would be when the howitzer started to drop shell and canister into the crowded wagon park. The shelling started about 01:30 and it produced such a commotion we had little trouble in gaining the camp perimeter. The pickets and camp guards were shot down as we ran through into the wagons. A section of mounted troopers were riding around towards the front of the camp and taking a heavy toll on those of the enemy cavalry who had been on vedette duty. The Yankees were in a state panic this was being made worse by the frightened draught horses and mules some of which the Bluecoats had been hitching –up just as the gun started to deliver the early morning barrage.

We mounted now as the horse holders ran up with our horses. There was the Captain shouting us to form on him to attack a group of more determined Bluecoats who had organised a defence line behind a stone wall. These were now shooting badly aimed volleys at our lads. We rounded onto their flank and rode towards them. They hadn't put out any flankers and we shot them down as we passed to their rear. It was all over by 06:30 including the time it took us to search the wagons and select around a hundred of them loaded with food and ammunition. Jacob had been missing for some thirty minutes and I was pleased the Captain hadn't asked me about his whereabouts. Just as I was getting more concerned for his safety he appeared around the end of a burning wagon. "There's a strongbox in a wagon back there and its padlocked with a huge lock and steel straps." He said and I blurted out. "Show me quickly." The lad led me between the burning wagons to where there was one partially up ended and it looking like it had been caused by the Bluecoats trying to get it away, but in their haste they had driven it into some bad ground. The team had been unhitched and probably led away by our lads but they in their haste had missed the box inside.

I climbed up into the rear under the canvas and immediately recognised a Paymasters chest I levelled the Remington revolver and fired at the padlock. It was still fast so I give it another and with this it dropped open. We both lifted the lid and to our astonishment there inside was thousands of Yankee dollars. We quickly emptied the chest stuffing the notes into our saddlebags. We had just finished when Chapman came and shouted at us to set fire to the wagon as soon as we'd taken off all the ammunition and food rations.

The Captain joined us but I had sworn the lad to secrecy, and we kept our mouths firmly shut although I couldn't help smiling at the lad, as he couldn't keep his body still from trying to stop himself from laughing. The wagons numbered around one hundred and these were filled to overflowing with supplies. There were also two hundred cattle and over five hundred horses which the Yankee army of General   Sheridan would be deprived of. We had also captured around two hundred prisoners and these in company with the cattle and wagons were put under escort and sent to the west bound for our home counties. This would make a difference to our forces with Old Jube.

That night as we entered our own territory I told the Captain of what we had found. At first I thought he was going to strike me, but as I reasoned with him and used the excuse that the boy had found the chest, he changed his mind and told me we should hide the bags containing the loot, for if the others ever found out they would shoot us.

We were continually being hounded by the Yankees and my heart goes out to all those people who gave us shelter and fed us from their own meagre food stores. We helped them as much as we could but as the bluecoats got more and more active the reprisals were getting worse. If they raided a farm or a homestead they would arrest all the male occupants of the household and take them away to imprison them. In late August Mosby was wounded in the thigh at Annandale but within three weeks he was again back in the saddle and leading us again.

As you know we were engaged from time to time with Custer's regiment and in September we were to learn of another war crime committed by the Yankees and this one in particular, carried out by Custer's men.

Six of our rangers had been taken prisoner and were being held at Front Royal. We had naturally presumed they would be treated as prisoners of war but we found out through our network of spy and couriers that the order had come from Washington that these men were to be executed as Guerrilla fighters, and as such were not entitled to be treated under the articles of war covering the fate of captured combatants. In fairness they would be imprisoned or could be exchanged for Yankees held by our forces. In this case it would not apply as they were to receive a death sentence.

To make matters worse this sentence was not carried out, by any means in accordance with any standard military execution methods; normally for spying or being captured in a uniform of the enemy a soldier would be sentenced to death by firing squad. For two of the men their fate was both unjust and against all laws of decency and humanity. Two men were shot, another two were hung by the neck and the worst incident was two more of our men were strangled up close and personal. This enraged the whole company and Mosby swore to us that we would get even with these murdering bastards.

We had talked it over many times and I had to admit it sounded very grand. The prospect of blowing up a train and robbing the cars was appealing. If this train was carrying military supplies or rations then this would render it a legitimate military target. In any case the Yankees were not playing by the rules anyway so why should we.

However in September Mosby was wounded again, this time in the groin. We were extremely concerned the Yankees would find him and every precaution was taken to hide him for it was a foregone conclusion if the Yankees got him he would probably face execution. Even though this was a bad wound in the groin, it didn't keep our leader out of action for long, and as he got stronger he wanted to know what we thought about the train raid. Joe and I had been working with a good scout called Jim Wiltshire and we had shown our Captain the area we had selected for wrecking the engine. This was a deep cutting where the rail bed cut through a long thin ridge of high ground. The idea would be to dismantle the rails for about two lengths and then wait for the train to come along and derail. This section was on the Baltimore and Ohio railroad in Jefferson County at a little place called Middleburg.

We rendezvous at Rectortown again and mustered around eighty men. We rode out and crossed into Jefferson County. Having forded the Shenandoah we then travelled west till we cut the Martinsburg – Winchester turnpike. We hid ourselves and waited. Mosby ordered out pickets and wanted every traveller on the road to be stopped. If they were civilians then they would be questioned and if their allegiances were in any way suspect then they were taken into custody. We were so engaged on the 11th October and watched as a trooper wearing a grey overcoat came along the pike. As we observed another came from the opposite direction and they stopped and talked together. This made us suspicious as none of us had seen these two men before. In our company there was a trooper who had been with Mosby since 1863 and it was on his assurance we took action. As we moved out of the tree line the two men started to make their escape. Our horses were fresh and this proved no contest for them putting the horsemen in our care after a few minutes chase. The Captain had now come up and he questioned the two riders. Suddenly one makes a break for it. He had made about twenty yards when a bullet from the Captain's revolver took him in the back. I dismounted to see if he was dead. The trooper was still breathing and as I felt around for an exit wound his coat came open. To my astonishment this trooper was wearing a Yankee shell jacket underneath. I took out my revolver and shot him in the head.

The other trooper was a bit more talkative and was begging us not to shoot him. Our Captain didn't hesitate as this rider also was wearing a confederate uniform over the top of his bluecoat. He still had the Remington in his hand and he merely raised it and shot the man in the head. We took their horses and buried the bodies in a secluded position off the road.

We reported to Mosby and he told us there was a train due at around 02:00 the following morning. He detailed a working party who had found wrenches and pry-bars in the trackside huts to start dismantling the rails. We were detailed to flank the workers and ensure they were not disturbed. The work done we rested and brewed some coffee and ate the rations the Yankees had in their saddle bags. At 01:00am we moved out and took up positions overlooking the rails. This is always the worst part as the waiting can really get to you if you allow it to. The only way is to think of something nice, warm and cosy like your house back home where your family would be waiting for a letter or some other news that would at least stop them wondering if you were safe or not. I hadn't had any letters from my family since we joined with Mosby and it was just the worry of not knowing that eats away at your insides, just the same as it would be doing to them. The Captain comes up now and says it will probably be here in a few more minutes. The time is 02:20 on the morning of 12th October. We are freezing and the snow underneath my uniform has turned to ice where it has been melted by my body heat, but then it has turned to ice, and I shiver with the thought of being wounded and left out here in the open waiting for my body to freeze. Without warning a rider comes in on a steaming, lathered horse. He leaps from the saddle and sprints over to where the Captain is talking to another officer from Mosby's command. The train had been sighted coming down the track from the east.

We move around now to try and gain some feeling into our frozen limbs and just as I am regaining a little feeling back in my legs we all hear that unmistakable noise. "It's here boys." The Captain says and we double away now to be ready to run up and jump onto the railroad cars when they come to a halt. The engine is in sight now and you can hear a definite change as it comes to the bottom of the grade and the smoke bellows out again as more pressure is delivered to the driving wheels. It trundles by where we are hiding tucked into the cutting at the side of the tracks. There is a grinding and the sound of steel wheels screaming as the friction between them and the dismantled rails is reduced. It cannot take the angle it has been forced to take and the top weight overbalances it and the loco slowly tips onto its side. The wheels are still spinning around at a fantastic rate until the safety valve opens and all the head of steam is vented to atmosphere and slowly they slow. The steam is making a horrendous racket and it's hard to take my eyes away from the dying, huge mechanical monster. I feel the Captain's boot in my backside as he comes up at the side of the railcars. "Get inside and take care of the Yankees." I leap up for the footplate of the last, eighth car in line and fling open the compartment door. I am met by a Yankee officer levelling a pistol at me and have to shoot him. Other officers are surrendering and the rest of the lads have joined me and we take them prisoner. We move from car to car and there are no more attempts at retaliation. The lads have lined the passengers up now having forced them to stand in the walkways between the seats. There are women with them, probably wives or family and I tell them to treat them with respect. However the youngsters of Mosby's command are a law unto themselves and they start to demand jewellery or valuables from the women. This is not good and it promotes a panic as the women start to scream. A Yankee officer steps forward and demands we treat the women with respect. Before I know it a young Lieutenant answers him by striking him a vicious blow across the face with the barrel of his pistol. "Is that the same respect you show to the residents of Loudoun and

Fauquier Counties?" he roars. I try and intervene but it's too late as the Majority of the passengers, military and civilian had been relieved of all their valuables. The Captain didn't interfere as this would have rendered our position within the command in further jeopardy.

We move the passengers off the train and down onto the track, Jacob is with me as we clear the coaches of any passengers and are just running through the freight car when he stops me. There in front of us is another strong box. I shoot the lock off and as we open the lid there inside is another large amount of Yankee 'greenbacks' I shout the nearest officer and we slide open the freight-cars door. He quickly organises for saddle bags to be thrown up to us and we transfer all the notes over.

The train and the locomotive are set on fire using the hot coals from the firebox and the cord wood from the tender. As it blazes we allow the disgruntled and irate passengers to walk up the road toward Middleburg.

We took all the officers and men, prisoners with us except those who were accompanied by wives and families. Among these were the Paymaster staff of Sheridan's army but they had no money left as they had paid our lads instead. We treated them with courtesy and respect befitting their rank and passed them over to the military at the first opportunity. Old Jubal had been defeated in early August so the taking of prisoners and transferring them to military prison of war camps got more involved.

The command of around eighty officers and men shared the booty we had taken from the train. This amounted to over $2000 each. The Captain didn't accept any of it and informed Mosby his share was to go to me.

At the beginning of November at Rectortown we were handed a situation which none of us wanted to be involved with. The opportunity for the table of fate to be turned had presented itself and this came in Mosby's promise to avenge the unjust treatment and murder of six of our men. Our command had taken twenty seven prisoners and Mosby's men were determined to execute a like number. The Captain and some of the other officers were against execution. And a compromise was agreed upon. This amounted to a raffle where by three soldiers would be selected from drawing a ticket with a cross on it. Each man being required to draw a ticket from the box containing 27 tickets, one for each soldier.

Three individuals were selected by this process but one was a young drummer boy. A Yankee officer objected and the ticket belonging to the boy was put back amongst the others. The very officer, who objected, drew the death ticket, a case you could call a definite tempting of fate.

We were present when the three soldiers were hung by the neck at the rear of the Methodist Church in Rectortown. A label being attached to one of the bodies saying this would be the fate of all of Custer's men, a curse that may have followed him throughout his military career.

Chapter 37

This paved the way for the most shocking series of war crimes we had ever witnessed; as in December the Yankee Gen. Wesley Merritt's troopers launched themselves without mercy on to the civilian population of Loudoun and Fauquier Counties.

People's livestock was driven off, hogs were slaughtered sometimes being tossed still alive onto fires from burning barns and outbuilding. Crops were destroyed and harvest and stored produce taken, anything that was considered could be used to offer sustenance and support to Mosby's men was either taken or destroyed. There were no exceptions, and the residents of these counties were lucky if they were left with a dwelling they could shelter in. This was the last straw and when Meritts troopers left, herding and carrying all their plundered goods, it left the land looking as though a plague of locusts had landed and destroyed everything. Any of you that believe in the Bible could relate to this as a pestilence brought down by a higher force. As far as we were concerned we could not continue to operate in this country and we explained how we felt to Mosby. He understood and admitted he was thinking hard about the future of the Battalion.

We spent a miserable Christmas in the mountains and hid ourselves in a secluded hunter's cabin far from prying Yankee eyes. Mosby's men had done well as they had succeeded in drawing away man power from other campaigns but at the end of the day the command was being worn down from persecution. The Yankees had denied us any shelter and made it extremely difficult for us to manoeuvre against him. In the end what amounted to Martial Law broke us. It not only broke our spirit but it reduced our numbers as the Yankees imprisoned all the men they considered to be connected with the Guerrilla activities. At least the unlawful executions were stopped and this meant that our boys that had been taken would get the chance to come home when it was all over.

When the snow had melted a little, we risked coming down out of the mountains to seek out Mosby. We found him by contacting his agents and were able to arrange a secret meeting. He explained the situation and the Captain sadly agreed that we would help him and what was left of his command. There was to be a last effort by Lee to break out of the strangle hold which Grant and Sherman had placed around the army. We were to act as a cavalry screen again and watch the country around the Yankee positions at Fort Stedman. This we did and sadly observed his army retreat south west.

We scouted for him in the armies dying last attempts to make the Yankees suffer. The plan now was to combine with Johnson's army coming out through North Carolina but this ended in failure also. Our patrol rode into Amelia Court House to inform him the railroad had been cut by Yankee cavalry and there was no hope of receiving supplies from Richmond and Danville Railroad.

Finally we witnessed the disaster at Saylers Creek when a large part of Lee's army was cut off and forced to surrender. This finished it for us and we returned to Mosby and got him to agree with releasing us early on furlough in order to travel to Georgia.

We set off for the west mountains on 5th April having recovered our buried horde of banknotes. This amounted to almost two hundred thousand Yankee dollars as it included all the other money we had received from the sale of captured US army property.

The journey was uneventful at first, but the countryside had been ravaged by the tides of war and you had to go higher into the mountains to be able to avoid Yankee patrols and outposts. We were used to this and were able to avoid trouble. Joe was with us but Silas had been granted permission to leave the 1st Virginia back in 1864 to join and train a native Cherokee regiment who were keen to fight for the Confederacy. One day the four of us were slowly making our way along a high ridge on the Tennessee border when I heard voices further along the path. These paths were not much more than game trails but there was evidence here of mounted men having shared the route. I didn't have time to return to warn the others because turning the horse would have alerted them. I could do nothing except draw my carbine and cock the action. The Captain was next up behind me and I gestured with my head there was danger. Joe and the boy came along causing us to bunch up together in a bad position with nowhere to go. Each of us had now drawn either revolvers or rifle and we waited silently for those people to show themselves in a little gap between the trees. Suddenly they were there; we were slightly above them as the track changed height. Our Captain and I were already levelling our weapons on where they would be. Suddenly the rearmost rider shouted out and instinctively we both fired at the same time. I dropped the carbine onto its sling and grabbed the Colt revolver. A shot rang out from below and I felt the strike of a bullet as it hit me in the hip. There was no pain as yet and I was able to fire my weapon again. Joe and Jacob had fired now but we could not see if any of them had been put out of action. An empty horse walked back down the track but we had no idea what had happened to its rider. We emptied our revolvers into the area where we considered the 'bushwhackers' might be and then grabbed another loaded weapon. The Captain and

Joe leapt down off the horses and ran down the track. There were another two shots and then silence. I was feeling very faint and my vision was clouding; my head began to swim and I toppled out of the saddle falling badly with my head striking a rock on the way down. I heard Jacob talking and felt them lift me into the saddle having bound up my wound with a clean shirt and some equipment bindings. They passed a rope around under the saddle and tied both legs under the horse. They then tied my wrists to the saddle and allowed me to lay hunched over along my horse's neck.

For days we made our way slowly south but my condition was serious. Blood loss and a raging fever had made it impossible for them to continue with me in that condition. We had been forced to lay-up and go into hiding to allow Joe to doctor my hip wound and removed the bullet. There was no infection, as yet and the blood loss had been stopped after a day and a night. He changed the dressings every day adding an ample application of whiskey to the open wound before bandaging. On the third day we continued. The Captain had been forced to try higher trails and ridges but this must have worked in our favour and we came down without incident, out of the mountains near Hiawassee Georgia. These mountains were full of desperate men. Some were 'bushwhackers' who would cut your throat as soon as look at you. We had to lay-up somewhere and if I was to recover they would have to get some help. After a long decision we came upon the best solution being the Captain and Jacob make their way to the farm and summon the help of uncle. I had not had any word since we joined with Mosby so was completely in the dark as to what had happened to him. I knew he had been serving as a scout with a cavalry unit but they had been retreating east towards the coast being steadily pursued by Sherman's army. The Captain understood this but still he was our only chance as the war was not over yet and if we were caught by the Yankees we would probably be shot. He left us the following morning, discarding all recognisable articles of Confederate uniform and changing into the clothes we had removed from the six dead men we had just met. These 'bushwhackers' had been riding mounts which did not bear Army brands and were complete with civilian horse tack. This enabled our Captain and his servant to journey,   south east into the Georgia heartland without drawing too much attention as they would have done before on cavalry horses.

We found a concealed little glade in the woods high on a ridge. It had a natural spring which tricked out of the rocks and the water was sweet and cold. There was nothing to eat and it was up to Joe to provide for us. The squirrels were pretty unfriendly but we were lucky as Joe was able to bring back a small deer. He butchered it and we cooked a lot of it, having to force it down in the end so as to get as much protein into me as possible. Our camp was in a good position and couldn't be overlooked from above because of the tree cover. It provided us a position that was not easily reached and anyone coming in our direction could be easily observed and their intentions interpreted. Bears were our only worry, as this was a popular area for them, making it necessary to bury the remains of the deer. Any blood smell would bring them in from over three miles away.

My condition got steadily worse and on the third day of our camp I became delirious and came down with a raging fever. The wound was infected and if Joe didn't do anything about it in time I would die of blood poisoning.

We had a little whisky left and after a day of fighting with Joe as he tried to stop me from trying to get up and walk over the ridge, I became rational for a while. He boiled the last of our coffee and we talked quietly about what my chances were. "You will lose the leg if I don't stop the infection soon." I listened to him and just put myself entirely in his hands. He took a spare hunting knife from out of his saddle bag and placed it over the small flames of our 'snake hole' fire. I knew what he had to do and didn't envy him this task as he would be required to open the wound and without damaging any arteries he would have to cauterize the wound in the only hope the infection would be stopped. If he was unsuccessful then I was going to die as the poison would have spread too far and there would be nothing he could do for me except wait till the end and then put a bullet in my head. He waited till next morning until the light was full. I agreed to have my legs staked out and spread eagled so as he could work on me without me kicking him in the face, my hands were again tied together and raised above my head and fastened to a stake knocked into the ground.

We had finished the last of the whiskey the night before so all he could offer me in the way of comfort was to place a section of wood between my teeth and then bind my mouth up with a neckerchief. At last he was ready. I was ready to die and I thought I would be like our beloved JEB as when he went there was no goodbye for his wife and his children and the little one was only a few months old. She would never see her Daddy but he would always be alive in her heart and in a lot of other people's not only in this country but everywhere for the name JEB Stuart would be immortal. I wondered if my name would be Pete Schofield, Corporal in the 1st Virginia cavalry.

I felt the razor sharp skinning knife open my wound, the pain took my breath away but I knew there was worse to come. It was like I was being hauled up over a cliff edge and then when I was on the top they threw me off the other side and I would panic and struggle against the rawhide thongs that held my limbs. The pain would ease in time for me to draw a breath, my throat was sore from trying to snuff out my screams but something said to me "Ride it out," "you can take this." I began again and waited for the pain to strengthen itself to come at me again but this time I was ready. I matched it and arched my back against the binding and raised myself above it. "It's going to get worse now." Joe said. He told me he was about to apply the red hot hunting knife and with that the pain hit me again but this time it was stronger. I could feel myself going under and my senses seem to be leaving without me. The pain is coming in waves each new attack more intense than the previous one. My mouth is twisted around the piece of wood and my teeth have bitten so deep into the wood I can't get them out. I am screaming but there is no sound it's like when you are in a rifle position near to a twelve pounder cannon and it suddenly fires right behind and above your head. Your hearing is destroyed and even though you see people's mouths working as they speak, you cannot hear anything. It was probably over in a few minutes but for me it seemed it had lasted for hours. Joe worked quickly and used some of my clean shirt tail to bind up the wound. He had resorted to using his knowledge of natural medicines and the day before he had gone into the forest and collected what he wanted, moss and powder from a certain type of dried mushroom. These he mixed with water into a paste and allowed it to warm in a tin mug placed on the fire. When he was satisfied it was ready he took it from the heat and allowed it to cool, while continually stirring into a green looking paste. When the poultice was ready he applied it liberally to the open but cauterised wound.

I fell in to a tortured sleep but I knew he was still there as I could feel him applying the cloth to my forehead and under my arms and over my chest in an attempt to get my body temperature down.

We waited for five long days during which time my condition fluctuated from completely rational to that of a raging lunatic. Joe kept me calm as best as he could but occasionally when the fever took me, he would have to restrain me for my own good and probably his safety. All this time he would try and get me to eat and would prepare squirrel or sometimes rabbit cooked over the small fire. I couldn't bring myself to eat anything and in the end he would try and boil up some stew from using the coffee pot. Although this ruined the pot it served us well because I was able to drink the broth. There was no coffee anyway so that didn't matter much.

I was awake early as there had been little rest for me during the night. I thought at first there was something inside my skull which was not fixed as I had probably suffered a skull fracture and concussion would certainly explain funny noises and seeing things that were not real. But as I blinked to try and clear my vision he was there. The small trees completely masked our camp site and to gain access to where we were camped you would have to move branches aside. I saw them moving but could not hear any more sounds until they had both stepped out and were standing over me. He changed his clothes and was now dressed in cheap shirt and pants. Uncle was just the same as he had been for as long as I could remember dressed in his buckskins. Jacob was pleased to see me and I tried to raise myself onto my arm but there was no response from my muscles.

"Don't struggle, stay where you are lad."

I knew everything would be all right now, and that little warm sensation of comfort and safety came over me. It must originate from instincts you learn from childhood from a mother's loving care. Just as I was trying to sit up Joe came crawling through underneath some low lying branches on the other side. "Glad to see you Sir." Said Joe. Our officer wanted to know everything that had transpired while he had been away and instructed us to change out of our ragged uniforms. "We are back home now and it will not serve any purpose to be taken as prisoners." Generals Lee and Johnson had not surrendered at this point but it was a foregone conclusion the end was very close. Uncle was with him and they had opened some saddlebags to find the pot while Jacob started to mend the fire so as to boil-up a fresh pot of coffee." It's Yankee coffee lad, uncle has been hunting." They all laughed.

They explained the situation was bad, with military check-points on most of the roads and cavalry patrols on every back road between here and Marietta. "We have to get out of here and back to Roswell as soon as we can then settle into the farmhouse and get the doctor for you." Our Captain said. I could feel myself going again as my brain started to shut down. "He goes like that regularly, Sir." Confirmed Joe.

They took me down the ridge and collected all our belongings. The weapons were buried along with our military equipment, wrapped in the oil cloth and covered in protecting axle grease which uncle had provided. The Captain allowed us to take a revolver each but this was all that remained of our normal arsenal. They had left a wagon just off the road and I was now made as comfortable as they could on the wagon bed.

From this point on I have to admit I have no recollection of what happened to us on the journey home. I lapsed into unconsciousness and on reaching the farm, was bedridden for over a week. They had got the doctor to visit and he gave them medicine for the infection. He inspected the gunshot wound and confirmed there was no more corruption and that it would heal soon. There was a need to leave a drain into the flesh to allow it to drain. This he did with great care and gladly accepting the Yankee dollars they paid to him he departed giving assurances he would attend the patient at any time day or night.

Chapter 38

As the wound in my hip healed I became more and more agitated and eager to follow the trail that the poor unfortunate factory women would have been forced to take under the orders of that madman. My uncle had tried his hardest to come to terms with his own grief and my overwhelming anger at him for not getting himself killed in the attempt to save my sister from her terrible ordeal.

As the days around the farm became too much for me to bear the Captain lectured us on the worsening situation in all the Southern States. South Carolina and Georgia had suffered terribly and the people were now being subjected to martial law. The counties were divided into military districts each one having an army officer acting as a Governor. All residents could be expected to produce identification documents and any ex serving soldiers of the Confederacy were to prove they had sworn allegiance to the United States Government and had surrendered with either Lee or Johnson.

This fact did not help our situation as we, like hundreds of others in our regiments that fought in Virginia who had simply spirited through the Yankee lines around Appomattox and never surrendered. We therefore needed to obtain some documents and especially travel papers which would allow us to make a train journey out of Georgia. People were being arrested daily, civilians, officers, soldiers and even ex Confederate Government politicians. We needed to obtain some false papers and then work out a plan to work out a route that would allow us to get to Louisville. This city was where we had been told some of the women had been taken too. There was a family only just reunited from Roswell and the women had been able to tell uncle of her hardship under the loving attention of the Yankee military. She explained my mother and two sisters had been with her, but just before the Confederacy surrendered she was offered a chance to return with a Yankee officer's family as he was being posted to a military district around Chattanooga and they would require a nanny to look after their children on the trip south. The information was vital and would be where our first search would start.

Beth's father was in a position to help us as he was still well connected in political circles. The Governors and ex Senate members who proved their allegiance and demonstrated their willingness to assist the new military regime were given some trust and position in local government. This level of authority although limited, would however enable us to obtain the necessary documents we were going to require for our journey. I mentioned before about the Captain and myself, being able to lay our hands on a ready supply of Yankee currency. This money you will remember, we relieved from the Army of the Shenandoah's paymaster. Wagon trains were our most popular targets when we served with Mosby and we became very wealthy in the last year of the war as all spoils were equally divided among the boys that were involved. We were not all fortunate but we enjoyed some luck in being in the right place at the right time. It was these spoils of war that were now enabling us to pursue this search for my missing family. Our commander Mosby had given us leave of absence to leave the regiment just before Lee's surrender and we had made our way south using a very similar route to the Captain's, when we first left Georgia to join JEB Stuarts regiment. Uncle had really come through for us as he had found out where we could expect to find military checkpoints and garrisons.

My friendship with Beth had blossomed and I found myself wanting to be in her company more than ever. Every opportunity that presented itself I would find myself hanging around her as she was either working helping her mother, or trying to prepare food for the four of us. I tried to make her like me and I never knew if I was doing any good, but every day I would talk with her. We were interested in a few similar things, reading and some poetry being the nearest. I would talk to her about Ivanhoe and the Knights of King Arthur. She would sit and listen to me and I sensed there was a change, small but definitely different, in the way she looked back at me. I would always pretend she was the lady of Shallot and I the gallant knight come to save her. I sometimes thought she would probably think I was still suffering from my wounds and she had simply to humour me. This didn't bother me though as it seemed something was working.

One day I was pestering her as usual, stopping her from completing her chores. She didn't even mind this now so I knew something had happened, or more like I was living in hope. She had been to Jacob's Store down Burnt Hickory road and had been driven there by one of the Negro farm hands. Here was now a wagon bed full of boxes containing groceries and fresh produce that needed to be carried into the farm kitchen. The driver had been told to finish another job first and had left her, promising to return as soon as he could. Her mother however needed the supplies inside out of the sun right there and then. Beth took it upon herself to start carrying the heavy boxes in to her mother. I felt awkward as I didn't know what her mother's opinion of me was. Beth was wearing a pretty dress and I didn't want her to get it dirty on them crates and boxes so I stepped in and grabbed a box from out of her arms. She seemed to stumble and it was as if everything had been slowed down. I didn't know what to grab first, the box or her.

Anyway I ended up with my hands around her waist supporting her full weight. She started to smile and allowed me to help her but as she came back onto her feet her lips were merely inches away from my face. Something just took over and I kissed her so gently on the mouth. It was the first time I had ever kissed a female apart from my horse or mother and maybe my sisters when they were little, but this felt different.

She seemed shocked and started to blush but I think my face was hotter than hers was, although she didn't pull away straight away and I got the impression she had kissed me back. This was the best feeling I had ever experienced. It was like my heart would stop beating at any minute. We came apart and she turned towards the kitchen door, but as I looked after her I saw her mother had been watching, her face a picture as it was framed by the biggest smile, on that woman's face I'd ever seen. Our relationship grew from these small beginnings and every morning when I woke, she was the first person I thought of. My mother and sisters followed a very close second. My wounds were healed now and it was fast approaching the time when we would be leaving to follow the trail of the Mill Workers. Uncle had excelled himself as the Union military never bothered us and Beth's father had been able to use his influence with a local government official to get us all the necessary travel and identity documents. We would have to purchase new clothes to go with the new identities. The Captain had already worked it out as he instructed us to accompany him on a visit to a tailor in Marietta. He was an amiable sort of man who had cleverly managed to hold onto some bolts of good cloth right through the war. Fortunately our Yankee dollars were more than enough to persuade him to set to work in producing a suit of garments for each of us which would more easily confirm our civilian identities. Our Captain's servant Jacob was to come with us also, as it would be impossible to exclude him and more to the point, we had no desire to as he was now very much one of us.

The tailor measured each of us and recorded everything he needed to produce the clothes. We were to have shirts, underclothes and hats to complete the outfitting and the tailor was so delighted we had chosen his business to provide our needs he didn't even think to press us for information involving our backgrounds.

The clothes would be ready in two to three weeks and we would pick these up as we came through the town in order to board a train for Chattanooga. This left our weapons. When we came out of the mountains we had buried all our military equipment and small arms. We wrapped them in oilcloth having first covered them liberally with a covering of axle grease. It was a shame we had been forced to do this but to have been caught with these weapons by a military patrol we would have meant being arrested and sent to a prisoner of war stockade. The Captain explained we could recover the weapons later, but for now we would have to make the journey north unarmed. This time waiting for the tailor gave me the opportunity to concentrate my attentions on Beth. I couldn't help worrying about mother and the girls and I think that if I hadn't had Beth to occupy my mind I would have gone crazy. My state of mind was very troubled and the only relief I could find was being able to talk with my friends the Captain, Joe and the boy.

I couldn't tell Beth what the exact problem was; only that it was denying me a good night's sleep. She obviously knew I was going out of my mind with worry but there was no chance I could involve her with those demons of the night that would come into my dreams regularly bringing with them those faces, the noise and voices. You never get used to them and they would be the same over and over again but each time they would take away with them a little bit more of my sanity.

It was now May 1865 and the war had been over since April but uncle had found out that war crimes were still being carried out in Kentucky. Confederate prisoners who should have been paroled were still being imprisoned by the military. We served with Mosby's cavalry in Virginia and a lot of our comrades very seldom were totally dressed in Confederate grey. Our Captain had always insisted we would continue to wear uniform and even when we came back into Georgia we had right up to the last minute all been dressed as Confederate cavalry, though we had buried our arms and equipment.

The wearing of uniform towards the end became more and more difficult as we could not get re-issued and simply, either took clothes from dead comrades or simply wore civilian dress. However the Yanks were pretty cut –up about the way we fought them and would take every opportunity to take hostages and persecute civilians, if they thought it would count against us. This behaviour was still alive and it made us determined to find the people who still carried it out. I'll have to agree that some of our men were taken prisoners out of uniform and this cost them their lives because the Yanks hung them as Guerrillas. There were innocents also who paid the price. Regardless of being caught, in or out of uniform Custer's men would execute prisoners especially if they had been recently whipped by our boys. This resulted in repercussions and inevitably meant Yankee prisoners were treat exactly the same.

We all believed in the 'eye for an eye' solution and I never lost any sleep or had any bad dreams over this. To a man we were all of the same opinion; we were always justified in delivering this swift justice.

Unfortunately it had come back to haunt us and for me it was too close for comfort.

The journey was uneventful and after you had stared for hours out of a carriage window, sleep would eventually overcome you and the rocking of the car over the rails would lull you into blissful sleep. We were often required to produce papers and twice a Yankee officer questioned us about the purpose of our Journey. I had made conversation with another passenger in the coach over many miles in-between Chattanooga and Nashville and then on into Louisville.

He was a Yankee civilian, an official with the military garrison in Atlanta who was journeying to Louisville to meet his son, a Captain in the US cavalry. Over the following conversations where he talked very freely I was able to learn that his son's regiment was the 1st Kentucky. He went on proudly to inform me that Sherman himself was due to visit the Head Quarters and garrison in the city in July as there was to be a massive parade and huge celebration before the Army of the West was disbanded. I could not have hoped for any better news save that of finding out where my family was. Here we were en route to that city where there was to be a huge parade of over 70,000 troops being overlooked by Sherman himself and all his staff. I quickly informed the Captain and he gathered us on the footplate between the two saloon cars, where we could not be overheard, and informed us he was working on a plan that would probably satisfy our needs.

We planned our mission down to the very smallest details. It involved finding some military uniforms, then masquerading as Union soldiers to infiltrate into the camps and discover where the regiment we were looking for was located. Once we knew where they were, we would adapt every pretence of actually belonging in that regiment. This would involve obtaining any distinguishing items like badges or other insignia that only this particular regiment would have.

Once we were close inside and near to our enemy then we would plan our next move, to remove the guilty, forever. We arrived in the city two days later having had the most uncomfortable journey of my life. My body ached in every bone and muscle far worse than being on campaign with the General our beloved leader, JEB Stuart.

We were able to book rooms in a very comfortable hotel and I couldn't believe how the war had apparently missed this city. There was an underlying sympathy for the Confederacy and although we never admitted we were southerners it must have been fairly evident by our Georgian accents, but when the Captain spoke, people would be confused and assume he was a northerner, immigrant from Europe. This did work in our favour and enabled us to avoid some suspicion. Our hotel room was grand and we dined that night in a fine restaurant. Joe had been ordered to cut his hair and shave his beard, leaving only facial hair that was fashioned into a moustache. I also had been required to have my hair cut and beard fashioned, and when the barber had finished anyone that had known us previously would simply not have been able to recognise us.

After dinner we adjourned to the very fashionable saloon bar and lounge where there were seated some of the city's most prominent citizens. Elegantly dressed ladies were very much in abundance, every one of them wearing expensive looking gowns that I had little doubt had come from the finest fashion houses.

The Captain immediately reconnoitred the cliental and motioned me to join him while Joe and the boy were detailed to remain by the entrance and away from the most popular social gatherings. He was intent on striking up a conversation with a very smartly dressed gentlemen and his lady. I followed humbly and felt so out of place it reminded me of being in front of a bunch of senior staff officers. However the Captain was soon engaged in conversation, and subtlety delivering compliments to the lady. She was soaking up his attentions and with practiced style the Captain was easily able to captivate them both with his charm and impeccable manners. It turned out that this couple were parents of another Yankee officer who was part of the Headquarters staff of the northern army. As the evening dragged slowly and painfully by for me the Captain was able to secure an invite to dinner for himself. I was not considered as he made excuses for me and for this I was eternally grateful.

The next evening was the night of our Captains dinner invite and he spent a lot of time on his appearance helped by his servant Jacob. His dress was immaculate and you could not help noticing he was every inch a military man. We were instructed not to draw undue attention to ourselves but were given permission to visit the hotel lounge after dinner. This again was uneventful, but I enjoyed watching these people who had not had to go through all the misery and horrors of war. It was like a different world and they had been fortunate not to have suffered in the same way as our countrymen had. The Captain had explained there were many citizens of the City who had been for the Confederacy and indeed money, soldiers, stores and equipment had been sent to the south in their hour of need. It was the same now and although Kentucky never seceded from the union, there were still a lot of people here whose sympathies were with the South and probably would still support them. I was glad when the others had got bored and suggested we retire.

The Captain came into the room at around two thirty in the morning. He woke me and started to tell me we had dropped lucky, because the gentlemen was going to be involved with the preparations for the coming military review.

Chapter 39

It became regular occurrence that week that we were all invited to dine with this gentleman and his wife. He was eager for us to help him in his preparations and wanted so much for us to meet his son. The time came very quickly towards that night and we were invited as dinner guests to share a table with his son. We arrived early as was requested and were shown into a large panelled room. Drinks were offered by Negro footmen and small delicacies on silver trays were passed from guest to guest. I couldn't think straight as this was unreal, I had just recovered from a gunshot wound and comrades with whom I had probably ridden with under Mosby were being imprisoned and here I was nibbling fancies and drinking fine liquor.

I was still shaking my head when the double panelled oak doors opened and a liveried Negro footman entered to announce the arrival of our host's son and heir. Major Tomlinson. I recognised his cap badge on his best uniformed hat, just as he passed it to the Negro footman. It was the 1st Kentucky.

My blood seemed to rush into my brain too quickly and I could feel the colour in my face turning to blood red. The Captain broke the spell and introduced himself, 'Captain Robinson late of her Majesty's 11th Hussars.'

'These are my associates,' he was continuing, 'and we are in the business of buying arms and all surplus equipment which will hopefully be in abundance in the next few weeks after the US army is disbanded and the soldiers mustered out.'

It was beyond belief how the Captain and Joe so easily mixed into the conversations between father and son. It was like they had known each other for years. I was completely taken aback by Joe's knowledge of subjects you would never have dreamt he was familiar with. The evening was a success and returning home to our hotel in the carriage the Captain congratulated everyone on their behaviour and our fine theatrical performance. They had managed to get an invite to the camp of the Major's regiment under the pretence of inspecting the armourer and quartermaster store. I had heard him so carefully enquire about the Atlanta campaign and the action on the Chattahoochee river line. He was not involved, but as the Captain had put it, he was enquiring after a certain officer from the regiment, who had been wounded at around that time. He lied that this officer was an old friend and as they had lost contact with each other he was anxious to learn if he had survived the war.

The Major was helpful and promised he would make enquiries from another officer who was at Roswell and had taken part in the escort of prisoners to Marietta.

This was going too well, but the Captain was already thinking about getting uniforms and planning how we could spirit a Yankee officer out of Headquarters and dump his body in the river.

The next task was to try and find any information on the Mill Workers and whether anyone knew if there were any of these women in the city.

Our dinner hosts were very helpful, and when we explained that we were enquiring after a dear friend's daughter who had gone missing, the Lady of the house was insistent she would find out. Her housekeeper was friendly with another lady who also had a position with a wealthy family close by. The next day we were summoned to the house and on entering the library I couldn't help notice the two seated ladies. From their dress it wasn't hard to guess they were both housekeepers because of the style of their smart uniform dresses.

The Lady host had already explained our dilemma and that we were anxiously seeking this friend's daughter. Immediately one of the lady housekeepers started to tell us of a woman and her two daughters. They had come to the city by steamboat along with few other refugees from the south. They had been lucky as the proprietor of a house of ill repute had been looking to employ kitchen and housekeeping staff for what was a high class gentlemen's club. The establishment had earned a reputation among army officers coming through Louisville on route to duty postings in the south, and was famous for its elegant dining room and the obliging ladies who would join the officers at their tables. She continued to say she had not seen the mother for some time, but had noticed both daughters at the market on the previous week. This was unbelievable and I was anxious to find out if they considered it possible we could meet these two girls by visiting the market. They both agreed it was likely the daughters would be there on the Tuesday of the following week. I was excited and couldn't settle down or concentrate on anything else other than the future trip to the market.

The Captain brought me down to earth and insisted we had to focus on the Army officer and the Major hopefully being able to find something out from his enquiries. The next day was Saturday and we were again invited to our new friend's house for dinner. A message had been left at hotel reception with the invite and the news we would be again in the company of the Major.

The Captain now detailed exactly what we needed to achieve from this meeting. We were to gather information on this other officer but at the same time try and secure an invite to visit the Head Quarters and depot where we would likely find a surplus of Army equipment that could be purchased. The dinner that night went according to plan. The officer who we were supposedly looking for was unheard of but there was another with the regiment who had been involved in that Chattahoochee engagement. Not wanting to appear over enthusiastic we were careful to suggest it may help our enquiries if this officer would agree to a meeting with us. To our surprise the Major had already organised for us to visit the depot the next day and he had gone as far as having permits made out for us all. These he casually handed across the table while still in conversation with his father on the big parade in July when Sherman would be the inspecting General. The depot was a mustering out point for all the regiments in the Yankee northern army and over the next month there were going to be thousands of Union troops passing through.

This was going to work very nicely for us, and I could see our leader was far ahead in his preparations. "We need to get our hands on some uniforms without attracting attention to ourselves." He said deep in thought. We were all wondering what next he would come up with and couldn't wait to get back to the hotel room where we could make plans for Sunday and our visit to Headquarters.

We were driven through the city to the depot gates by carriage and the Captain had hired an impressive looking vehicle pulled by a handsome set of four horses. We were assisted down the carriages step by the cabby and walked confidently towards the large iron gates. The sentries looked bored and were not even interested with checking our identities. The officer of the day was called and he ushered us through into a duty room where we were to wait for another officer. My mind was racing as I thought this could be the very same one who was responsible for the war crimes that had been forced upon my family. A Captain rushed into the room making his apologies and confirming he had been instructed by the Major to look after us during our visit to the depot and quartermasters warehouse.

Nobody knew what the criminal looked like as the only person who had witnessed the crime was uncle and we had left him back in Roswell. I took it upon myself to enquire of this officer, if he knew the name of the person we were allegedly looking for. Of course this person didn't exist, so I felt confident enough to elaborate on the fictitious tale of how our friend had been wounded and that was the last we had heard. The Yankee officer didn't even seem suspicious and was able to inform us of the cavalry action involved to force a passage across the Chattahoochee River to outflank the rebel earthworks. I hoped I wasn't going too fast but the situation was secured by our leader mentioning Garrett and his orders to occupy Roswell. The Yankee officer seemed surprised but he confirmed that part of his regiment, about two troops, had been detailed with Headquarters duty which entailed securing the town and maintaining peaceful order.

He mentioned there were no incidents until they had received new orders to destroy the mills at both New Manchester and Roswell. The owners put up some resistance and broke out a French National flag stating the buildings were neutral and not in any way legitimate military targets. The Major in charge had sent a galloper to Headquarters for orders and when these were returned they stated in no uncertain terms, that the buildings and all the associated contents were to be destroyed. In addition, the work force of both the mills were to be put under arrest and transported north by the orders of General Sherman. It took a great deal of control for me to remain calm and not launch myself at this officer's throat. Both Joe and our Captain could see I was struggling, but the Yankee was brought cleverly into further conversation that divulged further details. "That must have been awkward for you?" The Captain said conversationally. The officer agreed and I got the impression he was looking for sympathy. "We heard there were a lot of women mill workers that had to be transported?" Joe asked, continuing with. "That must have took some organising, I Bet?"

We gradually were able to extract more information from him but when our Captain inquired into whether there had been any incidents where there had been a breakdown of discipline; I simply had to sit on my hands to stop myself from shaking. Although the Captain covered this up by quickly comparing a situation he had been involved with years ago in the Crimean, the Yankee's attitude seemed to change. Suddenly he was blubbering about how he couldn't stop them and they were supposed to have been in Marietta before nightfall but as many people were being forced to walk, I ordered a lot of troopers to take women up onto their saddles in order to ride double and allow the wagon train to make faster progress.

"I bet that had the opposite effect!" Joe said laughing. "It was all I could do to stop them," "even the Sergeants were man handling them."

This was it; I had found the man responsible but was not prepared for what he said in his next breath.

"One of them is here in the armoury, a top Sergeant."

"Well some people certainly had a lovely war." The Captain laughed, but I was not laughing.

Our leader then steered the conversation around to the possibility of purchasing some good quality rifled muskets. He disguised the real reason very well I thought but he was probably thinking there may be a chance to come away with some weapons, into the bargain. The officer agreed he had been instructed by the Major to assist in every way possible but that this may be going a little too far. Our leader must have thought it was time to offer him a 'sweetener' and a huge roll of dollars in large denominations came out of his inside pocket.

The officers face lit-up at the sight and he soon mentioned that the armourer Sergeant would have to be included. If he were brought into the deal it would be a simple enough matter for a case of the rifles in question being delivered to our hotel that same afternoon.

We followed him into the warehouse and up to a secure cage fence. The entry gates were locked and there was a guard on duty sat behind a desk just to one side. The officer requested entry and signed the register allowing us all to pass through the gates. We were soon introduced to the armourer. He was a big man and immediately my memory was working over and it returned to that night when uncle had described the scene of my sister being subjected to a sexual assault from a man resembling this one who was now standing in front of me. If I had been in possession of my

Remington then I had no doubt it would have been all over in those next few seconds.

The Sergeant was one of those men you could instantly take a dislike to. Regardless he may be the rapist but this aside, his manner and the way he talked made me hope he was the one we wanted and I could relieve this world of his presence forever. We talked of a deal where we would be able to obtain three rifles and they would receive a thousand dollars each. It was soon agreed and all that remained was for us to select the rifles. Joe realised that once we walked out of the armoury having passed over any money it would be a simple matter they could cheat us out of our part of the agreement. The arrangements were soon altered with these now requiring the delivery of the rifles to our hotel where we would inspect the weapons. If everything was satisfactory the money would change hands. The only other conditions were that both the Yankee Captain and this Quartermaster Sergeant would both be present when they were delivered. In order the money could be given to each of them personally and avoid any treachery between them.

Monday morning would be set for the delivery and with this organised we indicated there was no further need to be in their company. Our hotel room was a sanctuary and I was so excited I asked his permission to partake in a little drink at the bar downstairs. He was quick to remind me that any drunkenness would be dealt with in his usual manner and we all knew what this involved.

The evening again went very enjoyably. I was relieved we had not been invited to our new friends house for dinner as our own, private dinner appointment enabled us to plan the exchange.

We would have to organise some delivery space where the crate could be unloaded and give us the chance to open it and inspect the rifles. The head waiter was that sort of man who had his fingers in many pies and the Captain's judge of character proved exactly correct. When we motioned for him to come to our table and told him our requirements he was more than obliging. The passing of one hundred dollars sealing the bargain and filling us with confidence the delivery would be able to go ahead without a hitch.

The Captain then told us we would invite the two Yankees up to our hotel room and over a celebratory drink they would be drugged unconscious. We would then use the linen shoot in the corridor outside our room to deposit them into the same delivery area adjacent to where the crate would be unpacked.

Monday morning dawned but I had been awake most of the night, unable to sleep for thinking of what today would bring. The agreed time for the delivery was fast approaching and our leader had us dressed and ready for action well before time. He led us down the back stairway and into the lower laundry and delivery area that served the hotel. There was no one around and we had the whole place to ourselves. There was little to do now but wait for the delivery.

Chapter 40

A wagon was coming into the yard and I peered out from behind some packing cases. Immediately I recognised the two occupants sitting on the driver's bench, it was them and the fact it was about to begin settled my nerves. They sauntered into the yard and we opened the gate for them. The head waiter had done his job well as the lock and chain was not secured properly and fell away as I rattled the chain. They greeted us and asked if we could assist with lifting the crate down onto the floor. The big Sergeant manoeuvred the wagon further into the delivery area where it was now under cover and out of sight of any passer-by.

The Captain prised open the lid of the crate and there inside were the British Enfield rifles. You didn't have to be an armourer to realise these weapons were almost new. In fact one of them still had a liberal coating of protecting grease smothering its trigger and hammer mechanisms. The money was not exchanged as the Captain explained the two soldiers were welcome to join us in a drink in our hotel room to celebrate our business arrangements and to seal the transfer.

They both agreed, the look on their faces showing obvious pleasure in the prospect of drinking some fine imported French brandy. We soon assembled in our hotel room having entered the stairway from the loading area carrying the crate with us and luckily not encountering any other person on the way.

Our Captain had obtained some sleeping draught from an apothecary the day before and all this was ready and waiting to be added to the fine brandy. We made light of the story the Yankee officer had told us, and at first the big Sergeant was suspicious of our conversation.

Eventually after three brandies his tongue began to loosen. I steered the talk around to women and made up a story of how we had forced our attentions on a family in West Virginia when we had been with Custer.

He seemed relieved and started to swagger and even boasted of some of his conquests during the war. Joe drew him out saying how he would have loved to have been with that escort duty when they had all those sweet young women at their mercy on that road to Marietta. This achieved the outcome and on the fourth glass of brandy the Captain laced the drinks with the strong sleeping draught.

It was amusing to watch them first sit down on our hotel suite sofa and then they were struggling to keep awake. Finally they both collapsed into a deep sleep. Our leader quickly told us what he intended and we started to empty a laundry basket of its dirty bed linen. It was essential the soldier's uniforms were removed as we would require these later for the next part of our Captain's plan. We wrapped their unconscious bodies with the sheets and other bedding. The officer was less of a problem being of average build but his quartermaster was different story. It took all three of us to man-handle the Sergeant onto the lip of the chute. With a last combined effort we were successful and we smiled to each other as we heard his big frame crash down through four floors to the basement. I was concerned now because there was no way I had considered getting rid of these two without getting caught. He told us to run down into the laundry room and retrieve the bodies before the early shift came on duty. We were instructed then to load their sleeping forms onto the wagon and cover them with empty crates which were littered around in the outside yard.

This done, he climbed onto the driving seat and ordered Joe and I to board the wagon. We drove out through the city towards the river. The streets were busy as there were a lot of businesses already open but we arrived on the water front without alerting anyone's attention. The day before when the Captain had purchased the sleeping draught he had also bought himself a good fitting uniform from a military suttler's store. Unbeknown to us he had also reconnoitred the perfect location to hide the bodies. This was the secluded dock we were now making our way to. It was deserted because there had been a recent collapse of the wharf pilings making this part of the river unsafe to use. We came to a halt and our leader ordered us to unload the sleeping soldiers.

I immediately got the impression the Captain wanted them both dead but I even surprised myself because I spoke out in defence of the officer. He had told us of the breakdown in discipline, and the fact he had restored some order in the column made me think he had done what he could. The Captain however wanted no trace of our little operation to be left uncovered and warned the military authorities would be able to follow our trail through the Major and his father. We had to dispose of the two soldiers and then disappear as though we never even existed. He was going to purchase a new Yankee uniform from a military tailor and we were going to have to make ourselves look like Yankees using the uniforms we had just removed from these two criminals. I indicated I was not in favour of murdering these two men, but before I could gather my thoughts Joe had produced a barbers shaving razor and within a second had opened both these men's throats. Blood spurted from the wounds staining the white of their undershirts. I watched horrified as the blood from each of them intermingled on the dock making little gurgling sounds as it spurted from the gaping wounds. I was in shock but he kicked me into action shouting for me to pick up all the sheets and other laundry and place them back onto the wagon. He had already moved them away from the bodies to prevent any tell-tale blood stains.

Joe and he now quickly tipped the two dead men into the river and I watched still transfixed in horror as their bodies bounced away on the tide. We mounted the wagon and again the Captain was two jumps ahead. "This is not a military vehicle and we will leave it outside of one of those warehouses where I am sure it will be put to good use." "The linen we will leave outside that boarding house as I know there'll be no questions asked."

We accomplished all of this and then walked through the streets toward our hotel as though nothing of any importance had happened.

"The next step is to pay our account at the hotel and then move to another, closer to the main square where I believe there is to be a huge military parade this coming weekend." Our officer said.

True enough as we rounded a corner that opened up onto the square there were soldiers everywhere. The atmosphere was as though the entire city was celebrating. People were running through the streets hugging and kissing and we were soon caught up in the mood. Soldiers were being congratulated and everywhere women and girls were kissing them. Gentlemen were asking to shake their hands and most people were shouting their praises to God the war was finally over and it was time to rejoice. This was madness, we had just murdered two people less than a mile from here and now we were being swept up in a throng of people who simply wanted to congratulate each other.

He had already picked out the hotel and ordered us to take notice. He disappeared into the impressive looking lobby and we were left looking at each other in amazement. Finally we caught up with him and he was booking us in to one of the most expensive suites in the house. He was treated with much respect and I had noticed his accent had become more refined and his speech much slower. The hotel booking clerk was only too pleased to accept the large bundle of dollars the Captain placed discretely into his gloved hands and we were informed there would be porters to meet us on our return.

On reaching the hotel he ordered us to remove all regimental or other distinguishing items from the uniforms and we packed all our belongings and the soldiers side arms and uniform belts into our valises. We would be going downstairs to settle our bill and then walking to our new hotel where we would have the valeting and tailoring service clean and alter these uniforms to ensure we looked every inch the Yankee soldier. The crate in our room was to be delivered to our new hotel also and with more money changing hands no questions were asked. That afternoon the case was delivered by two Negro footmen and they too were rewarded with Yankee dollars. For two days we kept ourselves to ourselves and felt secure in our expensive haven. Jacob was given accommodation in the staff quarters and was happy with the arrangements. We dined in the very exclusive restaurant where only the wealthiest of the cities dignitaries frequented. I had never eaten or had to battle with as many knives, forks and spoons in my life but he showed me and Joe exactly what to do and in what order. I believed we did not show him up or in any way cause him embarrassment. The city was filled to bursting point with Yankee soldiers as we had learned many regiments had left Washington to come to Louisville for a final parade and then to be mustered out of military service. This was a big undertaking and the Yanks were going to make a meal of it by having another parade on July 4th when that madman Sherman would be presiding over the ceremony.

Two days later the tailor arrived with our new uniforms and I was impressed by his tradesmanship. Joe's uniform having belonged to the dead quartermaster was far too big for him but now it fitted exactly and was cut to fit every part of his muscled body. The Captain as usual looked every part the Officer and he had acquired a Captains shoulder bars to complete the masquerade. My uniform also fitted me like a glove and I couldn't help admiring myself in the huge mirror in our suite. Our Captain now explained we would not be requiring the uniforms until the morning of the Parade. We were to visit the market where we had been informed the two girls might be seen. Our leader was not happy about me visiting the market as he was convinced I would not be able to control my feelings and consequently draw unwanted attention.

Joe and himself would visit the market and conduct all the reconnaissance work while I cleaned the rifles. Luckily we had been given sixty rounds of ball cartridges and enough percussion caps so there was no concerns, the rifles would be fully serviceable after the cleaning. They left me to my chores and set off for the market. Joe would easily recognise my mother or either of the girls as they had met when uncle had invited him to the house. This was years ago and thinking about it I was worried if mother wasn't there then he would have no chance recognising my sisters as the last time he laid eyes on them they were only slips of girls.

In the early evening he came back to our room. Joe had seen mother with the two girls and had easily recognised her. The Captain also was able to confirm that this was her and that the two girls with her were indeed my sisters. I waited with baited breath for them to expand on the information but they seemed reluctant to go any further.

"For Christ's sake tell me what's wrong." I shouted. "Well there is a big problem." Our Captain explained they had bumped into the three women and immediately opened a conversation into who they were and that their relative was here to take them back to the south and their family home. Your mother broke down and it took a long time before she got herself under control again and was able to talk without sobbing. Your sisters were full of praise for you and stated that they had not had any doubts you would find them and bring them back home. I was crying now as this was all too much. I wanted to see them but the Captain calmed me down and went on to explain that the women were reluctant to leave the rest of the people they worked with and that if they escaped then it would go badly for the rest of them who were left behind. "They are no better off than Negros under an inhuman foreman." Said the Captain. "We are going to have to plan how we will get all of them out, as there is little chance of your family leaving without we take all the others with us."

He started to explain how we could make this happen and went on to describe his next idea.

We have the uniforms and we will use these to gain entry into the brothel. We have enough money to order anything we want in there and it will make things easier if Joe and the lad go in from the rear while we do the business from front of house I intend to use the roof of our hotel as a firing position to shoot at the podium where Sherman and his staff will be sitting on the day of the parade. We have a few days to prepare and we will be able to get your entire mother's people away and into our accommodation here with us. There is some Negros also and I will ask Jacob to organise a safe house for them.

It took us some hours to take in exactly what the Captain had said but we were all stunned by his power of reasoning and intricate planning. Tomorrow night you and I are going to dine in the brothels restaurant. You are going to request the chef and the staff who prepare those fine dishes are brought to front of house because you want to congratulate them on the food, its unique taste and the fine sauce.

We dressed for dinner with the help of our Captains servant Jacob; he had learned how an officer and a gentleman should be properly turned out and was now at the top of his game. It was customary for wealthy gentlemen and ladies to be accompanied by their servants and accommodation was allocated in these hotels for this purpose. The Captain had already talked to the hotel manager and arranged for my family and some Negro servants to have reservations at the hotel. The women would occupy a neighbouring suite and the servants would be found space in the staff quarters. It was now time and I felt nervous, he had told me I was to act like an arrogant Yankee officer but this did little, save remind me of that scene on the dockside of a fast spreading blood stain on white cloth. The building was a fine example of a colonial style structure with wide boardwalk and ornate pillars supporting verandas on every one of its four floors. I followed him through the grand entrance doors to be greeted by a huge Negro doorman. The Captain produced his written table reservation which had been hand delivered to our hotel that morning. All the diners were required to book in advance but this did not guarantee a table as the management exercised their right to refuse anybody who they considered unsuitable.

An elegant lady swept across the floor towards us, she was dressed in a beautiful gown and had her hair styled in the latest European fashion. This was breath-taking and although I had thought only of Beth over the last few days this woman caused my jaw to open as my eyes were drawn towards her.

She was wearing long satin gloves which covered her arms up to her perfect elbow. The gown was so cut low it only just succeeded in covering the lower part of her bosom. She offered the Captain her hand and he snapped to attention and taking it gently in his fingers he bowed before her saying how much of an honour it was to have been accepted to dine in this wonderful establishment. I was then introduced, and I made a horrible mess of mixing my feet up and attempting to copy my leader. It must have amused her as she smiled and linking her arms through both of ours she led us away across the crowded dining area. I must have resembled a halfwit as I knew I was staring at the other diners who were nearly all accompanied by elegantly dressed beautiful women. Some seemed they were only girls but all were similarly dressed in expensive gowns of the latest fashion. She indicated this was our table and we were seated by Negro waiters who waited for us to take the chair and then lifted it within reach of the table. She hovered around fussing over the Captain showing him the wine list and informing him there was some fine French champagne available tonight. The head waiter appeared and he offered us both menus for this evening's dinner. "Sir, can I make bold as to offer a recommendation." "The lobster is fresh and I can tell you, Chef specialises in this dish and has prepared a special sauce for tonight." The Captain was hidden in the huge menu but on reappearing he immediately inquired if the steak was tender. He continued by ordering two fillet steaks marinated in good sipping whiskey and served with the most expensive full bodied red wine. The head waiter appeared annoyed and stormed away having snatched up the huge menus. The lady came closer and bent over to whisper in the Captains ear. This must have caused an explosion in my brain as the heat from it burst like a shell. She was smiling at me now and I could not help gazing up at her, my eyes never reaching higher than her wonderful bosom. The Captain asked her if there were any ladies from the Southern states there that night and she again smiled and swept away through the dining tables where many high ranking Yankee officers and their dinner partners were enjoying each other's intimate company.

Moments later two ladies approached our table, one of them asking if the two gentlemen would like company for the evening. They were charming and very attractive, dressed much the same as the lady front-of-house manager. You would have had to have been a eunuch to refuse these two delightful women and we both invited them to join us for dinner. The head waiter materialised like a Yankee skirmisher and inquired what the ladies would like to eat. The Captain insisted they eat what we had ordered but gave instructions the meals were to be brought to the table in thirty minutes time. "In the meantime you will bring us a bottle of the French Champagne." He was in his element and I had gone to heaven fifteen minutes ago.

This was one of the strangest evenings I had ever experienced. Nothing could be real, we had only just, a few hours ago, murdered two Yankee soldiers and three months before I had been shot and had been lucky to survive. I had returned home to Georgia after five years of war to find my home land ravaged and its people abused and robbed. But here I was tonight, sitting in the company of a young woman trying to think of what to say to her next.

Chapter 41

The Captain was experienced in the workings of these types of establishments as he used to tell me when he lost his wife these places were where he spent most of his time. The ladies had excused themselves and gone to freshen-up their appearance, or so they said. He told me now would come the time when they would ask us to join them in one of the upstairs private lounges. He wanted for us to accompany them in order to find out where my mother and sisters were. The Captain was convinced they were here in this house and our next step would be to create a diversion to be able to spirit them away with their friends along with them. The ladies came back and true to form the Captains words became reality once again. We allowed the women to guide us across the dining room to an elegant bow staircase leading up to a balcony which overlooked the diners below. They showed us to a room and we followed them into a room of palatial grandeur. Quickly the Captain poured out our story and the two women were rendered speechless. In the continuing conversation the ladies told us their story and it was hard to believe this one was so intertwined with my own families. They too had been taken north from Georgia and had at first tried to get work anywhere they could but as the war dragged on things got worse. They were close to starvation when one day they met the businesswoman who owned this house. The City was a hub for many businesses and manufacturing works. The war had not seriously affected its residents and so they didn't suffer too badly. It was also a mustering point where regiments were mobilised and deployed onto the different battle fronts. Consequently this owner's business had grown and she had expanded it having to move to bigger and grander houses as the demand and popularity increased. Her house was so famous with the Army officers it was even talked about in Washington. They explained the girls were all treated very well being given fine clothes, all the food, and even paid a small percentage of the money charged for the women's services. There were four of them who worked the dining area but there were also three more in the kitchens. There were two Negro women also and these had come north with the ones now working in the kitchen.

These women I knew were my family. The two women looked frightened and they began to explain that if any of them tried to run away the others would be subjected to a savage and cruel punishment. Each of the remaining women had been beaten last year when one of the dining room girls had run away. The women that knew her best had received the worst treatment which consisted of her being spread-eagled nude on a large spoke wheel where she suffered for hours at the hand of the lady owner. The runaway girl was found and she was made to administer punishment on her friend. They would be forced to change places and punishment would continue. If she considered they were not entering into the spirit she thought it deserved then both would be bound to the wheel on opposite sides while she continued to carry it out herself. Men who would have paid dearly to watch were sometimes invited to take part or just as spectators. She was a sadist and enjoyed delivering punishment to both men and women. It was true they told us, that a lot of men paid her to give them punishment but the poor woman whom had run away was not able to return to work for a week. They assured us that through all this mistreatment and torture there was a doctor present and he would be called upon to treat the open wounds so as there would be hardly any trace of the blows. He was also a sexual fiend and would engage those pinioned on the wheel in intercourse at the same time punishment was being carried out. I couldn't listen to it any more but wanted to know if my family had been tortured in this way. They both burst out crying and after what seemed an hour were able to continue. "Your mother was, when she tried to prevent Sarah from having to go with a man she didn't like the look of." "What I want to know how many times." I said but the Captain calmed me down by saying this was enough and should my mother or the girls decide they want to tell you, and then it is for them to do so when we get them back to Georgia.

He explained that they could expect another fifteen minutes of privacy and then the owner would come upstairs to check on us and require paying. We had enough time as he had arranged for Joe and his servant Jacob to enter the premises from the rear and where the tradesman's entrance was located. They would force entry and find the point where the gas supply came into the building. They would then make an incision in the supply pipe but not so it would deprive the lights in the house of the fuel they needed. The room where the pipe entered the building would be sealed completely from any outside air and the entrance secured. A candle would have been used placed high up near the ceiling of the room. When the gas was allowed to rise in volume it would eventually reach the naked flame and there would be a violent explosion. Our job was to collect all the women and be in position to make our escape as the building exploded. The two girls agreed they would go to the kitchen and prepare my mother and sisters. They would also watch and wait till the other girls working the dining room visited the bathroom and then they would collect them all and wait for our instructions. I persuaded the Captain to allow me to follow the girls down to the kitchen where I could assure my mother we would be getting them out. He was reluctant, but in the end he gave in but told me he would expect me in ten minutes with our two working girls on the veranda.

My mother was a physical and mental wreck and I was not much better as I was talking with him a man in a tall chef's hat started shouting at them. My sister Sarah started to tremble and alarm bells started to ring in my head. Had they been beaten by this man? He rounded on me but as I was in uniform it slowed him down while mine were accelerated. I picked a large butchers knife off the counter top and as he came close plunged it in an upward ark between his ribs and into his heart. He died instantly and collapsed in a heap at my sister's feet. I thought she would scream but mother took her and placed her hand over her mouth.

We had to get out of there and I pushed them out into the kitchen yard. There in front of us were Jacob and Joe. They insisted we get as far away from the building as possible because the fuse would ignite the gas in not less than five minutes. I left them with Joe and Jacob and ran through the kitchens and out into the dining area. The Captain was talking to the Madame and was smothering her with his charm and complements. He had asked her if it would be possible to thank the girls and say hello to the other two who had joined their friends on the balcony overlooking the dining tables. She agreed and we went up the staircase two steps at a time. There were only seconds to gather the girls together and usher them down the ornate staircase. It was too late as the Madame had sensed we were not behaving correctly. She had collected the huge Negro from the entrance and they were both halfway across the floor. The room seemed to be illuminated in a huge orange fireball. Pieces of masonry had been torn from the wall and these were now being propelled like round shot into the packed dining tables. The blast now caught up with them and it was like a hurricane. Men were pitched into the air, furniture was blown to pieces and the ornate staircase collapsed around our bodies. I shook myself from under the plaster dust and broken pieces of cornice and timber mouldings.

The Captain was lifting the unconscious form of one of our hosts; she was breathing but not conscious. The others I rushed to and with relief found they were much shaken cut and bruised but none had suffered any injuries that would stop them walking under their own steam with my help. I snatched them up and made a run for the ruined kitchens. The blast had seemed to have been directed toward the dividing wall and the dining room, this was load bearing and I could see the whole wall and the balcony were tottering on collapse. The Captain had gathered up the injured girl and was now in front running with her in his arms towards the back entrance. The Madame had survived and was searching for us through the carnage. There were many Yankees sprawled on the floor many had been struck with flying debris and would not be dining anywhere anymore. Others had been flattened by the blast and had died very quickly. It had not accounted for enough of them however and the doorman came up behind me followed by the hysterical Madame. I turned to face him but in that split second Joe had appeared and he was levelling a Colt revolver at him. He fired and fired again and I had just enough time to put up my arms in defence as this madwomen slashed at my face with a long thin bladed stiletto blade. She had her skirts raised and had pulled the blade from a purpose built sheath attached to her stocking top beneath her garter. It slashed my hands and she was coming in again now intent on cutting up my face for a good Cajon stir-fry. I grappled with her and her face was contorted into a mask of horror as she whipped her long nails on her free hand across my unprotected face. The pain was instant but I managed to free my hand and grab hold of her wrist. I twisted with all my strength but this woman was in a rage and it gave her extraordinary powers, ones that were slowly getting the better of me. I could feel the blood pouring from the cuts on my hands and my grip was losing all its purchase. She came on again sensing I had been weakened. Without me realising, something told me to swing my cavalry booted leg up into her. Her skirts were still raised and her legs were open as she rounded on me for what I thought would be the last time. I had glanced over at Joe and even though he had shot the doorman twice in the chest he had not gone down but was picking him up like a child's doll. I had not thought it would end like this but I felt my boot strike her right between the legs. She gasped in pain and shock and something told me to do it again. I kept kicking her in the crutch and she was going down. She was screaming at me now, insult after insult but I couldn't stop. The knife fell from her grasp and I snatched it up, reversed it and then plunged it into her body. Her skirts had momentarily covered her face and upper body so the knife blow had been directed towards the only part of her body which offered bare flesh. I looked down in horror as I realised where the knife had ended up I must of stabbed her a dozen times as there was a line of wounds starting between her corseted crutch to reach up to her abdomen. I broke the spell as Joe was calling out with his last breath. I instantly took everything in and had just snatched the fallen revolver from the floor. I stuck the muzzle savagely into the Negros mouth smashing his teeth till it stopped two inches inside. I cocked it and pulled the trigger. Then again and again, until his big ugly head was no more, just a bloody mess all over both of us. We staggered out into the cool of the night and headed away from the carnage and death. The Captain was the only one of us that was not covered in blood and gore. He volunteered to get the working girls to the nearest hotel and from there get them into a carriage and finally to our hotel.

Joe and I were left to help my family and the two Negro women to safety. It would have been easy for anyone to have been suspicious if they had noticed us skulking through the streets, us in bloody uniform and them in kitchen aprons. I knew our hotel was not too far away from the wrecked brothel but we would be advised not to use a direct route. There were fire engines, police and military provost patrols converging on the burning building and I urged everyone to make for the back streets that would give us an alternative but indirect route to the hotel. My mother seemed to be suffering and she had to be assisted by my sisters. Joe would go on ahead while I brought up the rear. We both had forgotten about Jacob the Captain's servant and never even gave him thought until he ran up behind me carrying a heavy strong box. He smiled when I looked down at what he had but he said "They surely don't need this money now, do they Corporal?" I had to agree.

We made it back to the hotel and were met by the under manager and some of the Negro porters. He led us around to the rear loading dock and between us we got all of the women into the hotel stairwell. Our rooms were on the top floor but the Negro maids would be accommodated in the servant's quarters just off the rear stair lobby. Jacob took the initiative and took over leading the women to some rooms that had been prepared for them earlier. Joe and I walked my family up the flights of stairs to the bedroom corridor which led to our suites. I opened the doors to the suite and we got mother onto the bed. The girls just wanted to get her settled and in our confused and troubled state of mind we all had neglected to realise we were together again after five long years. We hugged and kissed each other continually for hours snatching at conversation but avoiding anything that was associated with the brothel or their transportation north. The Captain had installed the working girls in our spacious suite. They were so grateful I had no doubt that he would have not had to sleep alone that night. I wasn't concerned as my mother and sisters were more important. He explained in the morning that he was pretty convinced we would be safe for a couple of days here at the Hotel. He had bribed all the most important people, those who managed the separate departments and ruled them with a rod of iron. The only danger would be if anyone else were to offer a bigger reward for any information that would prove connected to the fire and the deaths of the owner and her guests.

There were now thousands of troops pouring into the city being transported by steamboat and the railroad. Everyone with a business was driven by making money from this influx of soldiery as these men would have been paid and would therefore have money to spend. This took away the seriousness of the fire and any suspicious thoughts of murder would be forgotten. The hotel was filling up and every room was taken by that evening. We had inspected the roof top and had located a firing position which would serve our purpose as it overlooked where the inspecting Generals would be seated to take the salute as the regiments marched past.

It was around 700 yards but this distance would be paced out within the next few hours as everything had to be worked out down to the finest detail.

The rifles would be taken up to the roof the morning of the parade and we were delighted when we learned the roof parapet was also going to be used for a firework display. This meant that there would be men visible on the rooftops and we could easily be overlooked as we would most likely be taken for men setting up the display.

I knocked on the adjoining door of the room where we had placed the girls and my mother. As Sarah opened it I slipped inside. Mother was sitting up on the huge bed, propped up by numerous pillows. I rushed to her side and took her hand; she opened her eyes and smiled up at me. "I am much better now son." She said and when I looked at her there was a difference, the colour had returned and she was more like the lady I remembered.

"The girls have been taking good care of me son so there no need for you to worry now." She asked about the girls from the brothel and the Negro maids and I was able to put her mind at rest. "They are in our suite mother," I said and watched the expression on her face change. "No mother, there is an adjoining door and they are on their own."

"We are going to stay here for a few days till after the parade and then we'll go back to Georgia on the train." I said and they all looked so relieved.

The next day we sent out the girls to buy clothes. The working girls were probably going to be missed and we persuaded them not to accompany my sisters. We had given the woman money to purchase some outfits for them all, and that would be suitable for the train journey. These purchases included outfits for the working girls also as they only had the clothes they were wearing when we escaped from the burning building. It would be too much of a risk for us all to dine together downstairs in the restaurant, as there was a good chance one of the girls may be recognised by an ex customer who most likely would be dining with his wife.

The risks were too high for the working girls to even leave the suite so we appointed Joe to watch over them and make sure they didn't give us all away. I feel sure he didn't mind in the least and the girls accepted the arrangement. That evening the Captain had arranged for a table to be laid in our suite for seven women and three men to dine together. The meal was delicious and we refrained from gulping it down, a habit we had picked up over the war years. The ladies were dressed for dinner and they looked so nice. My mother and sisters were wearing the clothes that they had just bought; they had taken advantage of the hotel's facilities and had visits from hairdressers and the maid service to get them ready for the evening. The working girls were also dressed in similar outfits and they all were grateful for being able to get out of the evening gowns they had worn for work.

Chapter 42

Jacob helped to serve the meal and he watched the Negro waiters and anything that was not to his liking was soon rectified. The evening was a great success and gave us the opportunity to celebrate and thank God we were all safely sitting around this table loaded down with many different dishes all cooked and served to such a high standard. The talk over dinner was at first centred on congratulating one another and the women thanked each of us for bringing them to the hotel and for hopefully being able to return them to their homeland. As the evening passed the talk came around to our plans for the parade. The women were worried and couldn't understand why we were delaying the train journey. The Captain slowly outlined his plan to assassinate Sherman and as this man's name was voiced it caused the ladies to gasp on a breath of air, making that distinctive noise. His name had become such a symbol of evil it created a shock wave that struck everyone at the table. We are going to shoot into the pavilion where the General and his staff will be taking the salute. This will be done on the evening of the 4th July which is tomorrow, I want you all to be ready to move at a moment's notice so as soon as the firework display has started move down to the hotel foyer where I will have arranged carriages to take us to the railroad depot. We will wait for thirty minutes to allow you to be seated in the carriages and have started your journey towards the station. After the shooting we will intercept the carriages and hail the cabby to get him to stop while en route. Don't worry everything will have been paid for in advance and all involved will have been suitably rewarded for their cooperation.

The next day was tense as each of us was tormented by their own thoughts and concerns. The women were melancholy and broke down in tears over the least trivial of matters. We were quiet and withdrawn as it was very similar to suffering from the feeling you get the night before a battle, when all soldiers withdraw into their inner self. I believe some of us can foresee the outcome for I have witnessed troopers who have said to me that they will not survive and ask you to deliver last letters or to visit their loved ones after they have been killed. I like to think it's a kind of foreboding which if you allow to gather strength it will take over and all your fears will become reality.

A light luncheon was served in our suite, and we dined together, but the atmosphere around the table was very solemn and conversations brief and full of anguish. There was a constant buzz of excitement and noise coming up from the street and I opened the window in the hope some of the happiness would spread into the room and change people's mood. The parade had started and the regimental bands were now in full tune. The sounds of marching soldiers reached our ears but I couldn't bring myself to watch as the noise from the crowd reached a fever pitch. Our Captain was looking out of the window and his gaze was directed on the raised platform. Several minutes ago the staff of Sherman accompanied by regimental and divisional officers took their seats on the inspection platform. There had been a lull in the marching order as there were no more men marching past. This I thought could have been a rehearsal. The crowd again raised their voices in greeting and when I glanced over at the rear of the platform there was a commotion as Yankees started snapping smartly to attention and saluting. The reason plain to see as there before us was the Devil himself-

Sherman. The band started again as Sherman took his seat while his officers fussed and tried to gain his attention. "Here they come again." Grumbled Joe, but the band music had done the trick. This was a distraction and the ladies were amused for a while and it seemed to ease the tension. However the evening finally drew close and the Captain gathered us in order for him to outline his instructions.

There was to be a firework display starting as soon as it was dark enough. This was to last for many hours and all the buildings in the square would set-off fireworks attached to either their roofs or the parapets. This would be our signal to get ready, and when the right opportunity presented itself we would fire on the Yankees. We assembled on the roof of the hotel where the rifles had been hidden earlier. I had just finished putting two cartridges and some percussion primers into my pocket when I heard a noise. I slowly raised myself so as to be able to see over a roof skylight. The Captain and the rest were busy doing the same and I let a warning low whistling sound which we always used to signal danger. Everyone froze and I had nothing to offer in the way of, what to do next.

The Captain was the first to realize the sound was from the firework display men and we watched as they attached long fuses to each different bank of their display. We looked now as they backed, stooped over towards the roof edge unreeling the reel of fuse chord. They now proceeded to throw a weighted line across to the adjacent buildings roof top. This was collected by another member of their team who then started to pull the chord which had been attached to the end of the fuse towards him. This done they checked the fuse was continuous across the gap between the two roofs. This must have been satisfactory as they disappeared through the roof door and into the stairwell.

This was to our advantage, as there would be little chance of anyone coming up onto the roof during the display because we heard them securing the door from the stairs with a padlock.

We quickly got into position and I pushed the barrel through an aperture in the base of the parapet wall. These were for draining surface water off the roof but now it served me well as a concealed firing point. I aligned the sights and adjusted for the wind which was blowing steadily across me from left to right. To compensate I set the Vernier on the rear sight two divisions to the left. The Captain checked our calculations and accepted we were as correct as we could be without having had the opportunity to fire at the target in practice. Below us there were thousands of people all clamouring to get as close to the barricades as they could in order to be afforded a better view of the parade. There were also many soldiers on duty and every street had a line of men spaced out every ten yards along the edge of the sidewalk. Provost Marshall's patrols were also visible amongst the crowd and patrolling along the other side of the barriers. This would have to be quick and we would have to be away and down in the street before the panic started. Joe had been detailed to break open the roof door and I was happy to see it now hung open at a peculiar angle.

The crowd was now at a fever pitch as there was some movement at the rear of the platform where many folding seats had been set out on the raised deck.

I immediately recognised the group of Yankee officers and saw there looked to be a lot from the General's staff. There was also regimental staff from the different regiments that would be on parade.

He had already made it plain we would try and shoot our targets as they were stood but if one presented itself with another directly in line of fire behind it then we should choose this one, I was to go for Sherman as they had all agreed it was chiefly my vendetta. It was getting dark now and the roof was getting cold as the wind was blowing through the gap where I was going to put the shot. We had been shown not to expose the barrel as it would immediately give away your position when the space all around you would be illuminated by the muzzle flash. The last of the daylight seemed to have vanished very quickly and it was now becoming hard to make out the men sitting on the platform. Suddenly the sky above the building opposite was illuminated by exploding starlight from a rocket fired into the night from somewhere on its rooftop. This was it now, and we got down behind the rifles. The people were all standing looking skyward as the display lit the sky and the buildings in the square were alternatively illuminated. The platform was in semi darkness but the General's staff had busied themselves with placing lighted candles on the tables and lanterns were attached to the corner posts supporting the platforms roof. "We have enough light lads," Our Captain said, "and look at how the chairs have been laid out." He was right for the officers were sitting in a straight line and we were looking right along it from the left flank. We could aim at the head of the nearest officer and with good placement the ball would pass straight through and enter the head of the next officer in the line. As we were spaced out it would be logical if each rifleman chose his individual targets in pairs. My pair was sitting in the centre of the line and Sherman was the seventh man. We moved around behind the parapet aligning our targets and selecting the correct position to achieve the best accuracy. The firework on the adjacent building had just finished spewing out multi coloured balls of light. This meant the next firework to be set-off would be on our roof.

The Captain reassured us and talked low and confidently. "Steady now boys, wait for it."

Suddenly the rocket shot into the air and seconds later we were treated to the "ooohs" and "aaarhs" from the crowd below. The order to fire took me completely by surprise but I was ready, my sights perfectly aligned on the devil head of Sherman. The rifles crashed out in unison but the noise was masked by the crackle and bangs of all the fireworks exploding above all the square's buildings.

"Leave everything and get down those stairs." The Captain shouted, and we flew to the roof door and took the stairs four at a time. We slowed as we reached the bottom stair lobby and the Captain checked us over as though we were about to go on parade. When he was satisfied he opened the door and we stepped out into the hotel lobby. It was deserted as most of the staff and guests were crowding around outside trying to see what all the screaming and shouting was about. He quickly turned us around and we calmly walked to the rear entrance doors which led into the service area. It was deserted, and this made it easy for us to walk through the delivery and kitchen preparation areas and out into the yard. There was no time to lose and we took a shortcut which would bring us into the street where the carriages carrying the ladies and the Negro maids would be travelling along, on its way to the rail station.

We ran down the alley, Jacob taking the lead and Joe bringing up the rear. We turned the last corner and there in front of us was the main street. A carriage was coming up towards us, but we had no way of knowing if this was the one intended for us. It drew level with the alley now but we could see the curtains were lowered and there was no indication the passengers inside had made any arrangements to stop and pick-up for four men. Had we missed the carriage? Panic was setting itself in and that old familiar gut feeling started to come up into my throat. "Don't worry lads, the girls won't let us down, you'll see." Our Captain said questioningly. There must have been someone looking after us that night and a thought flashed in and then vanished out of my brain so quickly it left me weak at the knees. I didn't have time to worry any more then as a carriage was drawing up level with us and the horses were slowing. The door blind was raised and one of the working girls put her head out of the window and said in her best Georgia accent. "Can we ladies offer you any assistance gentlemen?"

We didn't need asking more than once and crowded into their carriage squeezing in-between the girls and their dresses which seemed to possess a mind of their own. We had done it so far anyway, and all I wanted to know was, if the others were with us. The second carriage drew up with us now and we finished the journey together to the station without any further occurrences. Jacob organised some porters and all our baggage was taken to the waiting railroad cars. We had booked reservations in a private car and I settled mother and my sisters kissing them and hugging them till they must have been sick of it.

The train pulled out and we relaxed into comfortable furniture where sleep soon overtook and I felt myself drifting away peacefully. The train made steady progress through the night and by morning we were well to the south. There was a stop coming up and we were asked by the conductor if we would require anything. The Captain ordered a newspaper and some fresh coffee. We were brought the papers and all across the front page of each different broadsheet was the story of an assassination in Louisville, where Sherman had been seriously wounded. The General was now in hospital but there was no news of his condition. Seven other officers were dead having been shot by what the military consider to have been a team of assassins. They thought they had made their escape by river steamer and all efforts were being concentrated to stop and search all vessels that had sailed from the Louisville wharfs within the last twelve hours.

I couldn't help but smile at my Captain as he looked over at me. I was sitting with my mother and was holding her hand. "I thought I had lost you mother," I said "but now I have achieved everything I set out to do." Mother kissed me and fussed around wiping the tears that had started to run, freely down my cheeks.

"I must have pulled that shot for the sights were on his head when I squeezed the trigger." The Captain laughed and went off to find Jacob who was enjoying himself in the other car with the maid girls.

We made it back to Nashville, Tennessee and booked into a good hotel for the overnight stop-over. I wanted a drink and all I could think off was Beth. My sisters were fine and they had recovered from all their ordeals. We laughed and talked of things from a lifetime ago and from a time that was so simple and happy. I was going to marry Beth if she would have me and I would build another house for us and go into business producing tobacco. The Captain had advised me the market was right and as soon as I'd paid for the land I would make a start. The Captain said he would stay around and help me plan things. I was grateful and wanted him to be at Beth and my wedding. I asked him if there was enough money left and he opened a carpet bag and showed me the folding green banknotes. "Still enough for what you want," he said. I had to ask him if there would be enough to help Beth's father out, and he assured me he would make sure there was sufficient to pay off the land agents and still have enough left over to spend on his daughter's wedding.

We boarded the car again the next day and the conductor was full of talk about the assassination. "Seems they got one of those fellas from Louisville," he said, and then continued "they was pretending to be working on the firework display when all the time they going to shoot Old Sherman," The train rolled into Marietta and we got down onto the platform. Our Captain had telegraphed ahead to uncle and he was there to meet us with two carriages and a wagon. Jacob organised some porters and the luggage was loaded onto the wagon. The girls were eager to send telegrams to their relatives; all of which lived in the area around Roswell. The Captain and I escorted them to the telegraph office where they each sent telegrams requesting their family to meet them. The telegraph office would get word to their parents and I hoped there would a happy reunion in store for them and a warm welcome back into the bosom of their families. I gave one of the girls some money and at first she was reluctant to accept it but when I told her the story of how I had taken it from the Yankee Captain and the quartermaster Sergeant she gave in and took the money, thanking me with a sweet kiss on the lips which was considerably longer than any I had received in the past, except maybe from my horse.

For me I was more nervous than I had ever been on any battlefield, I was going to ask Beth to marry me and if she accepted then I'd have to get permission from her parents. I had no idea where I stood in their estimation and for all I knew they may think of me as a guerrilla murderer as news had obviously travelled the length and breadth of the country of the tactics employed by raider bands.

The Yankees will have surely attempted to blacken the reputation of these commands just to cover up their own war crimes.

Chapter 43

My stomach was turning somersaults as we arrived in the farmyard and I spotted Beth standing with her parents. She had made an effort with her appearance as she was wearing a pretty yellow dress. I wouldn't dare to think she had made this effort solely for me and would therefore keep my mouth shut. I jumped down and ran to the carriage carrying mother and my two sisters. They were so happy and my sisters were that excited I couldn't help laughing at them as they allowed me to hand them down off the step, but then they must have forgot they were now young ladies as they took off running to greet Beth and her family.

I walked to uncle and took him by the shoulders and wrapped my arms around him in a bear-hug. I had been thinking about what I had put him through in the past and all the emotion and shame he must have felt. It was now time to try and forgive him for; I knew what he had done when he volunteered to scout for our cavalry as they retreated in front of Sherman's army pushing towards Savanah. How he had managed to mount a horse from a standing position on crutches was one of the things I was going to get him to demonstrate. We were both crying, but I didn't care as these people around me were my family and I vowed there and then, that no one would ever take them away from me again while I still had breath in my body.

My duty was again plain to see and I walked up to Beth. She was standing on the porch but as I got closer she ran at me and leaped off the top step into my arms. I was taken complete by surprise and it took me all of my strength to hold her while trying to remain upright. She was crying her eyes out and I was so surprised there was no way I could speak. I regained some composure and set her safely down on the ground. I couldn't help myself and went down on one knee in front of her. "Beth will you marry me?" I blurted out. "Because I can't think of another minute spent in my life, without you." She took my hands in hers and I stood up, she put her face close to mine and whispered she would be very happy to be my wife but I would have to ask her father. I straightened up and with a smile as big as Stone Mountain I went up the steps to where her father was standing alongside his wife. "Please Sir," I started but he stopped me holding up his hand. "You have been more than a son to me for all these years since your father died and I have always hoped Beth would want to marry you."

I turned around and Beth had come up behind me without me hearing her, I took her in my arms and kissed her tenderly on the lips for the first time. It was like my heart would stop but it was all I wanted to do, and if I died right then it wouldn't have mattered. We had many arrangements to make and the ladies all fussed around with organising the minister, the reception and biggest of all things, the dresses. I was happy my Captain was going to be my best man but he told me he was going to live in Virginia and run a large tobacco plantation. He explained Beth and I would be welcome to accompany him and that there would be a position for me on the management staff.

I talked it over with Beth but she was not happy, as to leave her sisters in law and my mother would be more than she could stand, and so it looked like my Captain and I would be parting company. Joe had his cabin in the woods and would simply go back to what he did before the war. Jacob would go with the Captain as there was nothing that would stop him from being with his master.

Things had gone well for the family and even though we were still under military law, the situation had got a little more relaxed. We had false papers and had never sworn allegiance to the Union; nor would we ever, as there was so much hatred still lying very close to the surface.

I had made my arrangements with Beth's father as we had come to an agreement over the money I had given him to pay-off the land agents who were nothing more than official bandits engaged by the banks. They were foreclosing on all properties under mortgage agreements. I accepted he would put money into my account every month but this to me seemed unjust as the money had been stolen from the Union paymaster. He put my concerns to rest as he said that wasn't it only right that the money should go back to the Union for after all it was better for them to pay our debts for us, so we could go on living peacefully in our own country.